The Knights-Errant

By

Sam Humphrey

To my old and Dear Friend, John.

Best wishes

Sam

The Knights-Errant

Copyright Mervyn Robert Humphrey

Writing as Sam Humphrey 2014-2017

The Knights Errant text © Sam Humphrey 2017

2nd edition Published April 2017

This book is dedicated to

My wife Louise, who endured a stressed-out husband, made costumes, painted heraldic shields, was deserted every weekend of the summer, sometimes for weeks at a time, leaving her with two young children and a business to run.

Also to the wives and partners of the longstanding members of the Troupe who suffered in a similar way.

Finally, all the members of the Nottingham Jousting Association whose actions gave me the material for this book.

My thanks to

Dick and LIn Benson for proof reading this book, correcting my dreadful spelling and grammar. I would also like to thank them for their encouragement and helpful suggestions. I apologise to Lynn for ignoring her suggestions for replacing some of the swear words in the book but it really wouldn't be me without a bit of swearing.

Also to my wife for reading the book several times to tidy up the layout and search out those annoying typos that hideaway just waiting to pop up when you think you have found them.

A Knight-Errant

The definition of a Knight-Errant varies but commonly refers to a medieval knight who travelled Christendom in search of chivalrous action. It also mentions adventure.

The name is also given to the landless Knights who made a living travelling from one Tournament to another and winning prize money fighting and jousting in the lists. There was always much feasting and drinking during and after these events.

I think these definitions still hold true today when applied to the life style we lived as members of the Nottingham Jousting Association from 1970 to 2006. Hence the name of this book.

The Knights-Errant

Table of Contents

THIS BOOK IS DEDICATED TO

MY THANKS TO

A KNIGHT-ERRANT

TABLE OF CONTENTS

AUTHOR'S NOTE

CHAPTER 1	THE BEGINNING SUMMER 1970-71

CHAPTER 2	TWO TROUPES

CHAPTER 3	MAKING FRIENDS AND LEARNING LESSONS 1973-74

CHAPTER 4	ON THE ROAD 1975-80

CHAPTER 5	THE CRAZY YEARS 1980 – 1988

CHAPTER 6	NEW HORIZONS 1989-2006

CHAPTER 7	 HORSES

CHAPTER 8   THE LAST HOORAH

EPILOGUE   WICKSEY

GLOSSARY

ABOUT THE AUTHOR

Joust Amazing Forward

I have written this book about The Nottingham Jousting Association because it changed my life. Every time I sit and reminisce about the Jousting years I always end up laughing and smiling. It was amazing!! How did such ordinary people from such diverse backgrounds gel, to create such stunning shows, have so much fun, and in the main get along with each other whilst living in each other's' pockets for so many years? In most cases the people that joined us were drifting in their lives when they joined us. I certainly was. A previous girl friend had convinced me that I should give up my life as a jobbing builder with my future brother-in-law, Bert, and get a respectable job. This was a life of hard work, very good money, the wages being approximately five times as much as most of my friends were earning, plus a fair bit of drinking thrown in for good measure. The job was at British Gypsum in their Research Dept. at East Leake. It paid a pittance but I had soon been promoted and my prospects, I was told, were very good. However, I was bored out of my mind! Then out of the blue Jousting came along. What started out as a "one off" took off like a rocket and very soon I had handed in my notice and become a full-time Jouster. This was much to the bewilderment of my Department Head who could only say "are you sure? We have just given you the highest pay rise in the whole of the Department". No!! I was not sure, but filled with emotion for the nice things he had said about my work I said goodbye and stepped out of the safe corporate world and into the complete unknown.

****

Looking back, I see different eras in the Jousting and loosely they relate to the generations of the Humphrey family

1970-72 Dad's generation

1972 -80 my generation

1980-92 my bothers generation

1992-2010 My sons' generation

2010---Knights of Nottingham

There is of course no exact date for these eras, as they slowly evolved over several years from one era to the next. With each era came a different show as the new main characters played their own interpretation of a character. This is something I always encouraged and I think it is one of the reasons the show has stayed so fresh and popular for so long. I always saw the show as theatre and stole a lot of ideas from West End musicals and remakes of films such as "Robin Hood" which have constantly reinvented themselves. I have been lucky to have worked with or been associated with some very talented people who freely passed on their crafts and talents to me.

****

Many people have joined us over the years. Those who joined for only the money or stardom soon left. Those that "got off" on captivating an audience and manipulating it to their wishes and enjoying the harsh camaraderie of the troupe stayed for years. They put up with early mornings and late nights, together with the hard monotonous setting up and de-rigging the show equipment. But boy! Did they have some great times! This is what this book is about.

****

Finally, what has been the greatest buzz of all is seeing rudderless souls develop into men of character. We can name amongst our ranks. The C.E.O. of a global corporation and there are at least two near or actual millionaires and dozens of lads who have become highly successful in their chosen careers.

Even after over 40 years, most us remain firm friends.

LET'S START TO RELIVE THE RIDE!

Author's note

As I started to assemble notes for this book it soon became clear that I needed a definite timeline of shows to put them altogether for a book. I thought it would be a relatively easy task to make a list of all the shows that had done. I had kept the files on nearly all the shows we had performed since the mid-70s. Boxes and boxes of them, or so I thought. However in reality I soon found that many files were missing. In some cases, whole years of records probably lost to office moves, floods, rodents, and the spring cleaning of the filing cabinets. So, it developed into a sort of treasure hunt, searching many diverse sources to nail down when shows took place.

In the appendix at the end of this book is a list of all the shows that we performed, I would like to make it clear that it is not a definitive finished. To make this list I have used various sources: - Correspondence files and contracts, random archived dates list for different years, press cuttings, old posters and souvenir programs that I have saved and of course contacting and tapping into the memories of old members of the jousting troupe.

Those shows that are listed on the dates and years are shows that I have definite documentary evidence for. The ones listed on their own without dates are shows that we can remember quite clearly but have no documentary evidence to identify them with a year. I'm quite sure that there are still a lot of shows missing and many of them will surface over the next few months as members of the troupe and friends read the date's list, jogging memories. It has taken over six months to assemble all these dates of past shows. T has also given me a bad home because our spare bedroom floor has been covered wall-to-wall with the old files, press cuttings, souvenir posters and programs. Having said that, it has been a very worthwhile exercise. It has bought back some very fond, and some very sad memories, a bit like a roller coaster ride, scary but thrilling.

The statistics show how the jousting grew very slowly during the 70's except for Gwrych Castle in 1972, then suddenly in the early 1980's it exploded to manic proportions and then as recessions came our fortunes faded and then revived again as money once again became more available. The figures also show what wonderful dedication the members of the jousting troupe showed. For 6 years, we averaged 30 plus venues per summer (60 performances most packed into 16 weeks.) We were bruised, battered and when you add on the days we were away from home travelling or preparing for shows, it was an amazing sacrifice to make. I know it cost some of the lads a lot.

Looking back, I'm just amazed how dedicated and driven they were.

Chapter 1   The beginning summer 1970-71

The offer came not directly from my Father but via my Mother. "I think your Father was wondering whether you would like to do some jousting at Wollaton Park this weekend?" said my Mother. "What!!!" I said. My mind spun; because at the time I was not really on speaking terms with my Father or to be truthful my Father was not speaking to me. I had recently left home and deprived him of his free labour. In his mind, he had bred me. He had spent a fortune feeding me and clothing me since my birth. Then just when I was becoming useful I had welched on the deal to pay it all back in free labour by leaving home.

Dad had become involved in the first ever jousting tournament for over a hundred years. He had been approached by Max Diamond, a famous film stuntman, to supply horses for his group of stuntmen. They had been contracted to recreate a jousting tournament at Wollaton Park, Nottingham. It was the brainchild of the Nottingham festival director, Richard Gregson-Williams. As part of the deal, Dad got to take part in the tournament riding his flashy palomino stallion, Ambre Solaire, who could rear and bow. Under the direction of Richard Gregson-Williams and run by a committee of councillors and private sector representatives, the 1970 festival presented an action-packed 16-day programme of events, drawing massive crowds and a Royal visit from Princess Margaret. During the middle weekend, more than 50,000 people flocked to Wollaton Park to watch attractions including no-holds barred jousting.

www.youtube.com/watch?v=ItRFAiKGj0U

Mum explained that there had been several injuries amongst the stuntman during the week of jousting. Saturday was supposedly the last day of the jousting and the Grand Finale´ day. The stuntmen were short of riders and were looking for local people to stand in for the injured riders. What they were looking for were riders who could dress up in costume and ride in the parade and salute the audience, there were still enough stuntman to do the actual dangerous riding and falls.

Looking back, this book and all the jousting, so nearly never happened. After Mum, had spoken to me I went up into the top field and paced around agonising over what to do. If I did the Jousting, then Dad had won; I would be drawn back into the Riding School and everything I hated. On the other-hand, if I didn't, I would miss out on the chance to do something I had read so much about and was really interested in. Three things were holding me back from saying yes: giving in to Dad, pride and the fact that I was incredibly shy, so much so that I would fake an illness and not go to school if anything theatrical was on the timetable. After much mental anguish for over 30 mins I finally decided to say yes!

With no rehearsal, off I went to the Festival. It was mind blowing for a 19-year-old country boy! There was security, with identity badges to get in. There were massive grandstands, Princess Margaret was coming to watch the

Show and I got to work with a group of film stuntmen who acted like super stars. The stunt guys did a lot of galloping around with lots of bravado but the jousting competitions and sword fights were very weak and hammed up compared with what we do today.

The Jousting was such a success that Gregson-Williams wanted to extend the show for an extra day to take in Sunday, the last day of the festival. However, the stunt men were already booked for another job and so bunch of complete amateurs turned out to perform. The horses were great, they had been doing it all week and knew the show a lot better than us. We were not bad at the jousting. The horses had been trained and most of us were seasoned mounted games competitors with good hand eye co-ordination. The weaker members of the team became our targets with them providing a good square shield for us to hit. The big thing that carried the show off for us was Dad and his stallion, Ambre Solaire.

Ambre was a natural super star, a stunning golden palomino stallion full of flair and testosterone. His rears were vertical to the point everyone believed he would come over backwards and to top it off he clapped his hooves together whilst pawing the air with his front legs. It always drew gasps from the audience, followed by spontaneous applause. His piece-de-la-resistance was to be able to drop down onto both knees and stretch out his neck to put his chin on the ground. It was a perfect theatrical bow that would evoke, wild cheers and applause with a standing ovation. This is what was to become the corner stone for our performances for the next two years, in fact as Dad taught Ambre (Fred, his stable name) more tricks, the show revolved more and more around Dad and Fred. The rest of us were more of a side show that packed out the show to 30 or 45 minutes.

The jousting at Nottingham Festival was a stunning success although we had not played a great part, Dad and Fred had been the star all week and received worldwide media attention. Everyone wanted a piece of the action; it was like a new pop group becoming a success, offers were coming from everywhere. The problem was that none of the stunt men or the Bunny jousters were in a position, to capitalise on it. The stunt men were literally a group of freelancers; many were contracted to film companies for forthcoming films. They also did not own any horses! The film industry was heavily unionised with strong demarcation lines, only stunt men on a stunt register could work on films. Horses were provided by a Horse Master, a separate department.

However, the stunt man who had put together the Nottingham tournament, Max Diamond, could see the potential to make money. Max formed the British Jousting Society and we formed the Nottingham Jousting Association. This was not a split or fallout. We continued to work and collaborate for many years to come but more of that later. The Nottingham Festival took place in August so there was not much opportunity to cash in on the success of the jousting that year although, we did several more press and TV. interviews. However, things were already brewing for next year, 1971.

The Nottingham Festival had been a great success with the public and media but had seriously over run its budget, ending up with Nottingham City council footing the shortfall. The festival had a strange makeup with private businesses running the festival but the city council covering any losses. A recipe that led to excesses and huge losses that would end in years to come with scandal and recriminations, but for now they had a huge success on their hands and everyone wanted more. Gregson - Williams was kept on as festival director and early in the New Year we were approached to run the jousting at the next Festival, but with a much-reduced budget.

Because of the festival's media coverage, the second festival, was able, to get companies to sponsor various parts of the festival. Dienhard Wines who had a knight as their logo offered to sponsor the jousting but to make it more appealing the PR Gurus came up with the idea of a multi venue challenge competition. Dienhard produced a large silver cup as a prize and covered the costs for all three shows. At this point in time, none of us were paid, it was just a hobby, free food and drink after the show if you were lucky. However just staging the jousting involved considerable costs. Horses, transport, props, medieval tents, costumes and chain-mail had to be hired from London at considerable expense.

All three shows were a success, with great local publicity, but lacked the international buzz of the year before. I have no lasting memories of these shows. I remember weeks in the workshop making helms, shields and breastplates, meticulously researched from history books in the library. These were great exciting weeks and much of the equipment we made in 1971 is still used today. Nobody had any great plans for jousting. A couple of local shows a year would do us fine with maybe something occasionally with Max Diamond on a grander scale.

In fact, Max's next show was already booked and we were invited to bring a small team. Dad, Brent Haddon, Brian Hinksman, a girl groom called Gail and myself. The three local shows had honed our jousting skills and we set off in good spirits to do battle against the stuntmen at Battle Abbey (built on the site of the Battle of Hastings by William the Conquerer). Max always did things on a grand theatrical scale. He had great contacts plus the charisma to attract wealthy sponsors and backers along with venues that would attract huge crowds and publicity.

Battle Abbey - http://youtu.be/J2OfX8e3Sbw search YouTube 1971 festival of battle

The shows at Battle were to be as life changing for me as when I gave up my job at British Gypsum. It would cause the Nottingham Jousting Association to become a professional group and see the formation of a company called Medieval Entertainments Ltd to run the business side of our jousting shows. Battle was where I saw the true potential of jousting, learning stuntmen's skills and tricks. But most of all we made contacts that would be instrumental in eventually turning a small group of amateurs into an international professional troupe. I would also learn very hard business lessons at the hands of some of the people I met at Battle. Like a lot of pop groups landing their first record contract, only later finding the small print robbed them blind. So much happened at Battle - it was a whole new world.

The opening ceremony was a night parade through the town to the Abbey led by the knights. The knights who were stuntmen all carried flaming torches on horseback -stunning!! I was speechless. They formed a flaming guard of honour at the Abbey gates for the sponsors and VIPs who swept past in a fleet of Rolls- Royce's, to be entertained at the Abbey. They included comic Charlie Drake and ITV newscaster Reginald Bosanquet, a great ladies heart throb at the time. Charlie Drake had been at the first Nottingham Joust and, along with Reggie was wheeled out as guest celebrities for all of Max's jousts long after their celebrity status had faded.

The jousting next day was an eye opener. We had been used to jousting as friends (still dangerous enough), but this was hard-core jousting against people we did not know with very large egos. We had been brought in as a necessity to make up numbers. We were to be cannon fodder. My first joust was very nearly my last. After two bone crunching strikes my third strike ran down my opponent's shield into his groin. I had no knowledge of this and on the fourth and final run all I remember was a huge bang and a flash of blinding light, then being helped off my horse at the end of the tilt and being asked if I was OK. I could not understand what had happened to me - I remembered having a good shield and my lance about to strike my opponents shield then, blank!

Apparently, the guy thought I deliberately struck him in the groin so aimed for my head in revenge, taking my helm clean off my head with his lance, sending it flying into the air. Our team were in more shock than I was. They had seen my helm fly 20 feet through the air and for a moment they thought my head was in the helm. My Father, not prone to showing any emotion other than rage and profanity, was silent and white as a sheet. The incident soured our relations with the stunt men, each blaming each other for the incident.

Unlike the first Nottingham joust this was much more of a show and included some choreographed foot fights. At first, I didn't realise they were staged and I was enthralled by the speed of the blows and the ferocity. I truly thought they would kill one another. It wasn't till the next day when they did the exact same fight that the penny dropped. Another great trick was to have a stuntman planted in the crowd. Nosher Powell, a huge strong man who regularly played the thug in British films, would fight several knights at once and when he had defeated them would cry out to the audience "is there no man here who dares to fight me". The stunt man in the audience was a very little guy, so it looked like a David and Goliath contest. He would shuffle out looking weak and a bit dim, but he was really a skilled Cornish Wrestler. Nosher would throw him all over the place until the crowd were booing and calling for it to stop then, as Nosher got complacent, the little guy would catch him unawares and after a flurry of quick moves defeat Nosher, to rapturous applause from the crowd. This was to become the basic script for the end of our show substituting the Good knight and the Black Knight. But that was in the future for although I rode as the Black Knight of Nottingham we had no characters in our jousting troupe as it was still a real sport as far as we were concerned. Not having been involved with the Nottingham joust I believed we were all competing in a championship, the Knight with the most strikes winning. However, it soon became clear that Max was going to win come what may as he had done in Nottingham. The judging was so blatantly biased in favour of Max that even the audience started to grumble when he was given strikes that missed by several feet. Another trick the stuntmen used was to cross lances. The audience would hear a crash and the lances would spin out of their hands, the knights wobbling all over the place and the judge proclaiming a massive double strike when there had been no strike at all. But this was the stuntmen's world of fantasy and deception. I do not know if it was true but I was told that Max kept a zip on arm plaster cast that he would wear for interviews to bolster his claims of how dangerous jousting was. There was nothing we could do about this. We had been paid our expenses and were treated like extras in a film. They were the stars! Even in the bars at night we were given the cold shoulder when we tried to socialise. The cheating and the arrogance hadn't gone unnoticed by some of the organisers who were not happy as it turned out about a lot of things. They had, however been impressed by our riding skills and the way we conducted ourselves.

We were invited to use an exclusive members-only dining club in the centre of Battle. We dined there every evening, meeting with some very wealthy and powerful people who were to help us make a quantum leap from raw naive amateurs to naive professionals. It was in the Battle Club that I learnt about fine food and fine wines, thanks to Brent Haddon. My friend Brent had had a wealthy upbringing and had received a substantial sum from his father when he sold his business. I had known Brent and his brother since childhood on the local Gymkhana and show jumping circuit; they were great riders and had top class horses to ride. As soon as they could drive they both had sports cars (E Type Jaguars I think) and women dripping off them. They knew how to live! The idea of the Battle club was to provide top class food and wine without profit. Their wine was sold at the cost they paid for it when it was laid down, plus a few percent. Brent introduced me to 20-year-old Chateaux bottled Margaux, Latour and Gevrey Chambertin. They cost us the princely sum of 10/- a bottle. We dined like royalty! To Brian and myself 10/- was indeed a princely sum as a week's wage for us was about £5, however we rarely paid for anything on this trip as we had found generous patrons. I remember meeting a merchant banker in the bar whose passion was an old pre-war fire engine. He was so excited about being able to drive it around the arena and clang its bell, we sat and listened to tales about his engine and never paid for a drink all night. It has never ceased to amaze me that extremely successful people can be so passionate about small simple things.

It was here at Battle that we met people that would change so many things in our lives. We met Terry Goulden who would find us many shows including Cyprus, and several lucrative TV & and Film contracts, but most importantly he would supply us with film quality chainmail and costumes. However, all this was a long way in the future.

The other man we met who led us to many other very diverse contacts, was Sir Trevor Lloyd - Hughes. Sir Trevor had been Prime Minister Harold Wilson's press secretary (spin doctor) and he now ran a Public Relations and Publicity Company called Lloyd Hughes Associates, based in London not far from Downing Street. He was involved in the Battle joust and his daughter Katie plus boyfriend Graham Lucking were down at the show helping on the gate with the money. They were very excited and enthusiastic about jousting and saw it as a major entertainment; we spent long evenings eating, drinking and talking about the future. Although the big ideas excited me I dismissed it as just social talk. By the end of the show I had become quite good friends with Katie and Graham and like with all holiday friendships parted saying we must meet up again.

The show ran its course and I have no other memories of incidents except that Max won by a large margin, and we never came anywhere, according to Max's judges. What I did decide was that we had little or no future with Max or the stuntmen. We had become a threat to them and they had closed ranks and shut us out. They wanted all the money and all the limelight. We were just a necessary evil they had to put up with when they could not make up the numbers. We were just thrown a few crumbs to keep us happy. The same thing was to happen to us when we got into Film & Television work. That got really nasty, but more of that later.

While Brent and Gail, his latest girlfriend, drove down in style in the E Type Jag, Dad, Brian and I trundled down in an old Bedford TK Horse box with lollipop front indicators. Dad was driver and Brian and I were squashed in on the bench seat.

Whoever sat next to dad had the job of filling and lighting his pipe which he smoked constantly whilst driving.

Driving horses down to Brighton was a major trip for us. We had never travelled more than 30 miles in a horse box before. Preparations were intense - fan belts checked along with tyres, lights got working, we even got the indicators working and they had never worked since we purchased it several years ago. I think we even changed the oil. A large tool box was prepared including a stick to tap the lollipop indicators that were prone to stop working spasmodically, but soon rectified by leaning out of the cab window and tapping with the stick. We decided also that as budding celebrities we should travel in style, so Brian riveted a pub bottle opener onto the metal dashboard and installed two cases of Home Ales Robin Hood IPA on the shelf behind the seats in the cab. When you think of the drink driving laws we have today, it's frightening to think that we had consumed almost four dozen half pint bottles by the time we arrived at Battle. When Dad smoked his pipe, he used to drift off into a sort of daze or trance. There was an advert on TV for Condor Pipe Tobacco where a man would take a puff of his pipe, sigh, look up at the sky and say "Aagh that Condor Moment ". Dad would be quite deaf to conversation when he was having one of his "Condor moments" as we called them. You would have to shout extremely loud to break him out of his trance. As we drove south of London the roads got much better with lots of dual carriageway and even bits of Motorway. Brian and I were the map readers. We calculated that soon we would have to turn off the Motorway. Unfortunately, Dad was having one of his "Condor moments". He had also moved into the outside lane because there were no cars in it and as the steering was a bit dodgy it was easier to cope with the wobble. He was totally oblivious of the cars under taking him and blowing their horns.

As we neared the junction we started to prep him - "Dad, we are turning off in minute" - "Dad, junction coming up" but he was still in the outside lane, foot flat to the floor (or what was left of it most of it had rotted away). We arrived at the beginning of the slip road and I screamed "Dad! turn off NOW! ". He jumped out of his trance, hauled on the wheel taking us across three lanes of the motorway scattering cars all over the place with horns blaring. By the time, we had crossed over we were past the exit. Undeterred he continued up the beginning of the embankment, over the criss-crossed curb stones that separated the slip-road from the motorway and onto the slip-road just before the traffic island. Ashen faced Bri & I stared at each other wondering how we had survived. Dad calmly turned to us and said, " bloody hell lads, you could have given me a bit more notice. I think you've been having too much of that beer". Brian and I were already reaching for another 2 bottles, shaking like leaves.

On leaving Battle we returned with several souvenirs. Dad was given a sword blade from the owner of the Abbey and a rustic three-legged stool - the seat being a whole round of a tree. I think my Mum still has it somewhere even after 40 years. We still have the sword blade which our armourer, Paddy Dolan, fitted a hilt and cut 6 " off the length of the blade which was over 4' long. Something I now regret but again I still have it, along with a First Day Cover from 1966 franked in Battle to commemorate the 900-year anniversary of the Battle of Hastings. Our other souvenir was two cases of canned Long Life beer that we purloined from a stable next to ours that was stacked to the roof with them. Those two souvenirs never made it home. Thirsty work driving! On my return home I phoned Midland Wine who supplied our Bar at the stables and spoke to the owner who I knew quite well. I asked him to get me a few cases of that nice Chateaux Latour. I heard him splutter a bit, he replied, "I don't have it in stock, I can get it, but do you have any idea how much it is?" I had to admit I didn't but when he told me I nearly died of shock and immediately cancelled the order.

During the Winter of 1971, things moved quickly Our new-found friends in London did contact us and Dad and myself shuttled back and forward to London for meetings. We were dealing with a strange group of people; some were extremely well groomed and educated (pinstriped suits, carnations in button holes), the others were Arty/ Hippy types but still well-educated and wealthy. It was all very overwhelming. Dad loved it. We had lunch at fashionable restaurants and dinner parties at flats in Knightsbridge and Chelsea. At one of these dinners there was a discussion about a failed attempt to recruit a SAS style mercenary force to free the then president of Kenya, Jomo Kenyatta who had been imprisoned by the British in the early 60s. I never understood whether the aim was to assassinate him or make him president for their benefit. It was during this period that I was very grateful to my old British Gypsum Boss, Chris, who had educated me in what was the fine dining of the late 60's. We would divert to London for expenses paid meals at top restaurants on our way to visit the Rochester Plaster making factory. Sir Trevor Lloyd - Hughes, Katie his daughter and boyfriend Graham Lucking featured heavily in all these meetings. By early 1972, things were starting to crystallise. Sir Trevor was starting to line up some top venue shows for us. The flagship of these was an appearance at the Royal International Horse Show performing 2 shows a day for the duration. Another ground-breaking show was at the Preston Guild, a once every 25 years event. The guild was staging a production of "Camelot" and the Director had the idea to stage the jousting scenes with real knights and horses in front of the main stage. It was at

Preston that another legendary story of Dad's character came about. Dad and Brian were sharing a room. On entering the room for the first time, one of the beds was missing its pillows. Dad immediately said to Brian, "Hey Bri, look your bed hasn't got any pillows". A few minutes later having stretched out on the bed he decided that there was a draught from the window and demanded that Brian swop beds with him. "Great, thought Brian. At least I get a pillow even if there is a draught". No such luck - Dad picked up the pillows and took them to the bed without pillows. Poor Brian ended up with no pillows and the draught. Although we teased Dad many times about this, he could never understand what was wrong about it.

Another high-profile event that gained massive publicity in national press was the re-enactment of the Eglington Tournament in the Royal Burgh of Irvine, Scotland.

(for more information search Eglington Tournament Wikipedia)

Then came the big daddy of them all! A group of investors called Scotia Investments had bought a castle in North Wales and planned to turn it into a Disney- style medieval theme park. What was a theme park? We hadn't even heard of Disney-land. Not a clue what they were talking about but HEY! they wanted a summer of jousting in a Welsh castle by the seaside. What could be better? We said yes straight away. (Bad move!)

CHAPTER 2   **Two Troupes**

Gwrych Castle and Dad's Shows

Copy and paste the links below to see videos of Gwrych Castle

http://youtu.be/FW_XzLQf3w4

http://youtu.be/1UX-dxYKntk

So, in early 1972 we agreed with a shadowy, multi-national company to perform for 16 weeks 2 shows per day 7 days per week. The show cast was 6 mounted knights, 6 squires-foot soldiers, plus a couple of reserves. We hadn't seen the site; only artist's impressions of the finished medieval theme park. It looked out of this world!

Having secured a large bank loan on the strength of the contract, we set about producing a second set of kits, buying more horses and recruiting the staff. The staff we recruited were a very mixed bunch. I think the only common denominator was a desire for fame and excitement. Most were running away from something, parents, school, relationships or just a boring life. Reading this now, I realise that this was a recipe for disaster but this was the beginning of the 1970s-anything was possible!

Dad and Graham Lucking; who was now working as our manager, were first to go up to see the castle and came back full of excitement. Work was just starting, but they had bought the dream. They returned with tales of us all actually living in the castle. All the rooms were being refurbished, new stables and a new 2,000 seat grandstand being built. The jousting arena was just as grand. It was sighted on a terrace just inside the main outside wall with sweeping views down to and across the sea towards Colwyn Bay.

 I think it was early April when I finally got time to visit. I had recently started to date my future wife, Lou, so decided to impress her by taking her to the exotic country of Wales and book into the best hotel in the exciting holiday playground of Rhyl!! I think the Hotel was called the Grand or something like that. Sadly, there was nothing grand about the hotel; it was basic and much in need of refurbishment but hey! I don't think I had ever stayed in a proper hotel before and certainly not with a pretty young girl who had told her parents all sorts of stories to enable her to come away with me for the weekend. We decided to go out and take in the sights and pleasures of this famous seaside town. Gale force winds and rain lashed the deserted seafront, everywhere was closed and dilapidated. The plan of impressing my girlfriend was not happening. Oh well never mind. We were going to meet the manager of this "Disney Land" castle where I was going to live and run the impressive main attraction. I was not sunk yet! We finally found the gatehouse entrance and a huge new sign with a galloping knight in its centre and the words GWRYCH CASTLE CROESO! This was more like it but what the hell Croeso meant, I had no idea.

My excitement was very short lived. Passing through the gate house the road carried on across a field and started to rise. Slowly out of the swirling mist appeared a dark and foreboding Victorian mock castle. It looked more like Dracula's Castle than a medieval summer theme park. Eventually we reached the main castle gate. It was wide open but no sign of life. We edged forward slowly in the car but still no sign of life. After some time, we parked the car, and walked around shouting, "hello is anyone there?". We found a guy who said he was the caretaker. I proudly announced who I was and asked to be taken to the manager who was expecting me. "Sorry there is no one here" he explained, all the workmen had gone home because of the bad weather and the manager had been summoned to London to explain the delays. Yes, he knew we were coming and left his apologies but when the board of directors summoned him he had to go immediately. He had left instructions for us to have a look around and contact him next week if we had any queries. The caretaker announced he himself had urgent business so could we show ourselves around. We wandered around a wet dripping building site full of half-finished joinery and painting. Most of the living area was locked and out of bounds and much of what I wanted to see was not built or we could not find it. Fed up and demoralised, I decided we should have a slap-up meal on expenses. Although the trip had been a disaster on both the business and romantic front, over the meal that evening we both found we had a common love of dining out with good food and sorting out life's problems over a good bottle of wine.

It was early May when Graham and I moved up to Wales with the advance party and started to receive the rest of the people we had employed to become jousters and squires. On our arrival at the castle we had been expecting an enthusiastic welcome but received anything but! The problem was complex but basically the castle staff and building staff had been working together for several months to convert the castle into a jousting theme park. They were behind schedule and along with the weather, our arrival was just another spanner in the works. Our first problem was that none of the accommodation was ready and so we faced living in derelict rooms with no heating. Next morning things got a lot worse. Having spent a cold, damp first night in the castle we were looking forward to a good hearty breakfast. Part of the contract was that we were provided with 3 meals a day. We arrived at the canteen about 7.45 am as we had been told that breakfast was between 7 and 8am. We were greeted from behind newspapers by a mixture of surly "you are not welcome looks" and sniggers, indicating they knew something we didn't. After waiting for about 10 minutes and no sign of anyone coming for orders I decided to go to the kitchen and let them know we were here. I entered the kitchen to be confronted by a thick wall of steam, burnt fat smoke and cigarette smoke. From out of this fog appeared a man with a cigarette hanging from his mouth. He was dressed in a greasy, once white tee shirt, arms covered with tattoos and black hair plastered to his head with grease. He glared at me and growled at me in a thick Scottish accent, "Whattt dah yoo wannt ". I explained that there were ten of us waiting for breakfast and thought perhaps he didn't realise we were there. "Yarr too fucking late, yarr long haired twatt" came the reply. I then tried to explain that we were told that breakfast was between 7am and 8am. " Aye stoop cooking at 7.30, everybody out bah eeght. Aagh hav tooo prep farr lunch". I decided further argument was futile so retreated and went in search of a cafe in Abergele with the rest of the lads (my first of many unexpected expenses). Over breakfast in Abergele we hatched a battle plan for next day. Although not used to rising before 8.30-9.00, as boss, I volunteered to get up and wake everyone at 6 am so we could all be in the canteen before 7.00. Next day, by ten to seven, every table in the small canteen was taken by jousters and slowly we were served our breakfast, with a menacing glare included. The first breakfasts had just started to come out as the site workers started to arrive and finding the canteen full, things turned quite ugly, but the jousters eventually all got fed. The site workers were not so lucky. They downed tools and went on strike as the chef still refused to cook a single bean after 7.30. The castle manager didn't start until 9 ish so for about two hours we were on the edge of open warfare. The manager was not sympathetic to our cause as his main priority was to get the site workers, who were already behind schedule, back to work. I reminded him that in the next few days our numbers would be more than doubling, it was part of our contract to be fed and that this was a serious problem for all parties. The outcome was that feeding times were extended by the manager keeping everyone happy except our Scottish friend, the chef, who a few weeks later disappeared to be replaced by a far more competent and pleasant person.

The opening date drew nearer and things were still way behind schedule including the training and rehearsal of the shows. The arena was a shambles - except for the sand on the floor of the arena, there was nothing. No tilt, no grandstand, no power, no commentary box, no sound system. Elsewhere, the stables weren't finished, we were still living in squalor and the concession shops didn't exist. Eventually we went over the head of the castle manager and contacted the director who had originally engaged us.

The result was an in depth visit by the directors who checked into every aspect of the project including our show. They were not happy at all. Everyone got a bollocking and were told things would have to change and fast, we would hear from them very soon.

They appointed an overall site manager with a festival background and was used to making things happen fast and to a tight deadline. He was a great guy! Overnight people were sacked, and new people came in who were prepared to work day and night to get the jobs done. The outcome of the director's visit for us was fantastic as we got a troupe of medieval musicians with authentic instruments, a script for the opening speech written by a Shakespearean actor which we still use to present day and two comedy sketches (St George and the Dragon and Dredfal David). Plus, we had lots of creative help on how to turn a basic jousting tournament into something truly entertaining. Unfortunately, this all came at a high cost and the bill came out of our fee! Another unexpected expense!

The week before we opened, the arena and grandstand were finished. A grand press day was arranged which attracted press and television from all over the world. By the end of the day we had done so many stunt falls for various television crews and photo journalists, we felt we had already done a month's jousting! We were totally exhausted and black and blue. Our biggest scoop from the press day was a complete full front page spread in Sunday Express. The amazing thing was that it was in colour. It was stunning and the first-time colour had been used like that in a newspaper. Except for later royal occasions, I don't think one item has since filled the front page in colour without any other subject being mentioned.

Finally, the opening day arrived. A full house of 2,000 greeted us including many dignitaries, press and television. For many of the troupe it was their first public performance; if they bottled it and the show was a failure it was all on my head. Every level of management constantly reminded me that if this show was not a success it could wreck the viability of the whole project. I was "shitting" myself!!! As it turned out the audience loved the show, although not a great show by later standards, the old hands that had come up to Wales to help us get started carried the show and covered up the weaker bits. We got great press coverage and everyone concerned was on a high. The opening had been timed a week or so before the Spring Bank Holiday so by the time the holidaymakers arrived we had a slick show running with the new staff becoming more confident every day. We were all learning how to manipulate the audience and change its moods from anger to ecstasy, and draw out cheers or boo's. It was during this time of great enthusiasm and innovation that the format of the show started to become the blueprint for all the shows we would perform for the next 40 years. One of the suggestions from the theatre director had been to change the jousting from individuals competing against each other, to a show with two camps, one good and one bad. Looking back, it was not rocket science as nearly every film or story had this as its theme in one guise or another. Over the past 2 years, the jousting had started to drift from a true competition towards a show. After Battle Abbey, we started to stage a couple of foot fights. Dad had also started to demand that he should always be Champion Knight, like Max Diamond. This was the prima donna syndrome that would be a constant problem during my 36 years in charge.

The biggest change involved me - it would seem ludicrous today. The change was to make the Black Knight leader of the Bad Camp and an evil character. If you ask anyone today what sort of character someone dressed in black would portray they would instantly say bad, evil and treacherous. That was not the case in the 60's and early 70's as there were several films and television programmes that portrayed black masked men as heroes, for instance, Batman, The Lone Ranger, Zorro and several swashbuckling Robin Hood spinoff films where the champion knight hid his real identity by dressing in black to defeat robber barons or those plotting to overthrow the King. It was this Black Knight that had prompted me to take the name The Black Knight of Nottingham. It was now being suggested that I become anything but a chivalrous hero.

Although this was a big shock that I had not considered, the idea of a good and bad camp was intriguingly good and I was quickly won round. The next big task was to decide who would be good and who would be bad. Surprisingly there was no enthusiasm for being a bad guy so it fell to me to choose the two camps. This proved relatively easy as it happened. I started by considering who would not be suitable to be bad. I started with Dad. He always wanted to be the winning hero loved by the crowd so there was no way he would consider being bad, not in a million years. Next was Brent Haddon, perfectly groomed, mild mannered in every way and with a charming public school accent. Then came Phil Middleton, a new recruit, ex jockey, light framed, fresh faced, with blond hair. He just could not portray bad if he tried. Having got the main characters, it was a simple task of looking at people who were working together on jousting or foot fights and splitting them up into good or bad. Eventually I inherited a bunch of surly people to form the bad camp, all of whom believed that they had been downgraded. Some were so upset they considered leaving the show and quitting.

Thankfully everyone stayed and after a few shows we started to realise that the "boos" we got from the audience were in fact our applause and that drove us on to become even more despicable. By the end of the first month the boos overwhelmed the cheers. People were coming to see the Black Knight with his band of evil and treacherous followers. Part of our contract was that the main characters had to sign autographs on photographs of themselves that were sold in the castle gift shop. Very quickly I was signing double the number of photos than the good knights were signing. Suddenly the feeling of being second best vanished; the Bad Camp had become stars of the show. They now walked with a swagger and started to take on a different persona. Their hair was unkempt; they grew beards or skipped shaving to have stubble. In the show, they rubbed mud on their hands and faces. The more wicked and nasty we became the more the audience loved us.

However, playing the Black Knight did have its downsides. My first humiliation came at the hands of my black horse Charlie. I had taken to making my entrance into the arena at the gallop without holding the reins, my hands high above my head to take the acclaim from the audience. On this occasion, heavy rain had made the entrance very boggy. To improve this, we had spread straw over the affected area, nice bright yellow straw! As I entered at full gallop to the cheers of the crowd, my hands held high above my head, Charlie took a violent dislike to the bright yellow straw and stopped dead! I was catapulted straight over his head landing me face down in the mud. The cheering abruptly stopped and turned to laughter. To get up covered in mud, heavily winded and try to play a super baddy anti-hero was one of the hardest things I have ever had to do in my jousting career. The only positive about the whole episode was that, over the years many more show disasters would happen during jousting shows. This incident could always be drawn on to put things back into perspective.

Another similar incident occurred as we reached the climax and end of our show. The last fight was a poleaxe fight between the Black Knight and the leader of the good camp. It was usually a stunning fight, honed to perfection by performing it twice a day 7 days a week. The finale was for the good knight to hurl his pole axe from about 6 feet away straight into my stomach. I would catch the head of the pole axe just as it struck my body, double up and let out an agonising scream as I died. End of show! Good Knight wins to standing ovation.

However, this time we strode out to meet each other, the crowd cheering and booing. We came to the on-guard position to start the fight and I stamped my left foot forward. I'm not sure what happened but an excruciating pain seared into my knee. I screamed and fell on the ground clutching my knee. Steve Harrison who was playing the good knight, just stared open mouthed. He later told me he initially thought it was a prank I had thought up. Eventually as I was stretchered off and it slowly dawned on the audience and cast that it was a real accident. After a minute or so of stunned confusion the commentator brought the show to a muted end. No cheers, a few claps and the audience left muttering and shaking heads. The doctor thought I had probably stamped my left foot into a depression in the sand arena and partially dislocated my knee cap. Luckily with a bit of manipulation and some strapping I was fit for the next day's show, although very sore.

The poleaxe fight seemed to be jinxed because not long after the knee incident we got the ending horribly wrong. We never worked out what went wrong as is the case when dealing with split second timing. Steve threw the poleaxe at me but I failed to catch it. The poleaxe sailed through the air, and I suddenly realised at the last second I was not going to catch it. I dived to my left to try and avoid it but the point hit me high on my right arm. Luckily my dive sideways and backwards took some energy out of the impact but it pierced my bicep leaving a neat round entry wound like a bullet wound. Bandaged up I was back doing the next show but my nerve had gone for catching the poleaxe and so had Steve's for throwing it. As hard as we tried rehearsing we just couldn't make the ending work again. I think this was the first time I had to face the fact that I had lost my nerve. Taking steps to get it back was difficult and emotionally traumatic. It was during these tough painful times that I started to understand the process that must be gone through to regain your nerve. Little did I know then that I would use the techniques I learned at Gwrych much later in my life to help riders regain their nerve to ride or compete.

It was now well into the second month of our summer season and problems were building. First was the weather. It was the wettest season in Wales on memory. The regime of two shows a day seven days a week was taking its toll on both horses and riders. When we set out we had reserves both for days off and injuries. The horses started to get fed up with the impacts of lances on the rider which would pull on their mouths, also people falling off them with all the clatter of shields and lances was unnerving the horses. Many of the horses were refusing to move forward the start of the joust.

Injuries to the knights were mounting as well and we could no longer give people days off. Our battered bodies were not having time to recover. Trying to convince your brain to let you throw yourself off a horse at the gallop or get whacked across the chest with a sword when your body is in severe pain already, is not easy. This led to hesitations, minute but lethal, when performing stunts. It became a vicious circle - the more we hurt, the more accidents we had. So just a quarter of the way through our contract we had four major problems. Low visitor numbers, high injuries, horses that would not take part and very low morale. I felt like a First World War officer leading his troops over the top. "Come on lads we can do it, one last push, it will get better". It never did!!! The castle manager who understood our problems and we understood his problems was sacked. Crowd numbers were below expectations and building work for a restaurant and bar plus other essential renovations were way behind due to appalling weather in Wales. However, to make matters worse, the rest of the UK was having a drought and a heat wave. The constant horse and staff problems continued. Dad, always the horse dealer, was tasked with finding replacements and with a constant revenue stream, he was able to source replacements. However, finding horses that would do the job was not easy and took a lot of time. Dad also helped ease the staff shortages, by bringing himself and other members from Nottingham to work at Gwrych at weekends. This gave some of the walking wounded much needed time and rest to recover. However, the stress put on Dad was immense and although I didn't realise it at the time, I am now sure it was a major factor in him suffering a heart attack later that year.

Although things were difficult and stressful we did have lighter moments. One of the fun things we did on a regular basis was to ride the horses down to the local beach which was wild and deserted. It was a great relaxation for both horse and rider although it did have its own dangers. The Welsh coast is renowned for its big waves and even in midsummer they can be quite severe. One stormy day we had taken the horses down to beach and the waves were slightly higher than normal. When we entered the water the horses seemed unsteady on their feet. Too late, we realised that the big waves had created a strong under tow and decided that is would be safer to leave the water. As we started to make our way back onto the beach a large wave struck Phil Middleton's horse and completely flipped it over on its side. We all found this hugely funny until Phil didn't appear as the horse clambered out of the sea. We quickly jumped off our horses and waded out to where Phil went down. Thankfully his head bobbed up, and we were able to grab him. The under current was immense, and we really struggled to get him back to shore. Once we had hold of him we all started to laugh again but this was very short lived as it quickly became apparent Phil was in a lot of pain and unable to help himself out of the sea. When we had him safely on the beach I asked where it hurt. "Broke my f****ing leg, felt it snap" he announced in typical jockey matter of fact way. In those days, we didn't have mobile phones so someone had to ride bare back as fast as they could to the Castle which was about three quarters of a mile to call for an ambulance. It was about 45 minutes before the ambulance arrived and Phil was in a lot of pain. As the ambulance took Phil away it suddenly dawned on me the gravity of the situation. In less than an hour we had to do our first show of the day, we were still on the beach, and one of our main characters had a broken leg. We muddled through the show, but the castle manager was furious that we had lost one of our main characters and so banned us from taking the horses to the beach in future. Another nail in the coffin for fun!

During our first month at the castle we used to enjoy going down into Rhyl to eat drink and party but had to retreat from the town as our fame spread. I remember the first time being recognised and a cry of "Look it's the Black Knight" my heart skipped a beat. How wonderful it was for people to recognise me and I signed the autographs with relish. A few weeks later, battered, aching and exhausted in a restaurant drowning my sorrows in a bottle of red wine, the usual happened "look it's the Black Knight" and people approached the table for an autograph. I had tears welling up as I tried to summon up a smile and it was at that moment I knew fame was not for me. After that night, I never went back to Rhyl. Instead I used the local village pub the Pen-Y-Bont or travelled further afield to the Farm restaurant up in the mountains or to Colwyn Bay and Conway where we were still unknown.

Living in the castle was a rather spooky affair. It came with a long history of being haunted. Although I never came across a ghost personally, others told a different story. For me the castle was a typical Hammer House of Horror film set. At night, the only light came from a few old bare 60 watt light bulbs dangling high up in cavernous rooms. The hall and staircase were the worst. The staircase rose for 3 levels lit by a single light bulb, bats swooped past you as you walked up the stairs. At the bottom of the stairs in the entrance hall was a huge piece of furniture - jet black and covered with carvings of gargoyles and the devil.   It had a cold damp feel. Worst of all we had to climb the stairs every night on our way to bed. Stuck in the castle night after night with nothing to do, some of the troupe took to playing with a "Ouija board". Supposedly, it was possible to contact the spirits of the dead using the board and a glass with a finger of each participant placed on top. The idea was that you asked the spirit questions that were then replied to by the glass moving to spell out an answer. The session was to take place in the infamous round tower which had a long history of supposed ghost sighting. The group was a mixture of male and female. They had asked Lou and me to join them but I declined. However, Lou did later decide to go. They also persuaded Ty Benson, a solid Cornish Farrier in his late twenties, to take part as their protector, in case things went wrong. The story told consistently by the group after the session was that it started light-heartedly. "Is there anyone there?" etc. After about fifteen minutes the mood of the group suddenly became very tense. The movement of the glass became fierce and rapidly spelt out "you are not welcome". It was at this point that Lou decided to leave as she was getting really scared. Shortly after Lou left, Ty was suddenly thrown backwards out of his chair across the room. I still do not know to this day if this was a prank or the truth. However, Ty seemed to be genuinely shaken and had injured his arm.

Next morning, we had another even stranger incident. I was called from my bed early next morning by the castle manager. He was a good guy and we got on well. When I asked his assistant, what was so urgent he became very evasive and just said "the manager will explain". As I came down the marble staircase I noticed a bright light at the bottom of the stairs lighting up the hall. The light came from large opening in the wall, the early morning sunlight streaming in. As I got closer I realised that the hole was in fact a doorway. I must have walked past it every day but it was never used and blended in with interior of the hall. Passing through the doorway I was met on the small outside lawn by the castle manager and the building works manager. In front of them was a heavy oak door with a pointed top that matched the vaulted door opening. I assumed that they were about to start a new phase of the refurbishments and wanted my input regarding safety when passing through the hall. "So, what are we up to today?" I cheerfully greeted them. "It's more what you lot have been up to", replied the works manager. Bemused I asked him what he meant. He explained that his workmen had found the door laid flat on the lawn when they started work first thing that morning and that the jousters had obviously done it as a drunken prank. For a moment, I was stunned with shock. If this was true then the jousters were in serious trouble, this was a major act of vandalism. I thought back to last night, we had all returned from the pub together just before midnight. We were all tired and had two more shows to do the next day. There had been no mention of a nightcap in someone's room, everyone had just wanted to get their heads down. I relayed that to the managers but added I would immediately gather everyone together to find out if anyone knew or had heard of anything. As I said this I was subconsciously studying the door and stone frame. A year as a jobbing builder with my brother-in-law Bert had given me enough knowledge to confidently make a comment.

The door was big and very heavy. Two people would have struggled to lift it. The hinges were heavy blacksmith made and rusted solid. The lock appeared to be the same. The hinge hooks had been built into the stone work. It was the hinge hooks that had been ripped out of the stonework thus freeing the lock from the stonework. When I mentioned this the works manager immediately nodded in agreement. I might just have an ally. The castle manager also had construction knowledge and became more amenable. I suggested we look for clues of how this huge door had been ripped from the stonework. We all agreed that great force was needed to break the hinges out of the stonework, which was sound and in good order. We also agreed that the two most likely ways to achieve this were either to sledgehammer the door hinges from inside or to chisel the hinges from outside and then force the door with crowbars. Both methods would leave damage and tell-tale marks. We carefully examined the hinges and found no marks on the door or frame. We spent another ten minutes trying to come up with other ideas, but the only other plausible idea was that it had been winched off but there were no signs of this either. I said I would gather the troupe together and make enquiries. As I expected they were as bemused as me. They were resentful of being suspects but also some were frightened after what had happened to Ty Benson. Many were beginning to believe that the castle was haunted by an evil presence. When I reported my findings to Castle Manager I think he had had similar thoughts. He decided it would be in the best interest of everyone if we "forgot" about it as there was no logical explanation how it could have happened.

Again, to this day I have no idea how or why it happened.

As the season wore on we honed our acting skills and discovered how easy it was to deceive the audience. My romance with Lou blossomed and although still at college she would make the long arduous train journey from Nottingham to Abergele most Friday nights to spend a very short weekend with me. On Lou's first trip up to Wales she got stranded at Abergele station. This was the era of British Rail and punctuality was not it's best point. Lou was only 17 years old, so I had arranged with her to phone the Castle when she arrived and I would pop down to pick her up. It was just a ten minutes' drive to the station. Unfortunately, when Lou phoned the Castle the manager's secretary answered the phone. She was pompous, self-important and hated the jousters. She told Lou that I was in a meeting and it was far too important for me to be disturbed. Poor Lou was stranded in a strange place with no way of getting in touch with me. Luckily, being a small station the station manager quickly noticed a young girl left alone on his platform. He was horrified about what had happened and took pity on Lou. He phoned the Castle again and demanded to speak to the manager saying he had a stranded young girl at his station and that there would be trouble if she was not collected immediately. This message got through and I was dispatched post-haste to collect her, important meeting or not. When Lou's college finished in mid-June she moved up to Gwrych permanently where we happily lived and worked together. That was, until Lou returned from her required once a week phone call home to report that she was ok. She returned with a mortified look. Her parents were coming to visit her next weekend.

Lou had a rocky relationship with her parents. They held to fifties morals and values. They were keen golfers who always adhered to the jacket and tie dress code of the clubhouse. Lou's father also loved his cars, always the latest model, waxed and polished inside and out. Lou hated golf, hated school and just lived for riding and horses. She was happy to spend her days in jodhpurs and jeans. Having grown up in the 1960's her life values were from another planet. They had no idea we were living together.

We hatched a plan for Lou to meet them (I would be too busy organising the show) give them a quick whizz around the shops in the castle and then get them onto especially reserved seats in the grandstand. Lou was part of the show as all the squires were girls dressed in very short costumes and black tights styled on the female handsome prince in pantomime. That might come as a bit of a shock but hey it's theatre! That took care of the afternoon, then an early evening meal with them and my Dad. Then pack them off back to Nottingham. They arrived early, as was her father's mantra was to always arrive 15 minutes early for an appointment. The first thing they wanted to see was where their beloved daughter was living in this magnificent Castle. Lou always quick thinking, explained because they were early she still had very important things to do before the show started. Why didn't they have a look at the shops and craft stalls? She would be back as quick as she could as soon as she finished these very important jobs.

She dashed round to find me and tell me I had 10 minutes to get every trace of me out of our room as her parents were coming to inspect. I did suggest we just tell them we were living together but she said the shock would either kill them or if not her father may well kill me. A gang of friends, mainly girls, were quickly summoned and any sign of my presence removed. Within 10 minutes the bedroom was a perfect tidy girl's room. The room was inspected and passed with flying colours. Thankfully the rest of the day went without a hitch.

As our acting skills improved we found that if we showed confidence, we could convince the audience that something had happened when, in actual fact had not. My persona as the Black Knight grew and I started to develop more and more evil, fiendish things to taunt the audience with.

The first stunt we perfected was the kick in the opponent's balls. As I lay on my back supposedly defeated the good knight would chivalrously ask me to yield. As he stood over me legs splayed either side of my body I would deliver a vicious kick to what appeared to be his groin. The good knight would scream in agony and double up in pain whilst I quickly defeated him to loud boos from the audience. I had, in fact, pulled the kick at the last minute, missed the groin completely and delivered a light kick up to the buttocks.

The second trick involved a glove. The fingers were filled with round wood to make it look like the hand was in glove. There was a metal bar fixed across the palm area so that you could hold the glove without having your fingers in the glove. I would defeat the opponent and he would cry out, "I yield!". I would ignore the yield and announce I wanted to hear him squeal. I would then place the false hand on top of the jousting barrier (the lists) and one by one crush the false fingers with my sword.

Every time the sword came down my opponent would writhe violently letting out a blood curdling scream. This drove the audience wild. However, it was so convincing that several members of the audience passed out and needed medical attention. Because of this we eventually withdrew the stunt from the show.

 The third stunt was like the false hand. It involved a dagger that we made from a large syringe and some flattened stainless pipe that was formed into a pointed blade. A thin tube connected the syringe which was the dagger handle to the point of the blade. I would disarm my opponent, grab him by the hair and drag him to the lists with him facing the audience. I would announce that I was going to spoil his pretty face. I then dragged the point of the dagger down the side of his face. As the point slowly moved down his face I was pressing the syringe full of false blood so that it left a blood trail down his face. The audience were convinced I had sliced his face with the dagger and would go wild screaming obscenities at me whilst my opponent staggered off screaming and clutching his face.

This stunt backfired on me badly one day when after the show, I was doing the usual half hour autograph signing when I was suddenly assailed by a lady wielding a large handbag. She beat me from head to foot with great ferocity whilst screaming that I was an evil lout. Did I not realise, that I had scarred that lovely young boy's face for life? I think this was the best but most painful compliment I ever received for my acting!

When the theatre director came, and gave us advice, he explained that no matter how heavy the subject matter you still need lighter elements to break it up. Watching knights trying to kill each other is exciting. However, after an hour of only that, it gets boring. To solve this, he came up with two comedy sketches.

The first was a short sketch of less than five minutes. It was entitled "Dreadful David Dabbles his master's Dishes". After a big build-up, Squire David would appear with a stick and plate. He would be helped up onto the top of the jousting lists which were about 6" wide. After a few deliberate wobbles, he got his balance. Then balancing the plate on the end of the stick, he would spin the plate on the end of the stick. As soon as he had exacted a round of applause from the audience he would take a bow, letting the stick go down with his body to reveal that the plate was nailed to the stick. He would then be chased from the arena by his furious master accompanied by hoots of laughter from the audience.

The second sketch was longer and much more elaborate and was entitled St. George and the Dragon. The Dragon was fantastic. Built in London by a Theatre props company it was 24 feet long and built on a lightweight wooden frame covered with canvas just like the way that early aeroplanes were made. The head was a true work of art like the Chinese dragons used to welcome in their New Year. A man would get into the belly of the dragon and use a harness to suspend the dragon on his shoulders. His head would fit into one of the large fins on the dragon's back with discreet holes cut to see where he was going. On his legs, he wore a pair of padded trousers painted to look like the dragon's legs complete with clawed feet. Once inside, the puppeteer could move the dragon easily and open and close its mouth via a rope and pulleys.

He could even make smoke come out of his mouth by blowing cigarette smoke down a tube. It was beautifully painted with green scales, life-like eyes, red tongue and gleaming white teeth.

We took George and The Dagon on tour with us for many years after Gwrych until he finally fell apart. Below is the actual script used for the sketch which I found in a box labelled "very old jousting shows "St. George and the Dragon".

"Now I am sure you are well acquainted with the famous English folk legend of St. George and The Dragon. However, in our travels we have become acquainted with an older and more original version, which we feel has a ring of truth about it.

Once upon a time in the medieval passes of Snowdonia, lived a loveable but lazy dragon. His name was Glyndwr. He was a very wicked and very Welsh Dragon. He was also a valiant and noble Dragon, renowned for his patriotic pride.

He loved his native Wales and used to gleefully flop around the countryside. But he was also a very sad dragon. You see he had never fought a duel with a Knight over a damsel in distress for you see he was also a very shy Dragon, the reason being he hadn't got a mate. He often searched for talent in the local tilt-yards but whenever the Lords and Ladies arrived he would hurry away to hide behind the tilt.

(As the commentator described the dragon's character the dragon mimicked the description)

Now one day, came all the way from heathen England, a winsome knight called George. His title was inherited, and of it he was not worthy. It fact so lacking was he in courage that he could not even ride a horse, but shouldering his lance, he'd prance around the tiltyard on foot. George came to Wales thinking he could mislead the inhabitants with tales of his successes at the tournaments at Tewksbury, and so enhance his reputation.

One day he happened upon our tiltyard shortly after the crowds had left, and just as Glyndwr emerged from hiding. Thus, they came face to face. In his panic and terror George nervously started to laugh and leapt into action, immediately retreated and tried to climb the tilt. Thus, they began their fight until finally Glyndwr became accidentally entangled on the end of George's lance. That is of course, how they have always been pictured. The English version stated that St. George was thrusting his lance into the dragon's throat, but we know slightly differently. The truth is that Glyndwr was establishing himself as the symbol of the Welsh National Heritage, their honour, and their patriotic pride. Your support please, for our noble dragon and our bold St. George."

Nobody who worked the season at Gwrych left the same as when they arrived, it affected everyone differently. Some came as kids and left adults. Some found drugs others alcohol, others sex. Lou and I found good food and fine wine. We were all earning well over the national average wage, so we could all afford to buy whatever we needed to help get us through the hell of jousting seven days a week, week after week. When I mention drugs, it was only marijuana that was "grown locally" in the mountains. The main supplier was the "Potter" who had a craft shop at the castle. He even made a special dish for communal pot-smoking with bowls for the pot and another for tobacco, even holders for the cigarette papers. These special dishes were one of his best sellers at the craft shop. I remember a group of long haired, bearded builders working at the castle who smoked pot constantly and walked around with polyethylene bags of the drug hanging from their belts. Little wonder they were behind schedule with the building work! As the season wore on more and more of the troupe started to lunch at the pub to tank up for the afternoon shows. Looking back now I can understand pop groups who suddenly make it big time, going on a world tour, fitting in recording schedules and doing constant public relations appearances taking drugs or alcohol kept them going through the stress and utter exhaustion.

My best friend Brian gave up his job as a printing engineer at Boots to come to Wales. He couldn't ride well enough to take a full part as a knight but was great at stunt falls. His party piece was to fall flat on his face onto a concrete floor with both hands folded flat across his chest. We used to sit him on a horse dressed as a knight, whack the horse on the backside and send him full gallop down the tilt. He only had to stay on 4 or 5 strides until the opposing knight blitzed him with his lance sending him to on his way to a stunning crashing fall. Brian had always enjoyed drinking and wooing the opposite sex and always used to leave me in second place in both departments. I asked him once how he managed to pull so many girls. "Simple" he replied "I ask them to dance then ask them if they fancy a shag?". "How do you manage to get away with that" I asked "I would be killed if I said that to a girl". "Oh, I don't. Most slap me across the face and storm off, but usually somewhere during the night one will say yes ok". "You just have to go through a bit of pain to get there". Earning wages of four to five times what he earned at Boots and local star fame, allowed Brian to go into overdrive in both indulgences. He drove an old Ford Consul because it had a generous back seat; it's sides were thoroughly battered from trying to negotiate the narrow stone gatehouse into the castle after a long night on the town. His capacity for consuming alcohol was legendary. But he could sleep it off very often not waking until after noon. This meant I often had to go and shake him awake ready for the first show of the day. Brian had a unique waking ritual. After being shaken and struck to the point of physical assault he would eventually come around from a state of unconsciousness. His first reaction was to search the bedside table for his cigarettes - light one up and disappear under the bed clothes. Approximately one minute later he would emerge from under the bed clothes coughing and choking, then grasp the half-drunk drink he had left the night before (usually gin and tonic or dry martini) and neck it down in one, followed by a growl. Brian was now fit to face the day! His performance in the show was always impeccable, so we overlooked his indulgences. However, he did push it a bit too much a few times. Once after a good night out he uncharacteristically locked his bedroom door. After 30 minutes of banging on his door without response we broke down the door with an axe. Another time they had not returned from the lunchtime pub session so I phoned and asked the landlord to turf them out as it was nearly time for our first show of the day. When they arrived more lubricated than usual I was told that Brian had achieved a lunchtime record by drinking twenty-one gin and tonics. Although he started the show he passed out halfway through.

As I mentioned earlier Dad was still touring doing shows back at Nottingham and Brian would leave Gwrych every now and then to work with Dad. Also, Dad would come up to Gwrych to help us out when he had time. Dad and Brian were great buddies and got up to all sorts of adventures. Dad was renowned for his rages and fiery temper. However, such was their close friendship, that when Brian borrowed his new minivan, for a night out on the town and wrote it off returning home, instead of exploding into a rage, he merely commented "That's a shame! I really liked that car but I suppose someone will lend me a car to get around while I'm up here".

So, the season finally ground to an end. After the August Bank holiday numbers dropped from thousands to less than fifty per show. The weather worsened again, "bucketing" it down with rain and eventually making the arena unusable. We performed our last show to about 20 people on the small tarmac terrace. We had nothing left and were merely going through the motions to fulfil our contractual obligations.

Behind the scenes, relations with Scotia Investments were becoming more and more fraught. Yet another castle manager was removed without warning. Our monthly payments for the shows were getting later and later. Invoices were being sent back with queries such as how many phone calls we had made via the castle phone etc. Looking back with hindsight we should have seen what was coming but at that moment we were very busy with everyday problems such as shortages of serviceable horses, staff wanting to leave, and our naivety to the ways of big business. By the time we finished the contract, we were still owed £16,000, a huge sum even in today's money, which left us worse off than when we started. Although we started to try to recover what was owed through the courts we were advised that on investigating the company it was one of many companies in a shadowy international group and it would cost more to recover than the debt itself. As we had no money ourselves we had to bitterly accept defeat.

As we said our goodbyes to the troupe we all realised it was the end of a very special era in our lives, but we were also glad it was over and that we were leaving the castle and Wales. The Welsh locals had been openly hostile towards us all season. We never made any Welsh friends. I have never kept in contact with any of the people I lived and worked so closely with for 16 weeks except those who came with me from Bunny Hill.

Dad's Shows

Although I have already mentioned briefly that Dad and the founding members of the Nottingham Jousting Association continued to do other shows, it was not until I spoke to Brian Hinksman about the Preston Guild show during my research, that I discovered that he had been present at all the other shows that year. He gave me valuable accounts of the shows performed by the second troupe.

Preston Guild celebrations take place once every 20 years and date back to the reign of Henry the Second in the 12th century. Originally, they were to celebrate the next generation of guild members being admitted to the Guild. The Guild was abolished in the 1700's but the celebrations have continued to present day and attract famous artists from around the world to perform at these events. Each new Guild tries to outdo the previous one, often with ground breaking performances. The 1972 Guild was no exception. As part of the week-long celebrations they decided to stage the musical "Camelot" with a special twist. The jousting and sword fighting scenes would take place front of stage using real horses and knights! Dad and Brian spent the week there doubling for the main characters. Brian still feels it was one of the best shows he has ever done to this day. Beside the rapturous response from the audience and press, there was a lot of after show partying that suited the dynamic duo down to the ground. Even to this day Brian is very coy about what they got up to. This show along with all the other shows they performed that year came out of London, often with the help of Sir Trevor Lloyd–Hughes, and although not large in number of knights they were all top-drawer, blue-ribbon events. The second troupe consisted of Dad, Brian Hinksman, Brent Haddon, George Rayns, with Brent's wife Gail and girls from the stables acting as squires/grooms. One of Brian's foremost memories of that year was Dad and him having their pictures taken with two topless models at the Ideal Home Exhibition for a national newspaper. The jousters had achieved celebrity status and everyone wanted a slice of us that year. Dad and the second troupe were travelling far and wide.

Their next show took them deep into Scotland to the Royal Burgh of Irvine. No mean feat in an ancient rusting Bedford TK Horsebox. The Burgh was celebrating its 600-year anniversary and was home to the famous Eglington Jousting Tournament that was held in 1839. For more info on this: - search *The Eglington tournament 1839*

Again, hotel and food were all included. A novel experience for the early 1970s! Next on the list it was back to London for a joint tournament with Max Diamond at Syon Park. I didn't realise what a major coup this tournament was until I started to research this book. Syon Park is the London Stately Home of the Duke of Northumberland set in a 200-acre park that runs down to the banks of the River Thames opposite Kew Gardens. (Go to: - *http://www.syonpark.co.uk)* Not only was it an extremely prestigious venue but it was also another ground-breaking event as it was the first-ever jousting tournament to be held at night using floodlights. The floodlights were ex-Army and very bright. Unfortunately, they placed the lights at either end of the arena blinding the knights as they charged each other! The knights involved were Dad, George Rayns, Brent Haddon and Brian Hinksman.

The final show of the season for the 2nd troupe was the jewel in the crown for Dad. It was The Royal International Horse Show. An event that every horseman dreams of riding at. It was at this event, run with military precision so that it could be shown live on television, that we had to adapt our equipment to set up and be cleared away in a matter of minutes. This was something that became our trade mark along with starting and finishing a show to exactly the minute. This enabled us to secure lots more big shows along with Film and TV appearances in the future.

CHAPTER 3   Making Friends and Learning Lessons 1973-74

We arrived back at Bunny in mid-September and at first nothing seemed to have changed, we were back home; something we had been longing for.

But the reality was, it caused as many problems as it solved.

Lou went back to live with her parents whilst we found somewhere to live. Eventually we found a flat in West Bridgford but Lou couldn't stay overnight night because her parents still had no idea that we had been living together in Wales. I don't think it went down very when Lou finally got up the courage to tell them but eventually our relationship got back on track. However, I don't think her parents were over the moon about the situation!

Graham and I had no job, although we had earned enough to tide us by for a while. Dad, had suffered a heart attack from the stress of keeping us supplied in Wales with horses, weapons and men. We all knew that to go back to Wales for a second season was financial, mental and physical suicide. Graham had most to lose as he had quit his job at Ford. Dad and I could scrape a living with the riding school although that was the last thing I really wanted to do. I toyed with setting up a weapons and costume business to supply other medieval groups from the contacts and skills we had developed over the last two years. Dad was happy to go back to the riding school and horse dealing. However, it was Graham who pushed the idea that we could still make a living from jousting and announced he would go off to London to try for shows for the following year. He also convinced us that with his accountancy skills he could turn the stables into a profitable business. By the beginning of 1973 the offers were starting to come in from London and locally. Graham had negotiated a large bank loan on our behalf based on the Gwrych turnover of last year to buy us three new ford Cortina estates and a long wheel base transit van (just like all the pop groups had) which he had managed to purchase from Ford direct at discount prices. His reasoning was, if we are going to get people to book us, we had to look confident and successful. He had a point, however it took us nearly twenty years to pay off the loan and get back into the black.

The jousting association was starting to change also. Except for Brian, Brent and me, the other founding members were in their late forties and had joined an association that was going to give demonstrations or friendly competitions of jousting. Those of us who had worked in Wales wanted to carry on the action-packed stage show we had developed. Most of the founders were horsemen not actors. The thought of acting and working to a script was abhorrent to them. So, they wished us luck and bowed out.

During the past two years, we had had loads of local and national publicity and a younger generation were knocking at the door desperate for a slice of the action and limelight. The first show we did in 1973 was the London Lord Mayor's Easter

Parade. It was one of Graham's marketing ideas to get us national publicity. You had to pay to take part in it. The parade started early in the morning from one of the parks - I think it was Hyde Park. We left in the middle of the night. It was cold, wet, and very slow. When we finally reached the end of the parade we were all chilled to the bone and our bums were raw from sitting on chainmail for hours. Never Again!

The next show was another low earner. It was at my father's home village of Ravensthorpe in Northamptonshire and although it was only a small village show we were treated like royalty. We all had a great weekend despite Dad ranting and raving wanting everything to be perfect as we were performing in front of his family and friends. It was also the show where my two brothers made their first appearance in the show at the ages of 11 and 12 years old.

1973 was an important year for making new contacts and friends. So, important were these people that we worked with them for the next thirty plus years until I retired. The first person was Terry Goulden. We had briefly met him at the Battle Abbey Tournament in 1971 where he performed a quarterstaff fight dressed as an Errol Flynn" Robin Hood ". The Battle show had inspired him to branch out from his quirky archery shop called "Art & Archery" into becoming a promoter of grand medieval events. His first major event was a two-day show in the town of Hertford. He brought together many different medieval groups for the show including, much to our surprise, another jousting Troupe, "The Knights of Arkley" who also became lifelong friends and rivals. We all camped on site and got along very well together. I think it was helped along by some serious drinking around campfires. The show was loosely based on King Arthur with Knights fighting Vikings.

Although we did a jousting competition against the Arkleys, and the Vikings also did their own show we were also going to do a joint show. The idea was that the Vikings would show off their skills by forming a shield wall that was supposed to be capable, of repelling a charge from the knights. The rehearsal started well with knights galloping in and arraying themselves ready for battle. The 50 or so Vikings, after waving their swords and chanting threats, duly formed their interlocking shield wall. The knights prepared to make their charge, first at walk, lances held upright. The shield wall started to quiver! At about 60 yards we began to trot. The shield wall started to shake violently! At 50 yards, we lowered our lances. The shield wall collapsed, all we could see through our visors were Vikings running, throwing down their weapons and helmets. They went over the fence and through the stands as fast as they could, many never to be seen again. That bit of the show never happened! The Saturday show was a great success and we all hit the town to celebrate Knights and Vikings all merrily together. We hooked up with a Viking who seemed to have an even bigger appetite for beer than us. Somewhere along the night we lost him as we went from pub to pub.

As Brian and I drove back into the campsite, something very large jumped onto our bonnet. After what were probably only a few milliseconds we realised that we had a long haired naked man crouched on our bonnet grasping the windscreen wipers. Not only was he naked but he was also painted from head to foot with weird blue markings; it was something like you would see in a horror film! Brian braked hard and then accelerated swerving from side to side, finally throwing the beast off the car along with both windscreen wipers. We jumped out of the car and gave chase. As we approached the campfire and tents he came rushing towards us wielding a gas lantern which he hit Brian over the head with. He struck him with such force that the gas canister split causing liquid gas to spay everywhere and knocked Brian out cold. Just at that moment about 20 people arrived at the run like a hue and cry and overpowered him. Apparently, he had been running amok in the camp like a wild animal attacking people and trashing tents. The police arrested him and took him away. It was the nice friendly guy we had been drinking with earlier.

Brian spent most of the night in hospital and we had to go to Hertford Central Police station next morning 9 am sharp to give witness statements. Apparently, the guy had been on medication for a kidney problem and was told under no circumstances to drink alcohol. The booze had caused him to hallucinate. He believed he was a Viking Berserker. Berserkers were naked warriors who painted themselves with blue woad. They took drugs which they believed made them invisible and so were impossible to kill. The Vikings used them as shock troops, their appearance frightened the enemy and they would hurl themselves on the enemy fighting like demons with no fear of death. A night out to remember!

Our next show was the start of another long relationship that has lasted off and on for four decades. The show was Heckington Agricultural Show near Sleaford, just a small village that has an old fashioned agricultural show that attracts thousands of visitors every year. They loved us then and continue to give us a warm and rapturous reception every time they have rebooked us over the last forty years. We love their show as much as they love our show.

Again, the next show was something small but led to greater things later. The show was Scarborough. It was just a medieval banquet and they wanted some sword fights as entertainment. It was something we had never done before but I thought, why not, and took the job. The event was a great success even though I stabbed Clive Broadbent during one of the fights. It's a wonder we didn't have more accidents!

As part of the show we joined the banquet and then started the fight as an argument at the table at the end of the banquet. It was a very raucous affair with free wine and ale flowing all night. By the time, we started our fights we had all drunk, 5 or 6 pints but so had everyone else so no one noticed how wobbly we were. In fact, they were most impressed that we could eat and drink so much and then put on such a fine display. It would be a few years until the contacts I made in Scarborough paid dividends, but pay they did!

Our final event of the season was a very prestigious one organised by Graham Lucking. The show was for his former employer Ford Motor Company. It was their 3-day summer fair held at Bramcote Army Barracks just north of Birmingham.

The shows were very well received although we were driven mad by the red tape involved when working on an active Army base. The lessons I learnt from Bramcote were to stand me in good stead for working with other military establishments. We camped on the base for four days and although the days were intense we let our hair down every night at the Blue Pig at Wolvey. At this time, wives and girlfriends were still involved in the show. On the last night, we were thoroughly fed-up with all the military restrictions and other problems. So, after getting well and truly drunk in the Blue Pig we decided to have a competition between lads and lasses over the army's assault course. It was a wonder we weren't all killed. The course was a lot harder than we had imagined (attempting it in dark and being somewhat inebriated didn't help). Brian or possibly Clive got hung upside down in a net fifteen foot above the ground and then fell into water nearly drowning. It was a wonder no one had a heart-attack. Another great jousting night-out just like Hertford.

During the Bramcote event something happened that still haunts me today. It showed up just how naive I and the rest of us were to the ways of the world. At the beginning of the event Graham approached me and suggested that to get more such events, it would be a good idea to invite the Ford people organising the event up to the Riding Club back at Bunny for a night out where they could let their hair down away from their bosses. The Riding Clubroom had been a regular weekend nightclub until we went to Wales and we still used it for parties and discos. So, on the middle evening of the event we all trekked back to Bunny Hill for the party. None of us were really looking forward to it. We had invited some friends to fill up the room and girlfriends had made some food. A night with the jousters had been promised and we always kept our word.

The Ford people, about ten of them arrived with a self-important swagger. The first words uttered were, "is this it then?" We fixed them up with drinks and apologised that we didn't do the unheard-of cocktails that they demanded. We tried to be friendly and Graham went around making introductions, but they just stood in a huddle looking down their noses at us and the clubroom. It was not going well! After a few more free drinks things got a lot worse. One of them asked a girl to dance. Nothing wrong with that - they were our guests. When he got onto the dance floor he started to grope and fondle the girl. The girl quickly disengaged herself at the end of the record but things became very tense. It looked highly likely that our employers were going to get their teeth kicked in. I grabbed Graham and told him this was his do and to sort his friends out quickly before the local lads did! But it was too late the Ford group were all trying to grope girls as they came up to the bar. I was really worried. It's another story, but we had been forced to close the nightclub nearly two years ago, after a mass brawl that ended in a year-long court case. We nearly lost our bar licence. Any more trouble and that was it; the court had made it very plain. It was the girls that calmed things down. They said we were to leave it to them, that they could look after themselves and there'd be no need for violence if we got rid of them as soon as possible. We primed the DJ to start winding things down at twenty past ten. The girls stayed together and fended off the constant attempts to grope them. The men were treating the girls as if they were prostitutes! At 10:30 on the dot we cleared the place and shut down explaining to the Ford people we had very strict licensing around this area with regular police checks. The mention of police seemed to calm them down and encourage them to getaway as fast as they could. I breathed a big sigh of relief. They never showed their faces for the rest of the show and thankfully we never saw them again.

I am still bitter to this day about what happened and it soured my relationship with Graham and was the beginning of the end of Graham's involvement with the jousting. It was also the end of our London connection! It seemed everything we were involved with that emanated from London always left us with a sour taste.

The last big event of the season was my marriage to Lou at the end of September. I was 22 years old and Lou 18 years old. We had already experienced more life, both good and bad than people ten years our senior. We believed we had old heads on young shoulders and were on our way. We went on honeymoon to Ibiza 10 days for £39!! It was the first time I had been on a plane and the first time I had left the country. Another milestone was that we both gave up smoking. This was defiantly one of the better decisions I have made in my life!

Looking back, 1973 was the beginning of the touring jousting show that we still boast forty years on down the road. It has changed with the styles of each generation and matured slowly like a good wine. During the winter of 1973 I went in search of a Theatrical Agent to find us shows. To my surprise, I found one on our doorstep in Nottingham. It was called Temple's show and Gala Agency. After an initial telephone conversation, I was summoned to a personal interview at the company office. Dressed in my best suit, armed with a briefcase full of letters of thanks, photos, and past shows, I set off to meet "The Agent". In my mind, I had this vision of a quick talking stressed go-getter with two telephones just like the movies. When I arrived at the address it was a nice house in a well-to-do suburb of Nottingham. I was greeted by a demure grey haired lady who invited me into her lounge, sat me down and promptly disappeared. She reappeared about 5 minutes later armed with a tray of biscuits and tea. It was served in fine bone china and the biscuits on matching plates. We chatted over several cups of tea for about an hour and I left as a new member of the Agency. Although Mrs Temple retired many years ago, it remained a family business and I worked with them until I retired.

I'm mentioning every show of 1974 because, something happened at each of these shows which affected the performances and the way we did business in the future. The year 1974 was the blue print for the next 30 years. Our first show of the season was provided by Temples. It was at Cherry Hinton Hall, Cambridge. A beautiful venue which these days is the home to the world-famous Cambridge Folk Festival. The show was well attended and we went down a storm. We had trained hard during the spring and the new riders of last season had grown in confidence, putting on a stunning show. One of the main characters now was Steve Harrison who came with many talents. He was a good rider and between shows he worked at the stables, a brilliant swordsman, very at home acting in front of an audience and also a good jousting commentator. The reason he was so at home in front of an audience was he was the lead singer in an up and coming pop group. The success of his pop career eventually took him away from us. Some years later I met Steve at a point to point race in Oxfordshire where I was riding. It turned out the group's success was short lived and the pop world not to his liking. He was back working with horses again but this time with race horses.

Another recruit was Tony Edwards. Tony had just left the cavalry; he was a dashing horseman and a natural showman. He was also a great charmer, full of passion and enthusiasm. The ladies loved him! He took the role of second in command to the Black Knight and was called Sir Anthony D'Argentine because of the silver streaks in his hair (Argent is the Heraldic word for silver). Over the next few years he was going to have a big impact on our show.

So, at the beginning of 1974 the line-up of knights was as follows.

Commentator: - Graham Lucking

The Good End: -

Dad -Robert of Sherwood

Steve Harrison - Stephen of Bosworth.

Clive Broadbent - Guy of Goscote.

The Bad End: -

Sam Humphrey - Black Knight.

Tony Edwards - Anthony D'Agentine

Brian Hinksman - Frederick of Flawforth.

Characters were beginning to develop. Brian had changed his character from a young knight with a chip on his shoulder to a slightly tipsy jovial character who was building a sizeable group of supporters at every show. His falls were spectacular. Tony on the other hand played the "cad," smiling and courteous to The Knight Marshal but doing dastardly foul deeds as soon as the Marshal wasn't looking. He also was attracting regular supporters. Steve on the other hand played the epitome of a good chivalrous knight again attracting a sizeable group of supporters. The show was changing from the simple White Knight versus Black Knight to a much more rounded sophisticated show, and the public loved it.

After a busy May Bank holiday, we set off to what we thought was just another parochial show organised by Ashby de la Zouch Round Table.

Ashby is only a small market town but it is the place where Sir Walter Scott set the jousting tournament in his world-famous book "Ivanhoe". Regional television was just getting going with both the BBC and ATV launching a Midlands regional news service. Both picked up on the connection and broadcasted pieces on us recreating the Ivanhoe joust. Many regional newspapers also picked up on the theme - most importantly the Birmingham papers, which is only 20 miles from Ashby. The Round Table had optimistically printed

10,000 tickets. They sold out before lunchtime and still they flooded in! Luckily it was on a huge site. No one knows how many people came but all they could say was over 20,000. Newspapers claimed 40,000! People were still coming in at 5 pm. We left that show totally overwhelmed it was our biggest show ever.

What nobody knew was that the show nearly never happened. I had had spoken with organisers of two events for that date and told them we were available but nothing was finalised. I had just agreed terms with Ashby when promoters of the other show rang saying that they had all their posters printed and they were looking forward to us performing at their event. They had just taken it as read that everything was settled. I had the unenviable task of informing them that we had taken another booking. It didn't go down well and I felt awful. I realised that we needed to change the way we did business. Except for the big shows everything was done verbally on the phone and we hardly ever met the organisers until the day of the show. We had already had some problems with arenas and PA systems because organisers had misunderstood our requirements. I decided on a set of rules that were costly but very effective. I decided to visit every show personally and meet the organisers before taking a booking. Every show would have a signed contract outlining all the points agreed at the meeting. Often shows could not confirm a show immediately until they had had full committee meetings or gained police approval. I agreed that I would hold the show for them until the contract was signed. If another party wanted that date before the contract was signed, then they would have 24 hours to sign or lose the show.

Although this meant travelling up and down the country on an ever-increasing scale making presentations to committees, it had many bonuses. The main one was that that we got more bookings. Time and again, chairmen told me what had swayed the committee to have such a big expensive attraction was that I had taken the trouble to come and meet them personally. I also knew exactly where the site was, where to park, what the organisers looked like and so could smooth out any show day problems quickly. I used this format for the next 30 years and it served me well, bringing in lots of repeat bookings. As if to reinforce this our next show was a Temples Agency booking at Harwarden Castle in North Wales, the ancestral home of the great Victorian Prime Minister, William Ewart Gladstone.

When we arrived at the castle gate the horsebox was too high to fit through and the show site was half a mile away (should have done a site visit!). We eventually scraped through after letting most of the air out of the lorry tyres and with all the jousters hanging onto the back of the ramp to pull down the lorry an extra couple of inches. Again, the show was well attended and a great success.

The troupe was becoming a well-oiled machine!

The next show was at Ruddington - a large village just 3 miles from Bunny Hill; Brian's home village. Although we had achieved national success hardly anyone locally had seen us in action since 1970, and we were keen to show off in front of our friends. So, we did the show for less than half price, something that did not go down well with some of the members including Graham the commentator who all refused to perform for less money. To our amazement, Brian announced he would take over the commentary for the day. Dad and his stallion stole the show and covered up the cracks caused by missing characters. The important thing was although we didn't realise it at the time, we had found our new commentator.

Our next show was without doubt the most important show we ever did. Like so many things in this story it very nearly didn't happen. I had sent out a circular to local castles and historical sites saying that we were keen to perform at these sorts of venues. Belvoir castle replied and asked me to come for a meeting. I met a gentleman who was effectively the castle manger but had a weird job title of Comptroller that I had never heard of. His name was Mr Meek. He was a very correct gentleman of the old school; tweed suit, bow tie and wire rimmed spectacles. His attitude towards me was like a Lord listening to a serf's humble request. He referred to the Duke of Rutland as "Himself ". Having been invited, I had expected to be met by an enthusiastic supporter. Far from it. I soon realised he was looking for reasons not to do a show and that it was the Duke who was the supporter. During the meeting, I took a bold decision. Mr Meek didn't want jousting; he thought it too down market but had to have the ammunition to justify this to the Duke. So, I changed my sales pitch. Was Belvoir Castle big enough to accommodate us as we attracted such large crowds? Instead of selling our show, I focused on practicalities. Did they have a large enough car park? Where could we put the horses? Was there enough access for the public? I also made it clear I would write to the Duke personally outlining the reasons why we could not perform at the Castle. He started to change tack. Perhaps they could do this or that to accommodate us. Inwardly I breathed a huge sigh of relief. I desperately wanted Belvoir Castle. I thought I had won until we started to look at possible sites. Only one had any possibility and that had so many things against it I nearly said no immediately.

Belvoir Castle is built on the edge of a huge rift valley, called the Vale of Belvoir, hundreds of feet above the valley floor. On one side of the Castle a steep bank had been terraced. Mr Meek showed me one of the terraces as a possible arena. It was awesome! It perched just below the Castle walls with stunning views across the Vale. However, the problems were equally awesome. The banks between the flat terraces were 30 - 40 meters high at an angle of 60 degrees. The flat areas were just 15 meters wide and 60 meters long. Our minimum specifications at that time were 80 meters wide and 150 long. Could the audience manage to sit on such a steep bank? Would the horses slip over the edge and go crashing down into the Duke's swimming pool? Also, the only access to the arena was up a narrow foot path some 200 meters long, steep all the way and almost vertical for the last 30 meters. We would have to carry all the equipment for the show up that steep hill. I wasn't even sure the horses would make it up that bank. I couldn't give an answer. I said I thought it would be ok but needed to check with my father; the horse expert. I brought Dad over the next day; he was horrified and at first said no. I had had time to think about it overnight and put forward the argument that we trained in the indoor school which was slightly shorter than this arena. Yes, it was narrower but except for the melee we only ran in straight lines. The big worry for both of us was that possibility of going over the edge 30 meters down into the Duke's swimming pool. We had good horsemen and had well trained horses, after much debate we decided to take a risk and perform the show. It was only one show but it was going to be spectacular! Little did we know that that the shows at Belvoir would go on for thirty years and that the publicity and fame we got from Belvoir would take us all over the World and into films and television. But all that was in the future.

Following on from a very successful first Belvoir show we travelled down to Cornwall for a very ambitious show. It was also going to teach me some more hard and painful business lessons. The site was the Royal Cornwall Show Ground at Wadebridge, a joint show with the Arkley Knights plus a host of medieval groups. Four days' work, one day for rehearsal, then three days jousting, two shows per day. The travel costs, food and accommodation were immense. I also needed to find stabling for the horses and local vet cover in case of emergency. After talking to the Arkleys we agreed an identical fee and put in the tender. It was massive by our standards but to our amazement they agreed. We had hit the big time! I flew down to Cornwall from the East Midlands airport to RAF St Morgan in a turbo prop Viscount. My second time flying. I loved it. My honeymoon flights had been the norm for cheap package holidays, night flights, packed in like sardines. This time it was daylight and the Viscounts only flew at 10,000 feet so I had a clear view of England all the way to Cornwall. The only scary bit was landing and taking off from St. Morgan which was on the edge of a cliff. As we landed it looked as if we were going to crash into the cliff, and when you took off the runway ended at cliff edge and we felt we were going to drop into the sea.

I came off the plane suited and briefcase in hand. The organiser who was a lady met me at the airport and whisked me off in a shiny new car to view the site. We then went on to arrange accommodation and banking facilities. We sorted out the contract details over a good lunch. I then caught the afternoon plane back to East Midlands Airport. Life in the fast lane, just fab; I was on such a high.

We decided to hire horse transport from a farmer friend of mine as we were not sure our old TK Bedford would make the

13-hour trip. The shows were great and all the participants meshed together well. I was proud of these shows. We had two commentators - ours and the Arkleys; they worked as a double act providing a slick professional experience. There was the usual partying after the shows in the local pubs. The show actually gets a mention in Rick Stein's memoirs "Under a Mackerel Sky", though I hasten to add it was not anyone from our troupe who punched him. The Troupe was scattered around Wadebridge in local bed and breakfasts. I was sharing a room with Brent Haddon. One night after copious amounts of beer I woke up to the sound of running water. To my surprise, Brent was carefully peeing into one of his jodhpur boots. I decided not to say anything in case it affected his aim and went back to sleep. In the morning when the alarm woke us I ribbed Brent about getting in such a state that he peed in his boots. Brent in his perfect public school accent replied, "Don't be so ridiculous; I would never do anything as disgusting as that"... I cheerfully replied, "Well look in your boots, mate'". He was mortified to find both his boots filled with urine and even tried to blame me. The big problem now was how to dispose of it without the landlady finding out as the toilet was through the kitchen where she was working. There were no large opening windows in the room so we had to delicately manoeuvre the jodhpur boots through the small top window and empty the contents out into the garden. We then used the toilet and smuggled copious amounts of toilet paper back into the room to stuff into the boots and dry them out as they were his only footwear.

The shows, although top class were not well attended. As each enthusiastic audience left we hoped for bigger crowds but it just didn't happen. The same old lesson we had learnt in Wales, holidaymakers don't want to pay for expensive entertainment when they have free sun and sand. All the artists were contracted to be paid after the last show. However even the worst mathematician could not help working out that the takings were not going to pay the bills. After the second day, some were demanding to be paid up front and when that didn't happen they upped and left. The rest of us had a meeting and decided to honour our contract so organiser had no grounds to withhold payment. As soon as the last show was performed we went straight to the admin tent for payment. As we had expected they came up with excuses not to pay us. That's when it got like Robin Hood. Swords were drawn, axes raised and arrows fitted to bow strings. After much shouting and threatening they handed over the takings but saying that it was armed robbery and they were calling the Police. When we got back to the backstage area the reality of what we had just done hit home and we were on very dodgy ground. The money was in Barclay's night safe bags. Most of us agreed that if we cut open the bags we were going to make things a lot worse with the police. We decided that as I had also got night safe facilities at Barclays we would lock them in the night safe to show we were not armed robbers. Next morning, we went straight to the bank at opening time to talk to the Bank Manager. He was very sympathetic but explained that every night safe bag had a serial number that matched the key of the person the night safe pouches were signed out to. Not even the manager could open them.

We had lost. I got the blame from the hot heads. The only option was to camp outside the Bank till they came for the money but Graham pointed out that they would only pay it into an account so there would be no cash to grab. Reality struck us and we all decided to leave for home it was costing us a fortune to stay down in Cornwall. We took the lady to court for the money but she had already declared herself bankrupt and her house, "The Gate House" at something park turned out to be a rented council house. She had just made up the name for her bogus company. We had been done over good and proper. The costs to us were massive. Dad and I were now also facing bankruptcy. We had borrowed money to pay for the food and accommodation of the troupe for a week, together with all the troupe's travel costs. We owed a large amount to the farmer who transported the horses and stayed down with us for the week and wages for the troupe. Added to that was the loss in takings at the riding school from taking 6 horses and three instructors being away for a week. Finally, there was the solicitor's bill for trying to get our money back. It was Gwrych all over again! We avoided bankruptcy by Graham negotiating another bank loan. The farmer eventually agreed to accept just the fuel costs and the lads did the show for no wages. It was a bleak winter for all. Another London rip off; us northerners were such easy prey. During that winter, Graham left to pursue other business adventures, Steve left to pursue his pop career and Clive changed jobs and eventually relocated to America in 1976. His new job gave him little time for jousting. Dad started to do fewer shows but my two brothers Phil and Stu became knights. Brian took on the role of commentator. I gave up the role of Black Knight to play Sir Frederick and promoted Tony Edwards to Black Knight.

When I suggested the change, Tony was reluctant and thought it was too early to take on a major role. I knew he could handle the change with ease and his character of Sir Anthony D'Argentine was just how I saw the new Black Knight. My advice to Tony, as it has been to all the other new Black Knights, who also had the same doubts; "Don't try to copy the old Black Knight, play it as you see it and feel it, be your own Black Knight". I would miss being the Black Knight and as all that have played the part will say, it's like a powerful drug; if you are not careful it will take over your life, sometimes not for the better! The problem was, that as we became more famous people expected us to carry on being the show characters in public. I always said to the troupe, "You are actors when you put on your costume, you are that character. When you take it off you are back to being yourself". It was not easy; Brian as the tipsy Sir Frederick had already found that if he went to the bar in costume after the show he could drink for free all day.

The part of the Black Knight would consume Tony in a way so powerful that it is hard to comprehend. During 1973 - 1974 money became tighter and the big budget shows of six knights complete with ladies, jugglers, fire eaters, even a mounted falconer (George Roach) became almost non-existent. So, we developed a cheaper four knight show which, with all the new skills for entertaining we had learned, was a far better show than the old six knight show. We now had four strong, identifiable characters that the public could get behind. The show was fast and punchy. It had dashing knights with skill, violence, treachery and comedy; the perfect combination to entertain the whole family. It was in 1975 that we started to tour with a stable cast of main characters, a cast that would be added to, by my brothers' friends; they would in time, rise through the ranks, becoming knights or men-at-arms. We toured and toured. Slowly but surely, the crowds and number of shows increased; then things went crazy! Slowly we developed a secret world of pranks, so bizarre as to be unbelievable. We lived in each other's pocket 14 to 16 hrs a day; if you didn't have something to laugh about you would go crazy with boredom. If you were going to survive in the Jousting Troupe you had to take it as well as give it out and that included me the boss!

Chapter 4   On the Road 1975-80

My Birthdays

My birthday is at the end of May which meant that somewhere over the May Bank holiday most years my birthday fell on a jousting day. My first special birthday came at Newstead Abbey. We had been doing sword fights for a medieval banquet and were packing up at about 10 pm on a lovely summer's evening. It was still light; suddenly the lads pounced on me, pinned me down and started to rip my clothes off. When stark naked they grabbed me by the wrists and ankles and carried me off to the nearby lake. I was terrified. I could barely swim, I only learnt in my late teens when I got stranded by the tide at Mablethorpe and the lads taught me doggy-paddle to get back to the beach. I was screaming "please don't do this I will drown I can't swim". I screamed it repeatedly to no avail. They reached the edge of the lake, then it was a leg and a wing, and I was flying through the air, and then into the lake. The number of thoughts that flashed through my mind in that split second before I hit the water was amazing. I saw myself sinking into deep black water, arms and legs flailing to no avail, my lungs filling with the black stinking water. I hit the water! It hurt but to my surprise I didn't sink but found I couldn't use my arms and legs. It gradually dawned on me that I was stuck in about a foot of liquid mud and that the water was only about 6" deep. By the time, I had managed to stand up I was covered from head to toe in black slime. Just as I reached the bank, two ladies from the banquet appeared around the corner of the Abbey taking a quiet evening stroll. They stopped stared and then beat a hasty retreat. It took me half an hour sitting in the sluice stream to wash enough of the black slime off to put my clothes back on. I still smelt awful and needed a long hot shower at home to get truly clean.

Another year we were at Belvoir Castle. I had kept very quiet about by birthday and no one seemed to have remembered. We were in the Windmill Pub at Redmile just below the Castle and had been celebrating a great show for about three hours when someone remembered my birthday. In those days, we would have four or five pints at lunchtime before the show and then continue after packing up the equipment so that by the time they remembered my birthday everyone was well oiled. They decided to give me the bumps. We were in the lounge bar which had a low ceiling and old wood beams. The bumps got more and more enthusiastic and I crashed into the ceiling cracking my head on the oak beam. It was very hard and I let out a loud scream. This shocked the bumpers and they shouted "Sorry". Unfortunately, they also let go of me so I crashed to the floor from about nine feet in the air this time cracking the back of my head and hurting my back. Happy birthday Sam! People often ask me how dangerous jousting was. My reply was always not as dangerous as the parties. After this my birthdays got even more extreme. One year at Belvoir they stripped me naked, tied me up and hung me upside down in the stable yard at Belvoir from a winch about six feet off the ground. Then just before they all went off for lunch they hosed me down with the fire hose. It was quite some time before a passer-by found me and let me down. Like the lake incident the organisers were not pleased about the lads' antics.

The most extravagant surprise though involved a coffin that we had acquired with a hinged lid and castor wheels. Again, it was at Belvoir Castle. They again stripped me naked and then locked me in the coffin! I was then loaded onto the coach and driven somewhere. It is very hard to work out how far you have travelled when locked in a coffin. Eventually the coach stopped and I was aware of being unloaded then being wheeled a long way. The rumbling noise inside the coffin was deafening then suddenly quiet again. The coffin was being manoeuvred up down around corners and then put down. Total silence. Then the padlock was unlocked, I waited and still not a sound. Where the hell had they left me! My guess was the castle dungeon. Oh well! I flung the lid open and sat up trying to adjust my eyes to the bright lights. It was surreal. I was sitting totally naked in a coffin surrounded by old aged pensioners, all with drinks in their hands peering at me. I quickly laid back down and put my hands over my private parts, instantly a pint of beer hit me full in the face which made me instinctively bring my hands back up to my face. By this time, I realised I was in the lounge bar of the Windmill pub. I took a deep breath and ran out into the car park where I expected to find my clothes. No such luck. The whole troupe was there but no clothes. They eventually managed to overcome their hysterics and inform me that I would find my clothes at the edge of the village several hundred yards up the main street. Thanks lads!! There were many more birthday surprises but these were the most memorable!!

Happy Days 1975-79

The latter half of the 1970s were probably the happiest jousting years of my career. We were not yet famous but we had a good troupe that was turning out scintillating shows. The audiences were all new so we had to go out and win them over every show. Our desire to do better and better shows burned like a fire. Tuesday night was our practice night and after rehearsals we sat down and tore our previous show apart. We argued, screamed at each other and came very close to fighting. Every blow struck, every word spoken during that show, was analysed. Timing was everything. We learnt that a split second could mean the difference between a standing ovation or a muted round of applause. Even during the interval between our shows, we would criticise the first part of the show. Tony's constant mantra was, "we need more aggression! Must have more aggression" and boy did we give it. Our fight choreography and acting skills became so good that we frightened audiences; they really believed we hated each other and were trying to kill each other. We even received a letter of complaint from the senior paediatrician at Nottingham Hospital saying the show at Belvoir Castle was too violent especially towards the young squires and set a bad example to the public in the way we treated young people. The squires found it very amusing as it was of course, all acting. In fact, after considering the letter we unanimously agreed it was the highest compliment we could have had been paid. It was strange how different audiences from different areas and class backgrounds reacted to the show. In the more affluent south, the crowd would cheer the good knight and boo the Black Knight. However, in the working-class North the Black Knight would be cheered, and support for the good was knight much more muted.

I however enjoyed the same warm response as the roly-poly drunk where ever we went. That was until one show near Newcastle upon Tyne.

Everything I did and said went down like a lead balloon. I tried everything but not a single laugh, just a hushed silence. It really knocked me for six. So, when I went to get paid I mentioned it to the organiser. He told me he wasn't surprised at all. It was a very depressed area with very high unemployment and a big drink problem. It was common for the men folk to drink most of their dole money leaving their families short of food and rent. There was also a long history of drunken violence towards their women. I was starting to realise one had to tread carefully in this acting lark. We were performing to a complete cross section of audiences. In 1975, we performed a show at Codnor Miners Welfare Club on a small recreation ground at the back of a row of terraced houses. But next day was a show at a luxury country hotel near Accrington.

The show was at the Dunkenhalgh Hotel near Accrington in Lancashire, a lovely Victorian country house set in park land. I went to meet the manager/ owner in early spring and was overawed by the grandeur of the place. When I reached the hotel entrance 2 huge stone flower basins greeted me, full of crocus and daffodils set in newly turned soil, the polished brass name plate and door handles gleamed in the sun. I remember thinking how glad I was that I had recently decided to invest in a top-quality suit and briefcase for meeting clients. I was greeted by an immaculately dressed receptionist who apologised that the manager was with someone but would be with me shortly. I was ushered into an oak panelled sitting room overlooking the park and no sooner had I sat down than a waiter appeared with coffee served on a silver tray with matching coffee jug. I sat outwardly relaxed admiring the view sipping my coffee. Inwardly I was terrified, again very much out of my depth. A few minutes later the manager swept in and shook my hand vigorously. He was much younger than I had expected, probably mid-thirties. The joust and medieval banquet was his own idea and although he hoped to make money out of the weekend his main objective was to publicise the hotel. After discussing the banquet, jousting, and taking a walk into the parkland to find a suitable site, we had lunch in the hotel restaurant. The manager was very proud of his new menu and wine list that he had just introduced as part of the hotel revamp and was keen to hear my opinion. Battle Abbey and Wales had encouraged me to read a lot about wine, port, brandy and malt whisky so it was with some confidence that I complimented him on the fine French wines, vintage Ports and even the Armagnac brandy which, in the mid-seventies, was very rare. He was delighted to find a kindred spirit in food and drink and so started one of the best lunches I have ever had. I have had many wonderful lunches since but the one thing they all have in common is that they were never planned. Three hours later over coffee and vintage Armagnac brandy we had concluded all the finer details of the weekend. The whole troupe would stay in the hotel on full board, attend the banquet free of charge and would receive free drink, plus admission to the post banquet private party. For our part, we would stage fights at the banquet and generally act in a raucous manner. The jousting would take place the next day in the park. The banquet and show were a huge success but there were a few memorable moments at the banquet and the after party. During the banquet, I saw three of the troupe quickly leave the room. Something didn't look right so I followed them outside. When I caught up with them they were in a huddle but I could also hear sharp words. It turned out that one of the younger squires had had too much to drink and had announced that he was going to be sick. The lads next to him bustled him out as quick as they could, threatening him with all manner of torture if he didn't hold it until outside. Just in case he didn't make it they ripped his chainmail coif (headpiece like a balaclava) off his head and told him to use it as a sick bag. Unfortunately, the coif was just loose knitted string sprayed with silver paint. That's how I found him gently sobbing apologies holding a coif full of sick that was leaking out over his hands. The other two lads said, "its ok we will walk him around for bit then put him to bed. We will keep popping in to keep an eye on him". Looking back this was the start of the troupe becoming a family, a bit like the musketeers; one for all and all for one. Like all families, we squabbled and fell out but we were always there for each other and it is the same today forty years on.

I was drinking with the manager at the end of the bar at after party had finished and everything had gone supremely well, and he was very pleased. He told me that he had just acquired a bottle of very rare 1913 Armagnac brandy and would I like to taste it to finish off a successful night? I was deeply honoured, never having tasted anything so rare. I had only taken a couple of sips when Tim Badder, one of the men at arms staggered towards us to thank the manager for a great party. After thanking the manager, he asked me what I was drinking, "Armagnac brandy," I said "Oh good I'm on port but I don't like it. Here you have it it'll go lovely with your brandy" and promptly deposited the contents of his glass into my glass, turned and walked away! I just prayed for the ground to open and swallow me....

The main knights had special costumes for banquets. Brian, now the permanent commentator had persuaded his mother, a talented seamstress, to make him a Richard the Third style doublet with matching hat in dark green velvet. He was going to wear it at the banquet but it was also going to be his new commentator's outfit. His mother had worked many late nights to finish the costume in time for the banquet.

As usual Brian first consumed a large amount of alcohol and then set about wooing the ladies. Towards the end of the party he was seen sneaking out with a female in tow. Next day we were busy setting up for the show and it was not until we were about to get changed that someone pointed out Brian had still not appeared. As usual it fell to me to go and track him down. My first port of call was his room. Luckily the door wasn't locked and there was Brian still sound asleep. I roused him and repeatedly told him to get into costume as we were about to start the show. He was wandering around lifting the bed sheets, in and out of the bathroom. Just as I was about to explode he announced, "she's nicked my costume ". Apparently when they got to the room Brian had disrobed and suggested that they got into bed (always straight to the point) at which point she announced that she was a lesbian and just wanted to talk about medieval things and at which point he had lost interest and passed out. I couldn't resist the jibe that it was obviously the costume not him that was the attraction. I don't think he ever dared to tell his mum that he had lost the costume.

We came home from the weekend with a new confidence that we were professional entertainers. The new lads had bonded with established members. We were on our way.

Our name for quality crowd pulling shows was starting to spread, and 1976 was a year of shows at great venues. Belvoir Castle was drawing ever larger crowds. Our banquets at Scarborough had paid dividends with three major shows at Scarborough Castle drawing in huge crowds spreading our name throughout the North East. It also brought us our first involvement in a television show. The Dave Allen show was huge in the late 70's and part of it was about people with weird pastimes. We certainly fulfilled that category! After a full day filming we asked if Dave and the crew would like to join us for a drink in the Riding Club Bar. We all crowded into the tiny lounge bar. Dave seated himself at the end of the bar and announced he was buying the drinks and then with a cigarette in one hand and a whisky in the other hand, just like he did on television, he started to reminisce and tell jokes. This continued for several hours. He paused only to buy more drinks for everyone and firmly refused offers from us to buy any drinks in return. Finally, the film director put an end to the festivities, and ordered a stop saying they had another early start in the morning. He was one of the most charming and unassuming men I have ever met and I think he would have stayed until the early hours if the director had let him.

Appearing on the Dave Allen show gave us the publicity which we badly needed. Although we were now performing at much bigger and classier venues the number of shows each year only just covered the running costs. The main reason for this was that in the second half of the 1970's the economy was in recession, money was tight and inflation high. People were reluctant to risk big budget shows especially with the fickle British weather. However, we stumbled on a group of people who were prepared to take risks. They were the Round Table organisation. Their members tended to be young successful business people, they raised money for charities, they were well respected in their communities, and they could get venues for free and rely on volunteers to run the day. In the late 70's and early 80's they became our regular clients. Their committee meetings were usually at a hotel or large pub and would involve a meal around a single large table. I would go and make a pre- dinner presentation which was an 8mm film of the jousting followed by a sales pitch and questions. Many of the meetings were so far away that they required an overnight stay in the hotel. Although this was a drain on scant resources it was money well spent as a night spent drinking in the hotel with the clients formed a close personal relationship and certainly helped with recommendations to other Round Tables.

1977 saw Belvoir Castle increase its number of shows to three and a new show that was going to become a rival to Belvoir in crowd numbers. The show was at Bosworth Battlefield and it was our first taste of working for a Local Authority, this one being Leicestershire County Council. It would turn out to be a long and successful partnership.

Every now and then we would get a show that had real community spirit. Usually they were celebrating a special date in the town's history or raising money for something that would benefit the whole community. Everyone was part of the event and everyone was so grateful that we had done them the honour of performing at their special day. Montgomery was one of these shows. Once an important medieval town it was set high on a hill on the border between England and Wales. It gave its name to and was the administrative centre of Montgomeryshire, now renamed Powys. Unfortunately, its good defensive position was its downfall. In the 18th and 19th centuries both the canals and the railways bypassed the hilltop town. A new town quickly developed in the valley a few miles away around the canal and then the railway called funnily enough, Newtown. Montgomery was left in a time warp not much larger than a big village, nevertheless a lovely place. It was a two-day festival to celebrate it being granted a royal charter many centuries ago. There was no money in the budget for accommodation so we camped in tents, horseboxes and caravans. The only excitement on the night that we stayed there, was the young squires being chased through the back gardens of the town houses by the police, after getting into mischief with the local lads. They all evaded capture, eventually returning to campsite. At that time, we had two lads that did an axe and mace fight. They were good lads in their mid-twenties and had been with us for two seasons. One had a steady girlfriend who came to all the shows with him. We had tried to teach them to sword fight but their reactions were not quick enough, hence the slower axe and mace fight. Try as we may we could not get them to spice up the fight. Everyone in the troupe acquired a nick name and theirs was Bish and Bash taken from the sound they made slowly taking it in turns to hit each other's shield. The fight is still called the Bish Bash fight thirty years on. It was painful to watch, we were constantly at them to speed up, show more aggression and put in new moves. They were always the first fight of the show, it made all the other fights look better.

That fateful day Brian announced their fight and both strode out purposefully banging their weapons on their shields, this looked more hopeful; they bowed to the audience and then flew at each other. We all stood mesmerised as they rained down blows on each other, at last they had taken on board our criticism. I think it slowly dawned on us that this was not a choreographed fight. A blow to the helmet floored one of them. I realised at that moment this fight was for real! I quickly sent two lads from our end to stop the fight. The other end had also realised what was happening and sent men out to help. By the time they got to them, the one who had struck the helm was trying to throttle the downed man with the shaft of his weapon across his throat. Brian skilfully covered up what had happened asking for a big cheer for such a great contest. We found out after the show that Bish had found his mate Bash in bed with his girlfriend and they admitted it had been going on regularly for some time. We never saw any of them ever again.

At our next jousting practice, we discussed the Bish and Bash episode and we all agreed that it was very lucky that neither was seriously injured or even killed. Everyone was asked if they had any knowledge of the secret love affair but nobody had the slightest inkling. However, we concluded that given the age group of most of the troupe and their ever-changing girlfriends there was a real possibility of it happening again. We unanimously took the decision that in future no women could travel with us to shows. We accepted that there was a possibility that something similar could happen in the future and we would have to be vigilant. This rule would at least provide a cooling off period. However, it didn't go down well with wives and girlfriends who already disliked the tight bond between all the members of the troupe. Most saw it as a chauvinistic way of hiding things from them. We eventually softened and allowed wives and girlfriends to attend the Belvoir shows. I was able to persuade Belvoir Castle to give me an allocation of free entrance tickets for each of the events, which helped make them feel a bit special as they could bypass the queues to get into the Castle.

The beginning of July was a heatwave and we were off to Hastings Festival. It is funny how certain events can have far reaching effects for the future and looking back, this little, tight budget show certainly did just that.

We set off on the Saturday to travel down, stay Saturday and Sunday nights performing our show on the Sunday, returning Monday. The plan was to have a few hours on the beach as a bit of a bonus. Everything went well until we got south of London then we hit gridlock; everyone was going to the coast to enjoy the heatwave. The temperature soared into the high 80s. We were stuck for three hours either standing still or inching forward. The horsebox was made of aluminium with side flaps for ventilation, fine for when you are traveling at speed but useless standing still. Also, aluminium is one of the best conductors of heat. The lorry became a sweat box, the longer it went on the more distressed the horses became. They quickly drank our emergency supply of water and then we could do nothing for them. We were somewhere in rural Kent trapped in stationary bumper- to- bumper traffic; even we were suffering dehydration, (no air con in those days). When we finally reached the livery stables late in the evening it was all locked up but luckily the owners lived on site and being horse people were very sympathetic to our plight. The horses staggered off the horsebox and were in a dreadful condition, ribs and bones sticking out. We felt so ashamed and kept telling the yard owners they didn't look like this when we left home. The horses drank buckets of water and quickly started to look brighter but we really didn't think they were in any fit state to joust next day. We trudged off exhausted to find our digs, a shared room for six at a B&B. We were crammed in like sardines - two proper beds and four camp beds as it was all we could get in high season at the seaside. All the pubs had stopped doing food so it was a couple of swift pints before closing time and a fish and chip supper. There were several heavy snorers in our party and I hardly slept a wink in the stiflingly hot room with no ventilation and quadraphonic snoring. Next morning, we went to the stables with trepidation. I was already rehearsing my speech to the organisers as to why we couldn't perform. To our astonishment four sets of pricked ears greeted us over the stable doors (always a good horse sign). They had recovered remarkably well and looked in reasonable condition.

The show was being held at Hastings Football Club ground an ideal location with readymade grandstands. Unfortunately, on the down side it formed a cauldron for the sun and the ground was baked hard like concrete. The afternoon's entertainment was very varied, so as we set up our props for the joust, we were checking with other entertainers that we would not interfere with their performances.

One of the acts was a high wire acrobatic group, two men and two women in their mid-twenties. They were travelling in a new long wheelbase Mercedes van. We were fascinated by the way they had fitted out this van, because not only did it carry an extensive array of equipment, but it also had extra seats, beds and a small galley kitchen. What appealed to me was the fact they could drive straight into the arena to set up. We on the other hand, had to lug our equipment from the horsebox which was often several hundred yards away from the arena. If we wanted to sleep, we had to curl up on the parcel shelf behind the driver and on top of the very noisy Bedford TK engine. It was obvious that if we were going to keep trekking up and down the country we needed a better way to travel.

The show was very successful but it was a killer. The intensity of the sun and ground like concrete, wiped us out. The only consolation was that the football dressing rooms had been made available for the entertainers. In those days, footballers would all take a post-match bath together in a huge bath big enough for the whole team. Brent had discovered the bath in an ante room and set about filling it for an after-show soak. It took nearly an hour to fill but was well worth it. After the show, we stripped off dived in and soaked our exhausted bodies. It was heaven sitting in the bath, can of beer in hand joking about funny things that had happened over the weekend. Suddenly the door opened and in walked the acrobats including the girls also suffering from heat exhaustion. "Corr that's just what we need. Mind if we join you?" Brent replied in his best public school accent, "not at all, but you see, the problem is we were not expecting female company, and we are all totally naked." "No problem, we are not shy" replied one of the girls. All four casually undressed in front of us and climbed into the bath as if it was an everyday occurrence. They were much more relaxed about being naked in front of strangers than the four macho jousters already in the bath, who were now worrying about having to get out of the bath in front of them. Especially as sitting in cold water for 15 minutes shrinks your manhood to an embarrassingly small size! We delighted in telling Dad about what he had missed with a great deal of embellishment just to rub salt into the wound.

Travelling home we set off at dawn to save the horses from the heat of the day. As we crossed the Kent hills at sunrise we were treated to the most spectacular phenomenon. Cloud had formed in the valleys but as we climbed the hills we broke through the cloud into bright sunshine just like flying at high altitude; it was truly amazing!

I returned home from Hastings with two goals. Neither of them would happen immediately due to a shortage of money but both came to fruition a few years later as we became more successful. The first was to build a horsebox that was insulated and well ventilated; the second was to have a separate vehicle to transport the lads and equipment.

As the Seventies ended we chugged along with the shows at Belvoir and Bosworth keeping us going with ever increasing crowd numbers. Although I only record under ten shows a year, there were in fact several more from the unrecorded list.

There were several moments that deserve a mention from this unrecorded list. Goodwood House was a two-knight show. We were to be the warm up act before a Sealed Knot civil war re-enactment. It was a long trip down to Goodwood as it is just north of Chichester on the south coast. We arrived about 6.30 in the evening, found our stabling at the famous racecourse in the Estate and our own accommodation in the jockey's quarters that were above the stables. It was about 7.30 by the time we thought about eating, but when we enquired about the location of the nearest pub that did food, we were told that there were none. However, there was an excellent restaurant at the entrance to the park. Luckily, we had packed some going out clothes, so a quick change and we were off for some "Scran". "Good" was an understatement - a polished brass plate announced it was the headquarters of the British Ferrari Club. Did they have a table? We apologised for our casual dress and explained we were doing a horse display at the event tomorrow. Yes, they did have a table. The food and service was excellent so we decided as we had a long tiring journey to treat ourselves on expenses.

The wine, the sommelier recommended. was exquisite, the steaks were flambéed at the table, and after another bottle of wine, the sweet trolley arrived, then the cheese board Better have some port with the cheese we thought. By this time, we were on a roll and Dad asked if they had any cigars and brandy. A waiter appeared with a mahogany case full of Havana cigars followed by a trolley full of fine brandies. Reality kicked in when the bill arrived; it was well over the cost of what we were being paid for the whole weekend. Mum and Lou were not amused when I submitted the expenses for the show on our return. However, the night of surprises was not over yet. We wandered back from the restaurant feeling very content and at one with the world. Our accommodation was in the stable yard just to the side of the main house. As we approached the entrance a voice growled, "Halt who goes there".   We assumed it was a joke so replied, "Fuck off! we're off to bed" and carried on walking. Four strange apparitions appeared out of the dark and levelled pikes at us. "Password" they barked.

By this time, we realised that they were sealed knot cavaliers. The alcohol we had consumed changed our affable nature to belligerence in seconds. "We don't know anything about a password, we are not part of your silly society, and we are here to perform a separate show so get out of our way now and let us go to bed!" We screamed forcefully at them. At which point things became a shouting match bringing out their sergeant of the guard to see what all the noise was about. He turned out to be no better than the goons with the pikes. They really believed they were in the army and obeyed orders blindly. Things calmed down when we informed them that we knew Brigadier Peter Young the founder and now self-styled General of the sealed knot, and asked to see their commanding officer. That calmed things and we were quickly taken under so called "arrest" to the Captain of the Guard. The Sergeant made his report to the Captain. We explained our side again. "So, you claim to know the General"; we noted he didn't use the correct title of Brigadier. These people all lived as if it really was the 1640's. He then left the room for a few minutes. When he returned, he asked us to follow him as we were going to meet "The General ". He ushered us into a room and to our astonishment there were about eight gentlemen around a table all drinking port or brandy dressed as cavalier aristocrats swathed in highly embroidered clothes and bright silk sashes. The small rotund Brigadier with flowing silver hair and a huge matching flamboyant moustache stood as we entered. He appeared pompous but his voice was clipped decisive military. "Sorry about this mess but we were told that only the Sealed knot would be using this block. Nobody informed us about you. Please join us for a night cap as way of recompense, my staff officers and I have just finished dinner ". He went on to give his fellow officers a glowing report of our equestrian skills and offered us port or brandy. In addition to an affable end to the evening, we were also offered a part as cavalry in the siege of Newark planned for next year but more about that later

Our first trip into Scotland as a full troupe was for Kirkcaldy Round Table. The show was a great success and the organisers were over the moon with the larger than expected crowds. Things had not started so well. Kirkcaldy is North of Edinburgh so it was a long trip up in the old TK Bedford and we were exhausted when we arrived in the early evening. Some of us decided to stay in a hotel at our own expense and others camped at a site on the edge of town. The hotel was a grand old fashioned Victorian hotel. It had its own smart bar and restaurant. We staggered into the hotel exhausted and opted for the usual format - a quick drink, shower, change clothes and then food. The first culture shock was to find out they had no real ale, only fizzy keg beer, next no shower but a very grand bath. It was very large, took ages to fill, the water was brown and when I finally got in I nearly drowned in the brown water. The bath was about eight feet long and I was used to shorter baths that when I lay back my feet touched the end and kept my head above the water. When I lay back in this bath I shot under the water like a torpedo and came up spitting the brown water.

We arrived at the restaurant just after 7pm to find it closed. When we enquired at reception at what time the restaurant opened, the astonished receptionist replied that it had already closed. Shocked, we asked what restaurants there were in the town. She told us there were several but they all closed at 6.30 or 7pm at the latest. What about a fish and chip shop we asked in desperation? Oh yes, there was a chip shop but that didn't open till 10 pm for the drinkers! So, it was fizzy beer and late night fish and chips after a long exhausting trip.

After the show the organisers asked us to meet them in our hotel bar for a celebration drink. We met up at about 6:30 and soon noticed most of the locals were drinking Black Bottle Whisky a brand we had not come across south of the border. As the beer was not to our taste Brian and I decided to try the Black Bottle after Tony had announced how good it was. When in Scotland drink as the Scots do! A fatal mistake! Yes, it was very smooth for a blended grain whisky but to drink it for four plus hours was a very bad idea. The organisers came and went in a shift system never staying for more than an hour. Pride would not let us admit we were done for, so we stuck it out to the bitter end still drinking The Black Bottle. We crawled up the stairs and passed out on our beds. We were so hungover the next day, we had to stop at every service stations on the way home to rest up enough to drive the next ten or twelve miles. It took us an extra four hours to drive home and another two days to recover. Forty years on we still talk about the Black Bottle night.

Paddy Dolan

One practice night in the mid-seventies a stranger arrived and asked to speak to the person in charge saying that he had some weapons that he had made and thought they would be good for us to use.

We had spent a fortune on weapons but everything we bought just broke. I bought swords from many suppliers all of whom assured me their swords would not break but they all did. Eventually I found a small company in Sheffield that made Scottish Claymore, dancing swords, and the blades were just the right width and length. The first batch of blades were better than any other blades we had tried before, but they still didn't last very long. However, the owner of the factory was intrigued by our problem and after many changes in the tempering process, came up with a blade that lasted at least half a season.

I very nearly didn't bother even talking to him, as the troupe was in a heated argument over how to end a fight. The messenger however persuaded me to 'take a look', saying he was a really nice man and had some unusual weapons with him. So, it was with great reluctance I took time out to meet Paddy Dolan.

He was a short, stocky man; extremely polite and softly spoken. Very unlike anyone I had ever met on the re-enactment scene. He opened the back of his Ford Escort Estate and removed a blanket to reveal a fantastic array of weapons. I told him that they were beautiful, but we would destroy them in a matter of hours and that it would be sacrilege to his works of art. He smiled and said "I hoped you would say that, but that's just what I want you to do. You see I'm really interested in making something that really works for you. I've watched your shows and your fights are like nothing I have ever seen before. Take these, and break them, and I'll make you some that are better. It won't cost you any money - I just want to make weapons that you can use and won't break".

True to his word, he made and we broke, but by the end of the season he made and we didn't break!

He was always asking what other weapons did we fancy fighting with, and soon we had enough different weapons to make each foot fight in the show, totally different. This was so good for the show and gave it yet another exciting dimension. Having weapons that didn't break improved our safety record, and drastically reduced the time spent repairing and replacing weapons.

Paddy and his family became great personal friends, and he was a great inspiration in my life and to the jousting show. He loved nurturing creative people and would often present me with a piece of carved wood, or tooled leather, and just say I know you will appreciate the skill that went into making this. I still have many cherished objects that Paddy or his associates made in my house to this day

Paddy was responsible for giving us the tools to make another quantum leap with the development of our show. He was very wise and these wise words have stayed with me forever! He told me one day that he had been offered a big promotion but had turned it down. When I asked why, he said that he already earned enough money to eat and drink as much as he wanted, he loved the house he lived in, and could afford to go on as many holidays as he wanted. Why have a lot more stress and money that he didn't need?

I think these are some of the wisest words ever spoken from a man who was very happy with his life.

Tony Edwards The Black Knight

Tony joined us I think in 1974. He lived locally in the village of Thrussington where his family kept the very successful Star Pub and Restaurant. Tony had recently come out of the army where he had served in the Household cavalry. His cavalry training was ideal for jousting, he was an excellent rider and used to handling swords and lances. His skills meant he became a Knight in the show only weeks after joining us, playing alongside myself as the Black Knight's right hand man. At this time, we were still choosing our own character names and Tony chose Sir Antony D' Argentine. We came up with the name D'Argentine because it sounded dashing, which Tony certainly was, but as I already mentioned earlier also the word "Argent" is the heraldic word for silver, and referred to a streak of silver in his jet-black hair. Tony quickly developed his own character within the show and it was very much a "Harry Flashman" character from the novels of George MacDonald Fraser written in the late sixties. As Tony's confidence grew so did his character and the audience loved it. We became great friends. Tony was working in the printing trade and had quite flexible hours. We were the same age and both recently married. We both also shared a vision to make the jousting more exciting and become a major crowd pulling entertainment. Tony also introduced a jockey friend Malcolm Bastard to the jousting. He also quickly became a Knight taking over Brian's part as the Drunk, when he broke his ankle.

It was a time of big change for the jousting show. Graham Lucking was becoming more involved as a business consultant to other companies, having realised that the economics of jousting were not going to make him his fortune and wanted out of everything including doing the commentary, which Brian eventually took over.

Brian became a great commentator and made the role his permanently. Malcolm was a great stand in for Brian but after a season or so left to become a very successful international bloodstock agent. So, after less than two seasons of Tony joining us, I made the biggest decision yet in the line-up of the jousting show. I would stop playing The Black Knight and take up the part of Sir Frederick the drunk. It was a very hard decision I loved the role of Black Knight dearly but after playing the part for five years and following all the performances we did in Wales which was equivalent to another 10 years, I was ready for a new challenge. Tony would become the new Black Knight. Tony was reluctant at first to take on the role but I assured him he was up to it. I told him not to copy me but play it how he felt it should be played; advice I have given to every successive Black Knight. The role was to become like Dr Who. Each new Black Knight took some of the old but added their own individual character to the part. My brother Phil took over Tony's old part and used the name of Sir Richard of Gloucester. These three names and parts are still used in the show even after 40 years. Tony was always full of energy and ideas. I could imagine him as a cavalry officer leading the charge of the Light Brigade encouraging his men forward whilst being shot to pieces. Not long after taking on the part of the Black Knight he became landlord of the Blue Bell pub at Hoby. It had been kept by his grandfather for many years and was a beautiful thatched building with a large car park all set in the centre of the village. Just down the road from the pub was Brooksby Agricultural College which was full of thirsty young farmers and great for business. The regular shows we were doing at Belvoir Castle turned Tony into a local celebrity and the Blue Bell was often known as the "Black Knight's Pub". Tony was also a great cook and the food at his pub became admired by everyone in the locality again boosting his trade and work load. The jousting troupe would go back to the Blue Bell after shows, especially after Belvoir as it was almost on the way home and Tony's barbecued steaks were delicious. They were just what we needed after a hard days jousting. It soon became known that the jousters would be at the Blue Bell after a local show and especially after a Belvoir show. On these days, the pub was heaving with the outside courtyard full and people spilling out into the car park. We often stayed until the early hours of the morning and sometimes all night. Despite drinking whisky all night Tony would be up with the lark enthusiastically cooking breakfast for all those still there in the morning.

His army training bought a polish to our shows. We practiced our salutes that we performed to the audience at the beginning and end of the shows, until they were so crisp that they drew a spontaneous applause from the audience. The speed of the show was quickened, the next fight always armed up and ready to go as soon as the arena was clear. The audience was bombarded with yet more thrills. It was not to everyone's taste. Dad still thought of the show as a display of horsemanship that should be performed slowly so that the audience would appreciate the finer points.

Tony with his head-on approach tried to make Dad speed up by becoming more aggressive in their fights. This didn't bother Dad but it did bother Dad's horse Ambre Solaire (Fred) who thought the aggression was aimed at him. Dad warned Tony not to confront Fred head on but to only attack from the side. Tony was confident that he could beat anything a horse could throw at him and ignored the warnings. Not long after the warning, in the middle of their routine Fred quick as a flash sunk his teeth into Tony and lifted him off his feet. He then carried him the whole length of the arena like a dog carrying a bone and dropped him in front of the Black Knight's tent. After this incident, we decided it would be safer to muzzle Fred for the show.

Tony was energised by the audience. The more they screamed insults at him the more he loved it. He would throw his hands up for acclaim and stare at the audience and it would drive the audience into a frenzy; he could hold them in that state for longer than any other member of the troupe.

Being the Black Knight took over Tony's life. His many T.V. appearances and newspaper articles made him far more recognisable than I had been in Wales. However, unlike me who ran from the limelight, Tony embraced it with the same enthusiasm as he did with everything else. He happily switched into Black Knight mode anywhere and everywhere for his fans or the media, loving every minute of it. Tony even purchased a black Triumph Toledo sports saloon car and had his coat of arms painted on it and number plates that read BK-

1. When Tony joined us in the mid-seventies we were performing about 7-10 shows a season, as we went into the eighties that rocketed to the high teens and by 1983 when Tony left it was up to twenty-nine. It was the most successful touring season since we started. Our season was mid-May to the end of August, although we sometimes had the odd early or later show, which meant we were booked every Saturday and Sunday throughout the season. This put a lot of stress on all of us. We also had to try and keep up with the demands of our work and personal lives. I don't think I realised the stress this put-on Tony. He had his pub to run; he had also bought a very large farm house which he was in the middle of restoring and had horses of his own to look after. It was also a time of great financial uncertainty with interest rates rising rapidly along with super high inflation which was causing problems for everyone in business.

The week end of the 21st of August 1983 should have been the highlight of the season. Three days at Southport Flower Show. A very famous show - a sort of county show at the seaside. We arrived Thursday evening, with shows on Friday and Saturday, plus Bosworth Battlefield on the Sunday another big crowd pulling show. By the Sunday evening I was in hospital and Tony had played his last show for us.

It was a bizarre weekend, many strange things happened, it was like all the planets collided at once. Just remembering it writing this book brought tears to my eyes.

A very great weekend that ended very badly!

Jimmy Durrands

Towards the end of the seventies Belvoir Castle appointed a new manager. His name was Jimmy Durrands. Jimmy was a local guy and completely the opposite of his predecessor. In fact, it caused quite a stir in the old-fashioned offices of Belvoir Castle. The Duke was an astute businessman and I think he had decided it was time to modernise the image of the Castle. I got a call from the office at Belvoir saying that the new manager would like to meet me. I went over, rather worried that this new manager might want to pull the plug on the jousting as there was always an element at Belvoir that didn't like the disruption of large crowds invading their tranquil lives.

When I arrived at the offices, the usual format was to report to the manager's secretary then sit on a little seat in the narrow corridor for about 20 minutes. The secretary would then reappear and say the Manager will see you now, lead me down the corridor, open the door and announce, Mr Humphrey to see you sir. This time when I reported in the secretary whispered," I think you are in for a bit of a shock. You know where the office is, don't you? Go straight in. He's waiting for you". Bit of a shock; they really were going to ditch the jousting!

I entered the office with trepidation. What confronted me was such a change that I felt rooted to the floor. Gone was the neat office desk with the petit Mr Meeks behind it in tweed suit, gold rimmed glasses and bow tie. In his place was a thirty stone plus giant with an open neck shirt, sleeves rolled up and mopping sweat from his brow with a handkerchief. I felt decidedly over dressed in my suit. His desk was piled high with magazines and travel brochures all open at a page with a corner folded down. He greeted me as Sam not Mr Humphrey and thanked me for sparing the time to come and see him. He had watched several of our shows and saw them as central in making Belvoir a top tourist attraction!

Jimmy was instantly likeable and despite the impediment of his huge weight, was full of energy and enthusiasm. We talked for over an hour, about his plans for the future of Belvoir and the jousting. He made it clear from the start that I could be brutally honest about anything. He wanted straight facts and would not be offended about anything I said. Gone was the politically correct world of his predecessor. His first project was to encourage all the UK coach companies to run excursions to Belvoir, and in particular, excursions to see the jousting shows. This took time and we didn't see any significant change for well over a year. Jimmy was way ahead of his time with publicity. These days we are used to people being on TV chat shows or radio to plug their new book or film. In the late seventies, this was unheard of. We became known as the Belvoir Castle Jousters and over the next ten years we appeared constantly as guests on TV shows. We always appeared in costume which was hell under the hot TV lighting. Jim used every angle possible to get us on the box. The list of celebrities we worked with was phenomenal; Dave Allen, Jimmy Greaves, The Nolan Sisters, Deacon Blue, Durran-Durran, Jimmy Savile, Matthew Kelly, Sarah Kennedy, Jeremy

Beadle, Rod Hull & Emu, Chris Tarrant, Maggie Philbin, Mark Curry, Terry Biddlecome, Spit the Dog, Rosie and Jim and many more. We were never paid for these appearances by Belvoir but often received expenses from the TV companies but we benefited just as much as Belvoir. Many of the TV shows were for children, and we soon had regular fan mail arriving. Jim and I also embarked on a UK tour of the new commercial radio stations that had popped up all over the UK. One day I queried the value driving down to Bristol for just a few minutes on the radio. Jim's answer was that radio advertising was £60 per minute so even if we did only ten minutes, and often we did a lot longer, that was worth £600. As technology advanced, I was able to skip the travel and do the interviews over the phone. After every show at Belvoir Jimmy would be waiting to find out about any incidents that he could use for a press release. He was always delighted, in the nicest possible way, when someone was injured and had to go to hospital. His press release would begin, "Brave young knight viciously cut down defending a lady's honour by the evil and treacherous Black Knight at Belvoir Castle".

There was a really, soft side to Jimmy, as well as the publicity machine. When the temperatures soared, he would greet us as we staggered off at the end of a show exhausted with a box of ice creams. He hardly ever missed greeting us after our final show of the day, telling all the lads how good the show had been and always bringing the attendance numbers for the day with him. As a matter of personal pride, he also told us how many coaches had come that day. One day he phoned me to pick my brains for yet another press release. He was struggling for a new angle. "Have you done any really unusual shows?" he asked, and after racking my brains for a few moments came up with a show we had done for the American Airforce at Lakenheath Airbase in Suffolk. We had actually done the show on the grass area around the runway. Every now and then the commentary would be drowned out by the roar of an F111 jet landing or taking off. There was no fencing between the audience and the runway. Oh, for the good old days before health and safety!

A couple of days later Jimmy phoned. He had discovered that there were lots of American bases within two hours' drive of Belvoir. He told me that he had been in touch with all the Recreation Officers, at all the American bases and they would be sending coach loads of service personnel and their families to the jousting shows. Jimmy always knew which bases were sending coaches and would ask us to announce each base and formally welcome them to Belvoir Castle. The "Yanks" were very loud and enthusiastic spectators. When we called out their base name they would all leap to their feet waving shirts, flags, and whooping and hollering. They adored the Black Knight, spurring Tony on to become ever dastardlier.

They also brought with them huge cool boxes filled with ice and Budweiser or Schlitz beer. Neither beers nor these huge, ice filled cool boxes were available in England at this time and we were very jealous of their ability to have endless ice cold beer available on a hot summer's day. We soon discovered that if we signed autographs for them they would feed us with ice cold "Bud".

The Americans were great for me playing the part of Sir Frederick the Drunk. As I became more confident in my role I would leave the arena and go and sit with the audience until ordered back by the Knight Marshal. I would study the crowd during the opening ceremony and pick out a group with a large cool box, then at the appropriate time stagger out of the arena and sit amongst the Americans enjoying an ice-cold beer whilst everyone sweated it out in the arena. The crowd loved it, and it made the Americans´ day. I would always get a huge cheer when I staggered back to re-join the show.

The signing of autographs was a real novelty for us, and when I mentioned this to Jimmy he again got his marketing brain working. Very quickly he had photos of the main characters and a group shot for sale in the gift shop. The four knights plus Brian the Knight Marshal would rush off after the show up to the castle courtyard to greet the crowds as they made their way back from the jousting arena to the castle and sign autographs. Although it was very successful it was always a bone of contention with the rest of the troupe who were left to dismantle the props and manhandle them down the bank. They never understood that it was hard work signing endless autographs and to answer the same questions repeatedly. We were never paid for this extra but Jimmy agreed to feed the whole troupe in the tea rooms with tea, sandwiches and cream cakes. Often the lads had packed all the equipment on the coach, got changed and eaten all the food before we had finished signing autographs. The tea rooms were very set in their ways and did not take kindly to feeding a group of battered, sweaty lads at the end of the day. I always made sure that everyone thanked them for the food but we were never welcomed. For us it was great because it filled in the gap before the pub in the village reopened, and got some food into our stomachs before the post show drinking session.

The autograph signing slowly developed into a mini market. First there was a photographer selling photographs of the jousting and quick-development photos of us with members of the audience. This was followed by an artist selling ink sketches and oil paintings of the jousting. Finally, we had a man selling small wooden swords and shields for the children.

Again, although we didn't benefit financially from these add-ons but we did have access to good free publicity photos and the artist gave all the main characters an oil painting of themselves. The greatest benefit to us was making new contacts, and we picked up many shows by talking to people, whilst signing the autographs. It was a catalyst that got stronger and stronger. Media and growing crowd numbers led us to more shows all over the country which got us yet more shows and more media attention. Jimmy's greatest publicity stunt was when he wrote to the Pope to ask for his permission to hold jousting on a Sunday. How he had discovered a papal edict from the Middle Ages forbidding jousting on a Sunday, I do not know how, but he managed to get into in all the National newspapers, and he actually got a reply from the Pope to allow jousting at Belvoir Castle on a Sunday!

Then out of the blue in early July 1988 I got a call from Belvoir Castle. Jimmy was dead. His heart had failed under the strain off carrying his huge body. I don't know if he knew something, but the last time we met he seemed quite low and reflective, and it was the only time I heard him swear in ten years. A great friend personally, and to the jousters. Belvoir and the jousting were never the same again.

"Jimmy" greatly loved and sadly missed!

Lorries and Coaches

When people talk about the jousting they always refer to the great shows we have performed. But talk to members of the jousting troupe and they will, more often than not, refer to the endless hours of travelling or the waiting around to go out and perform. When a famous pop group splits up, travelling is more often the cause than artistic direction. Many a good member of the troupe left us because of travelling. Most shows of 2 x 45 minute sets would require a minimum of a 12-hour day and often 16 or 18 hours. To cope with this repetitive boredom, we developed endless pranks and stunts along with continuous beer consumption to keep ourselves amused.

Our first mode of transport as mentioned earlier was a very old TK Bedford horsebox with lollipop indicators that stuck out at the side of the cab. The cab on the outside was rusty with the odd corrosive hole. Inside the cab, the floor on the driver's side had a hole so large that you could put foot through it, and the road was clearly visible as you drove. For "Health & Safety" a bit of old floorboard was balanced across the ravine but there were still large gaps for air conditioning. This was great in summer but in the winter, you lost all feeling in your legs below the knee. To make things worse there was no cab heater. The cab was also very noisy and we had to shout and constantly repeat ourselves when trying to hold a conversation. We could squeeze three people in the cab. The one in the middle had the dubious pleasure of the gear stick sticking into their buttocks. Every time 1st, 2nd or reverse gear was required the one in the middle had to hutch up onto the outer passenger's knee. Strangely, any female passengers were always allocated the middle seat. We could also fit another three up in the luton, which is the piece the lorry body extends above the cab. The rest of the troupe would travel in cars.

The big problem with this for one day shows was that everyone set out at different times. The cars would often leave an hour later than the lorry. With this arrangement, I never knew if everyone in cars had left on time, and with no mobile phones I just had to wait and worry at the show ground until the cars arrived in dribs and drabs.

The lifestyle of the troupe meant that they were notorious for oversleeping; many times, we would be dressed and ready to do the first show but still have several main characters missing. Thankfully they nearly always arrived in the nick of time, and always with a plausible explanation as to why they were late. The stress for me was terrible. Show organisers would come around and ask me if we were ready to go on in fifteen minutes. I would be smiling saying "no problem" when I knew I was missing two main knights and a commentator. I didn't manage to solve this problem until the eighties.

We used TK Bedford lorries for carrying the horses until the nineties and I think I owned every model they made. They were very reliable, easy to mend and easy to maintain. They were also very noisy, hard work to drive and draughty. Most of them didn't have power steering so your arms got a good workout.

They did, however, have two mechanical problems - fuel injector pipes and tyres. The injector pipes were prone to fracturing with vibration, and the tyres would blow out due to overloading. After several problems with both I came up with a solution for both problems. We carried a full set of injector pipes and two spare wheels. We also carried spare fuel filters, fan belts, oil and lightbulbs. I became an expert roadside mechanic. I could change a blown-out wheel or injector pipe in less than 20 minutes. It was not uncommon to have to do both in one trip.

With regard to overloading, we were blissfully unaware that we were overloading and this was the cause of all our tyre blowouts. I always thought it was the dodgy second-hand wheels we got from the breakers yards. It was not until on one of our later trips to Belgium that the lorry was weighed prior to going onto the ferry that we realised we were overloaded. The lorry could carry 7.5 tonnes max and we weighed in at 11.5 tonnes, a full 4 tonnes over the legal weight.

Martin Brown one of the main Knights had a transport business and pointed out that was why we were having blowouts and that the Ministry of Transport were now clamping down on over-loaded lorries and handing out massive fines to offenders. Things had to change! So, I set out in search of a lorry that could legally carry more weight. Problem was, if you went over 7.5 tonnes gross vehicle weight you needed an HGV licence holder to drive which severely restricted who could drive. Although I had an HGV licence it was restricted to max 10 tonnes. I calculated that with a few changes we could manage with a 10 tonnes of gross vehicle weight and I had the reassurance that I could still drive the horsebox if necessary.

My dream was to have a new Ford Cargo Model lorry with its luxurious custom cab. I spent all winter searching for one, but by spring I still had not found one. The 10 tonne models were rare and all outside my budget.

We had a show booked in Southern Ireland for May, and Martin warned me that the ministry was having a crackdown on lorries travelling to and from Ireland. If caught we would be looking at a fine of several thousands of pounds.

By the beginning of May I still had not found a new lorry, and as a last resort Dad suggested Podder Lane Breakers Yard - owned by an old friend of Dads. I had been there many times in the 1960's but never since. The owner was a straight talking gruff old boy. He told me plainly, that for my budget I could not buy a decent Ford Custom and that old Fords were not worth a W****. He did how ever have a 10 tonne Bedford TK chassis cab with the big 500 engine and power steering in very good nick. Disappointed but desperate I brought yet another TK.

I now had less than 10 days to paint the cab and swap our horsebox body onto the new chassis. What could go wrong?

Well just about everything. Luckily, my good friend and frequent times saviour Alan Lane offered his workshop and facilities to make the change. Alan was a farmer who had very successfully diversified into steel fabrication and had designed and built our new horsebox body a couple of years before. Alan was away but my brother Stuart worked for Alan and he would be working with me. A couple of days to prepare and paint the cab and another 2-3 days to remove the old lorry and pop the body back on the new chassis cab, leaving us plenty of time to pack for a six-day international trip.

The cab painting slipped to 3 days. No problem, still plenty of time. The removal of the body took longer than planned. The first 16-hour day. The new chassis was too long so we had to cut a piece out and weld it back together. Somehow, we got the measurements wrong and had do it again. Lots of arguing and another 16-hr day. Finally, we backed the chassis under the body, and two more problems arose. First the fixing brackets didn't line-up so we needed to make a whole load of new ones and weld them on. The second was that the lorry cab was several inches taller than the old cab so it didn't fit under the Luton part of the body that goes over the top of the cab (whoops phone a friend). Not a problem says expert friend, you can put a wooden packer on top of the chassis to lift the body then bolt it all together. However, the wood must be hardwood like mahogany. So, started the hunt for suitable sized hardwood. It proved to be like rocking horse shit and the cost! It was way out of our budget. However, we finally found some second-hand hardwood. We would have to cut it to size, but that wasn't a problem we were saving hundreds of pounds. A day later and two burned out saws we had only cut one 6-foot length. Helpful knowledgeable friend says, "surely we knew you need a special saw to cut that sort of wood". Another very expensive 16-hour day. No progress but very much wiser and very worried. I spent half the next day trying to find someone who could cut the hardwood. Finally, I tracked down someone who can do it in our time frame, but the wood wouldn't be ready until tomorrow at 4pm-ish…

We should now be starting to load the lorry ready for Ireland, so we spend the next day getting everything ready for a quick load and buy a new set of longer, high tensile fixing bolts. To add to the pressure, we had the ministry vet coming to inspect the lorry and horses for animal health papers prior to leaving for Ireland. If we fail the health inspection, then we cannot travel. No show! It didn't bear thinking about!

The wood finally arrived about six o clock and we worked feverishly until about 11 pm. The body was now under and in place but we still needed to weld on all the new brackets and bolt the body down but decided to go home and get some sleep. We had done a week of 16 hour days and were getting the shakes along with cold sweats of exhaustion. We couldn't afford any more mistakes. A few hours' sleep and start again at 5am....

The next day went like clockwork. We were finished and back in the yard for 10am giving us an hour to disinfect the lorry for the ministry inspection. Thankfully horses and lorry passed and all paperwork stamped for departure that evening. Now all we had to do was load the lorry and pack our own bags.

We were to catch the overnight ferry to Ireland, and as we neared the port in the middle of nowhere just after midnight, a police squad car swooped in front of us with blue lights flashing, bringing us to an abrupt halt. We were questioned about our load and destination then they asked us to drop the ramp to check the number of horses. They then checked the operator's licence and vehicle-plating certificate to check the gross weight. Finally, they asked how much each of the horses weighed and then apologised for delaying us and wished us a safe onward journey. As we drove off Stu and I both breathed a huge sigh of relief and agreed that the last 10 days of hard work and stress had been well worth it. End of troubles! Or so we thought but that's another story for later in the book.

Along with Alan Lane, our other unsung hero of the N.J.A. was Dave Freer, mechanic extraordinaire! Tim Badder, one of the jousting troupe's long serving members during the eighties and nineties, was a lorry mechanic at a Ford main dealership in Nottingham. He stood watching in disbelief one evening as Dave cut 2 feet out of the middle of the bus front axle so that he could remove the engine sump to fit a new oil pump and then weld the axle back together again. The job took 4 hours! Done the normal way it would require a crane to lift the front of the bus and then remove the whole front axle. Probably two to three days' work. Tim shook his head and said, " I thought I was a lorry mechanic but now I realise I'm just a fitter of new parts, this man is a real mechanic". Dave started at tea time and finished about 10pm, and we set off on a long jousting trip at 6am next morning.

Dave had a full-time day job so could only come and work on our vehicles after 6 pm. One of the TK's limped back from a show running very rough. Dave diagnosed a broken piston ring which meant removing the sump and the cylinder head to remove the pistons. We would need a new set of pistons and valves. Next day we worked late into the night to strip the engine down and send the pistons off so that exact new replacements could be supplied. "We will send them off today and they should be with you Wednesday" they said. They didn't arrive Wednesday or Thursday and I was very worried. We had two shows at the weekend with an early start Saturday morning. They finally arrived at midday on Friday. I was trying to borrow a suitable replacement horse box but couldn't find one. I rang Dave who said he would be over about 7pm. He was sorry he couldn't get earlier but had to pick up children from a school function.

Things did not go well and at about 10 pm some major part snapped. My heart sank. That's it, I thought, "if we can't get to the Saturday show, and probably not the Sunday one either; I'm in big trouble". We were desperately short of money and Mum and Dad's house was the guarantee for the business loans. If both shows sued for loss of revenues, we could lose the stables and house. Dave saw my dejection, smiled and said, " Don't worry, I know someone who has a lathe, I'll go and make a new one, it will take a couple of hours, so you get on and grind the valves in. I'll be back before you've finished". Where he found a lathe that he could use in the middle of the night I have no idea, but true to his word he returned just after midnight with the new part. We struggled on, overcoming unexpected problem after unexpected problem. Just before 6 am we finished rebuilding the engine, filled it with oil and bled the fuel through. Would it start or had we made some stupid error from exhaustion? The lorry cranked over but no sign of life from the engine, the bottom dropped out of my stomach.

Dave was unperturbed, and announced we would re-bleed the fuel system. More cranking to purge the fuel system. Very worryingly the battery was starting to fade. Dave sensed it too and quickly told me to retighten the injector pipes. As I did so there was a great jerk from the engine throwing the spanner out of my hand. She was firing on one cylinder! I quickly retrieved my spanner and finished tightening the rest of the injection pipes as fuel sprayed everywhere. As I tightened the unions the cylinders started to fire and the vibration decreased. Finally, all 6 were tightened and the engine was running sweetly. I just laughed with relief. I was soaked in diesel and the lads would be arriving in 45 minutes. I thanked Dave and we just grinned at each other knowing we had succeeded against the odds but only just! I shot off home to shower and change and have a bacon sandwich. I arrived back at the stables 10 minutes later than the call time to be berated by the lads for having overslept. I was too tired to argue so I just apologised and off we went to do another show.

Some years later Dave was tragically injured when a tractor he was mending crushed him. It was late at night, as usual, and some time before anyone found him. He was in a bad way for a long time and one hand was badly damaged. Sadly, he was not able to do mechanical work anymore. We are still friends and he now owns a shooting and fishing shop in Loughborough.

Probably the truly unsung heroes of the jousting troupe have been our bus and lorry drivers. They have had to put up with constant latecomers who have overslept in the mornings, sitting in pubs till closing time or later, hundreds of miles from home, waiting for us to finish partying, and then driving us home through the night whilst we all snored soundly asleep. If that was not enough they constantly had practical jokes played on them and the "piss" taken out of them. Finally, as coach drivers, they were responsible for our behaviour. This was the greatest challenge of them all. Surprisingly all the drivers stayed with us a long time. I think that they must have all had masochistic tendencies to put up with it all.

In the early days, Dad then I drove the lorry with help from other members of the troupe on the longer trips. When we acquired our first coach in the early eighties we started to have regular drivers. Brent Haddon (Hairy Chest), Alan Lane (The Doctor) and our longest serving driver, Jim Mc Cartan (Scots "Jimmeh") who has been now succeeded by Stan Watson (Stan the Man). Although their nicknames are self-explanatory, Alan was not a doctor, although he did sort out a lot of serious problems for us. He acquired his name in the local Chinese takeaway. One evening Alan and a group of jousters had gone to the East Leake "Chinki" for a takeaway. They had been waiting a long while for their food to arrive and were getting a little agitated. To make matters worse a man came in and collected his food immediately. Tim Badder, not one for mincing his words, sprang up and demanded to know why this man was served ahead of them. The Chinese owner puffed his chest out and replied "He velly important man; he Doctor"! Never one to lose and argument Tim turned and pointed at Alan and said, "Well he's a Doctor as well!"

The owner looked aghast! "I velly solly Sir! I never knew you was Doctor" and then with hands together bowed several times to Alan. Food with free extras arrived rapidly with more apologies. Alan, never a man to cause trouble, thanked him and left never explaining he was not a doctor. Alan never thought any more about it until he returned for a takeaway a few days later, when again he received the Royal treatment. This continued for about two years until a local enquired as to why Alan was always referred to as Doctor. The China man looked puzzled and replied, "cos he velly important Doctor". The local replied "No he isn't. He is a farmer and I have known him all my life". The next time Alan went for his Chinese he was confronted by the owner who said, "Hey you no Doctor, why you tell me you Doctor?". Alan replied that "actually he never had", but was so embarrassed that he stopped using that Chinese takeaway.

These sorts of things amused the jousters greatly and from day one he was always known as "The Doctor" and still is to this day. Like every practical joke with the jousters they kept it going years. They presented him with all manner of doctor's equipment and even acquired a Belgium Red Cross sticker from the First aid unit at Horst Castle in Belgium, which they fixed to the centre of the bus steering wheel.

One of the worst and funniest things that the lads did to Alan was not actually intentional. As the old saying goes, what goes in must come out. The demands for Alan to stop the coach for a "pee" became endless and very time consuming. After a while he announced that he was only going to stop at proper services and that they would have to curb their beer drinking on the coach. About the same time as I bought the first coach, I also secured some sponsorship from Everards Brewery. They gave us free cases of beer for each show, which meant there was always plenty to drink on the bus. The lads came up with a plan. Rather than stop, they would open the bus door, get a mate to hold onto their belt, then lean out of the door and pee onto the road. This was pretty hairy when travelling at 60 plus miles per hour. However, an ex- police officer heard about our exploits and warned Alan that if someone reported this he would be held responsible and he could possibly lose his licence. Consequently, he banned any more peeing out the front door.

So again, the lads came up with another way to empty their bladders which was even more dangerous. At the rear of the bus on the floor above the back axle was an access panel about 2 feet by 3 feet. One night, as we sped home down the motorway, well loaded with beer, they removed the floor panel and "peed" onto the speeding road beneath. This was very dangerous. As most will know, it is not easy to stand on a speeding coach sober, let alone when you have a gallon of ale inside you!

What nobody expected was what happened next!

As they "peed" onto the road there was an extremely strong up-draught and all the urine shot straight back up at them. This, however, was just the start. It was like a huge industrial fan pumping air into the coach. The air had to go somewhere and its' only exit was Alan's open driver's window. Like some magical trick, the urine rose-up to the roof, and then travelled down the coach to the open driver's window. Alan felt something wet hitting the back of his head and assumed it was the lads flicking water at him for a joke. The lads were in hysterics. Alan shouted back, eyes still glued to the road, "come on lads it's not that funny". This had them rolling in the aisles and queuing up to keep the pee flowing. Eventually Alan chanced a glance over his shoulder to see what was so funny. Normally, very laid back, Alan was furious and I feared we were going to lose our long-suffering driver for ever.

Most of the time Scots Jimmy drove the lorry with the horses. To say he was a lorry driver by trade he managed to do some fantastic things that amused the lads greatly.

One of the first times he drove for us was to Alnwick Castle in Northumberland. We had driven up the day before and had a good night out in the town. The show was set in the parkland below the castle where the first series of "Black Adder" was filmed. I was trying to sort out a problem with the P.A. System when Jimmy approached me and announced that he had a confession to make. I was so absorbed in my problem that I failed to notice the lads waiting for him to tell me what he had done. He took a deep breath and announced he was very sorry, but he had driven the horsebox under a tree, and hit a "wee twig". I distractedly thanked him for telling me and not to worry, we all have little mishaps. He thanked me for being so understanding and left. It was not until later that one of the lads remarked how disappointed they were that I hadn't exploded when Jimmy told me about the damage he had done to the horsebox. It turned out Jimmy's wee twig was a huge low bough of an oak tree that he had tried to drive the lorry under, caving in the front of the Luton and twisting the whole body out of line by four inches.

Jimmy's cock-ups became legendary. Although he was a professional lorry driver he knew very little about the workings of a lorry. One day, Dave Freer and I had just finished a major rebuild of the TK Bedford's engine when Jimmy appeared and asked if there was anything he could do to help. It had been a long hard day so I said "yes, can you fill the engine with oil while we go and have a cup of tea" (or in Dave's case a cup of hot water). When we had finished our break Dave and I returned to start the engine. To our amazement, Jimmy still had the oil jug in his hand. We had been gone 30 mins and it was less than a 10-minute job to fill the engine with oil. I quipped, "what have you been messing about at ". He came straight back at me saying it had taken over 20 jugs of oil to fill the engine. Dave and I looked at each other aghast! That was 3 times more than it should have been. Luckily, we realised something was amiss. If we had tried to start the engine with that amount of oil in, it would have blown it to pieces. Jimmy had literally filled the engine with oil until it came out the top of the rocker housing on top of the engine, where the oil filler cap was. We were dumfounded that he hadn't used the oil dip stick to check the oil level. We now had the job of draining the oil out of the engine and starting again. Jimmy just kept saying, "Well you said fill her up so I did".

Apparently, it turned out he never checked his lorry's oil at all. It was done daily by a mechanic so he just got in and drove.

A similar thing happened with our second coach. We had just bought it at the beginning of the season and had not quite finished overhauling it or fitting it out, but nevertheless decided to take it for a run out to Leicestershire County Show. We had performed there before, it was held in the first week of May and was notorious for being very wet. The idea was to use it as a changing room and a safe haven from the elements.

Early season shows are always a worry as equipment has been taken out of the horsebox and coach over the winter for maintenance and rehearsals. Every season we would discover we had left some vital bit of kit at home.

The day before the show we were all busy tracking down missing bits of equipment when Jimmy turned up and asked what he could do to help. The new coach had a faulty fuel gauge so I asked Jimmy to dip the tank. He reported back that it had about a foot of diesel in it. It was a huge fuel tank and that amount would have taken us to London and back let alone the 20 miles to Leicester.

When we arrived at the show we missed the back entrance to the show ground and ended up in a housing estate having to do a U turn with an 11-metre-long coach. This took a lot of shunting and bouncing up curbs. Just as we had nearly finished shunting, the engine petered out. The consensus was that we must have disturbed some muck in the fuel tank bouncing around. So, while our coach blocked off the housing estate, I began removing the fuel filters and bleeding the system. Forty minutes later, covered in and stinking of diesel, the bus was up and running again. We proceeded to the show and did two great shows.

On top of the world we packed up in glorious spring sunshine and discussed which pub should have the pleasure of our company on the way home. Our route home took us briefly up the M1 from the M69 junction, passing Leicester Forest East Services to the A46 junction, less than 2 miles further on. As we approached the Services the engine spluttered and died. It was about 100 yards to the services slip road when we coasted to a halt on the hard shoulder. The coach was full of about 20 strong lads so off everyone jumped and started to push the coach slightly uphill towards the slip road. Our first concern was to get the coach off the motorway and avoid a costly tow-off fee. It was exhausting, but yard by yard we pushed the coach off the motorway into the Services. Thankfully we managed to avoid any passing police patrol cars as I think they would have taken a dim view of what we were doing. Once in the safety of the services we found a stick and dipped the fuel tank. It was bone dry!! Luckily for Jimmy, he had taken the horse's home or else murder might have been committed. Not to be defeated, and more to the point waste valuable drinking time waiting for a tow truck, we decided to try and push the coach up the even steeper hill to the diesel pumps. It was very hard; we could only manage a few yards before needing a rest. We soon attracted an audience from the services car park and then people started to join us and help push. With extra help, we crested the top of the rise to cheers and claps as we coasted the coach down to the pumps. After filling up, I went into pay and was greeted by a chuckling cashier who enquired if we were one of these new cut price coach trips. Another half hour bleeding the fuel system out again and we were on our way home. It turned out Jimmy couldn't find a stick to dip the tank so had used a stirrup leather instead. He had pushed the whole length in and it had travelled across the width of the tank wetting about a foot of the leather even though the tank was nearly empty. We still don't let him forget that gaffe to this day over 30 years on!

Our next show after this incident was at Harpenden Round Table near Luton, and after the problems with our new coach we decided to take it out for a proving run before retiring the old coach. We hadn't finished converting it; in fact, all we had done was strip out the seats. It wasn't even taxed but we did stick a sign in the window saying Tax in the post (agh! the good old days).

So off we went to Harpenden with our two coaches. I felt so proud. There was roadworks on the M1, so we decided to take the A5 route instead (the scenic route). It was a beautiful day and all was going well. The new coach was zipping along leading the way. I was driving. I arrived at the show ground ahead of schedule and waited. After half an hour, I was worried as the old coach hadn't arrived. So, I found a call box and phoned the stables to see if they had any news (no mobile phones in those days). Nothing! After several more calls in fifteen minutes' intervals, to an irate Lou who was running the stables on her own on the busiest day of the week, the horse box arrived.

The coach had broken down on a steep hill near Dunstable. The lads had off loaded the costumes, weapons and themselves into a jam-packed horsebox. I went and explained the problem to the organisers and suggested we do a small show without jousting whilst we went back to the broken-down bus and got the rest of the equipment. They were not happy but understood we were trying our best.

So, with two others I set off back to fetch the rest of the equipment. It involved two hours driving plus about half an hour transferring the kit. We were in so much of a hurry to get back we took a wrong turn and ended up in a town. The only place we could find to turn around was a large police station. Not the best place to take an untaxed bus. Just as we were backing into the entrance of the police station a police car pulled up and the police officer got out and strode purposefully towards the bus. We all thought, shit he is going to do us for driving an untaxed vehicle. As he approached the door I pressed our new toy, the automatic door opening button, and smiled. Before I could say anything, he asked what we were doing trying to park a coach in the police car park. Having explained we were lost and trying to turn around he offered to help us back in, gave us directions to get to our destination and then stopped all the traffic to let us pull out! We laughed all the way to the show ground. We just couldn't believe our luck. As we pulled into the show ground it was as if Royalty had arrived, with the crowd giving us a standing ovation. The lads´ unscripted show had gone down well and they were dying to see the full show. The organisers really appreciated what we had done and paid us in full despite the delay.

All our coaches had to be modified to avoid a HGV licence to drive them. The law at that time was a bit vague about private coaches. I spent days on the phone to various departments of the ministry of Transport. Each department told me something different and invariably told me to contact another department for confirmation. In the end, there seemed to be two ways to get around the HGV problem. Just when we were sure we knew what we were talking about, we hit another problem. The MOT! Because of its size and weight, it needed a special Class 5 MOT. Finding a garage that did the Class 5 was like finding rocking horse shit and finding one that could be bothered to do one was well-nigh impossible. The garages, like ourselves, could not agree on what it was. Some said a mobile home, others a minibus. In the end, we decided to fill both criteria. We removed all but twelve seats giving us 13 seats including the driver's. thereby filling the criteria for a mini bus. We then fitted bunk beds, storage lockers which doubled as extra beds, a sink and a cooker. We now filled the criteria for a mobile home. As the bunk beds were the most comfortable, everyone wanted to sleep on them. However, they did have a problem when we cornered at speed, people rolled out onto the floor. Very painful if sleeping on the top bunk! We solved this problem with a sheet of plywood screwed to side of the beds. Being rough joiners we just cut a large hole with a jig saw to gain access to the lower bunk making it dark and private. This became known as the "Polecats Den" because of the smell of sweat and fart trapped inside it. It was quite normal to find three drunk jousters piled up on top of each other snoring happily away like basking seals.

The coaches were loved by the jousters. They could catch up on much needed sleep and we always had food and drink on board so there was no need to stop at services, drastically cutting down journey times. We finally solved the problem of "pee stops" after doing a joint venture with the Arkley Knights, who used a mini bus as transport. They had fixed a 5-gallon plastic drum with a large funnel in the top to make a mobile urinal. Some skill was required as to accuracy, because the bus bounced and swayed quite a lot at the back where it was fitted. The major down side was the smell and emptying it. The bus was like a greenhouse in summer not a good recipe for well agitated urine!

As we became more successful the travelling increased and what used to be an exciting day out became just another day's work. Boredom set in and different members of the troupe coped with it in their own ways. I personally never came to terms with it and that is why I used to drive so much. The two main ways the lads coped were cards and sleep, both fuelled with beer. Some lads could walk onto the bus, collapse onto a bed and not wake for four hours, with mayhem going on all around. The card school, on the other hand, was wide awake every moment of the trip. They would start playing even before the coach departed and continue until strong words from me forced them off the bus to start setting up. As the number of shows increased, so did their income, and so did the stakes they played for. It was quite normal for someone to have won £200-£300 on a one-way trip from the stables to the venue. A princely sum in the 1980s. On one occasion Harvey Broadhead won a car off Martin Brown within 10 minutes of leaving the stables. And, the debt was honoured. Whenever we arrived at a destination the players would change from their favoured game of brag to a few rapid hands of deadly £10 turnover. The great thing about card playing was the big winner used to buy the first round in the pub, leaving me to pick up the bill for the rest of the drinks.

There were also endless pranks and play-acting to pass the time away. Some lasting a whole season. There were so many you could write a book about them.

For a whole year, we carried a mobile coffin with us. It had many uses, mainly as an extra bed or for the initiation of some new member into the troupe by padlocking them inside for a whole journey. The funniest and probably the most dangerous prank was devised by Pete Webster commonly known as Satan. He would whiten his face and redden his eyes and lips so he looked like a corpse. He then got into the coffin which had been placed in the back window of the bus, clearly visible by cars following. He had an assistant who would tell him when a car was following behind. He would then slowly open the lid and sit up starring at the driver behind. His piece-de-resistance was a pair ghoulish eye balls that fell out of his eye sockets on springs, bouncing up and down with the motion of the bus. How this didn't cause an accident or heart attack I will never know.

Another stunt the lads used to do pull was to trigger the emergency stop-lights for the low bridges at Bingham and Tollerton. The lads had noticed that there were high sensors at the side of the road that were triggered by high lorries approaching these low railway bridges. By sticking a banner pole through the skylight in the coach roof they could trigger all the lights telling the driver to stop and turn back. There were flashing warning lights everywhere for about half a mile before the bridge. I'm sure the Police would have taken a dim view but the lads found it hilarious.

A simple well-meaning gift caused a lot of trouble. Paul Cooling aka Wicksey, went to visit his sister in Belgium. She was a military nurse stationed over there and it was the period when the AIDS epidemic was rife. As Wicksey said goodbye, his sister presented him with a polythene bag containing a 100 plus condoms, all loose and individually wrapped, and the parting words "If you can't be good be careful". Wicksey decided to share them with the jousters, so brought them with him when Andrew Ducker picked him up to give him a lift to travel on the bus. Ducker had a sports car and Wicksey stuffed the bag of condoms into the tiny glove compartment and promptly forgot about them. About a week later Ducker was driving with his fiancé Gaynor, when she decided that she needed a tissue out of the glove compartment. As she pulled open the glove compartment, condoms started to cascade out and into her lap. Ducker said that it seemed to go on for an eternity as more and more piled into her lap. To make matters worse Gaynor was on the pill. Wives and girlfriends of the jousters were always suspicious of the close camaraderie of the jousters and were always convinced they were hiding the truth if they used a fellow jouster as an alibi, so when Ducker said Wicksey had left them in the glove compartment it only made matters worse. The offending bag of condoms then made its way onto the coach where they lay on the luggage rack offending nobody until one evening coming home from Belvoir Castle.

Belvoir was the one show we allowed wives and girlfriends to come with us and the coach was overloaded with jovial people of both sexes after the usual 3-hour session in the Windmill Pub at Redmile. A chance remark by somebody that they had seen a person put a condom over their head and nose and then blow it up by exhaling through their nose, started a giggling debate. Would they stretch enough to fit on your head? Who had a willy as thick as a head? etc.!! The bag of condoms was suddenly remembered and within minutes everyone had an inflated condom on their head waving to following and passing motorists. They must have thought it was a bus load of Martians.

The next game after everyone got bored with scaring motorists was to see who could inflate the largest condom on their head. So now we had condoms exploding on everybody's head. It was hilarious and soon the 100 plus condoms had all been used.

The following morning our new PA started her first day working for us. Her predecessor Jill had been an old friend of Lou's and mother to one of the jousters. Although the job was primarily booking and manning reception, at quiet times such as mornings, she would also clean and perform any general duties that Lou or I didn't have time for. I wasn't there when Jo, our new PA arrived on her first day. Lou had no idea about anything that had gone on in the bus. Lou was unexpectedly tied up when Jo arrived to start work so asked if she could clean out the bus whilst she finished sorting out the unexpected problem and then Lou would do a proper induction with her. Poor girl. She was straight out of Uni. As she entered the bus, full of enthusiasm, she was confronted with the sight of what appeared to be a hundred odd used condoms, empty beer bottles and cans, plus the left overs of twenty odd fish and chip suppers, all warming up nicely in the summer sun. To make things worse, there were several nude books scattered around. She must have thought we had had a mass orgy. Apparently, she came back to Lou with a red face and very flustered. She announced that, "There is far too much testosterone going on in that bus for my liking" and she declared would never ever set foot onto it ever again.

Although I could tell hundreds more tales that happened on our Coach, I will leave this chapter with one more which I am sure you can easily visualise and hopefully make you chuckle as much as it did me.

In the early nineties, we did several shows in Kilkenny Eire, where I became very good friends with Jim Brennan and his Family. We met under slightly fraught conditions, more of which you will hear about later. Needless to say, it turned out we had many things in common. We both had two children; a boy and a girl of similar ages. Except for Jim, the whole family rode and hunted. We also shared a common sense of humour and had a great love of food and drink. The families have remained close friends ever since, visiting each other on a regular basis and holidaying together on many occasions.

It was September 1999. Jim's wife, Patricia, was visiting England with her sister Vivian and another friend. They knew all the jousters from their trips to Kilkenny so we decided to take them on the bus to a show we were doing at Wolverhampton Races. It was perfect, for like all Irish, they loved horse racing. Having heard so many tales about what went on in the bus travelling to and from shows, they were desperate to sample the fun. The show was at night, so we didn't leave Bunny until after lunch which meant plenty of time for a few drinks in the club bar before leaving. There was also plenty to drink on the bus including a bottle of Tequila, especially for the girls (old scores to settle). I had left slightly earlier with the horses knowing the bus was faster and would catch me up. I was past Birmingham on the M6 when I saw the bus in my mirror. The bus soon caught us and as they cruised past everyone was waving and making rude gestures, glasses in hand. They were obviously having a great party.

The bus settled down just in front of us to complete the last leg in convoy as usual. A couple of miles further on I overtook the bus again, which was not uncommon, as the lorry had different gearing. I glanced across to check with the driver that everything was ok and got the thumbs up. Not long after, we hit some heavy traffic caused by a very long steep hill. I could see the bus slowly gaining on us as we ground up the hill at about twenty miles per hour. Inch by inch the bus gained on us until it was alongside us and almost matching our speed. As they drew level I caught a wry grin from Scots Jim who was driving. Then like a slide show, one by one the large windows of the bus came into view, all filled with bare bottoms pressed against the glass. The whole bus was mooning down the M6 motorway on one of its busiest sections, all led by our two respectably married Irish guests. It was a wonder they didn't cause a multiple pileup.

Chapter 5   The Crazy Years 1980 – 1988

(Or the Golden years)

Although I have set a time scale of fifteen years for the Crazy Years, they evolved slowly and ended slowly and it's true to say that they probably lasted in some form for more like 21 years. It was my two younger brothers and their friends who took over the hell-raising from Tony, Brian and me. They took it to a new level. However, reading about what we used to do these day's might seem crazy now, but this was the Eighties and everything was outrageous! We were playing to huge crowds at both home and abroad, plus doing loads of filming and television. We were in show biz and it was expected that you drank a lot and behaved outrageously. Having said that, it was a salve for the constant punishment we inflicted on our bodies, for boredom, for loneliness, and provided a way to cope with the massive amounts of adrenaline we were pumping into our bodies.

As I started this chapter, I met Martin Brown at my brother Phil's eldest daughter Kayleigh's, wedding. We were reminiscing about the jousting and I told him that I had called his era the "Crazy Years". He replied "No! Not the Crazy Years, they were the Golden Years."

Thinking about it, probably it was Golden for most of them as they were all in their mid-teens or early twenties when we started to travel abroad. Many had never been abroad at all before they joined the jousting association.

I chose 1980 as the start of this era for many reasons. If you look at the lists of shows we performed in 1979 and 1980, there is a threefold jump in the number of shows for 1980. This happened for several reasons. The main one was that we had developed a solid base of customers up and down the country that were happy to recommend us to other prospective clients. Secondly, we were starting to appear on TV shows that gave us national recognition, and lastly Jimmy Durrands was constantly promoting us through Belvoir Castle. He was the best agent we ever had and totally unpaid.

It was from a contact passed to us from Jimmy that we got involved in a small promotional day at Warwick Castle for a carpet manufacturer called Illingworth Carpets. They had just developed a super, hard wearing carpet tile and the advertising slogan was "Illingworth the invincible". Hence the involvement of knights and armour. "Why" you may ask? We certainly did, but advertising agencies got paid for strange ideas. It was quite a nondescript day, but we got paid well and went home not expecting to hear from Ilingworth Carpets ever again. Just another day at the office.

Early the next year I was contacted by the advertising agency asking if I would be prepared to do some photographic work in a full suite of plate armour. I didn't have a suit of armour, nor did I have a horse that was trained to a clanky suit of full plate armour. I said, "yes no problem", without hesitation. The agency was trying to sell Illingworth's an advertising package, they wanted a rough quote so that they could come up with a budget to put to the company. It was a long, drawn out process taking nearly a year. All very hush hush. Finally, I got a date and a location for a final costing. We were going to do the shoot in Scotland by a loch, in January. I arranged to hire a fabulous, silver-plated suit of armour from Terry Goulden, who ran his film props and costume company called Arms and Armoury in Ware, Hertfordshire. Terry supplied all our chainmail and we had worked together since the early seventies. Then out of the blue I got a call asking if I would be prepared to go to Florida to do the shoot. Rather stunned and not thinking about the consequences through I said, "Yes". Apparently, they needed shots of a knight by a secluded lake surrounded by green trees and sunshine. Scotland in January was just not going to provide that.

I've taken time to talk about how this came about because although we didn't joust and only I went to Florida, we got a lot of publicity at home, thanks again to Jimmy Durrands.

We also got to put on our CV, that we had worked in the USA. It gave us credibility to work internationally. It also opened the door to all the other international tours.

But I'm jumping ahead, let's start at the beginning.

1980-81

Those first three years of the Eighties had a great influence on the next hectic decade and just looking at show numbers doesn't tell the whole story. The late Seventies were a struggle; the country was in a financial mess; money and confidence were in short supply. The number of shows dwindled and we almost stopped jousting. Most of our shows came from people watching us and thinking that jousting would be great for our fete or carnival. As the show numbers dropped fewer people saw us so fewer people inquired about shows. The standard 6 knight show was a thing of the past. Nobody could afford them so we started to offer 4 and even 2 knight shows just to keep our face out there. The 6 knight shows were either one 90-minute show or two one hour shows. Our new 4 knight and 2 knight shows were 2 x45 minutes or 1 x 60 minutes and 2 x 20 minutes or 1 x 30 minutes. We hated the 2 knight shows. They were so short that we never had time to develop the characters with the audience. They were also very hard work because you still had to set up all the kit but with half the number of lads. The 4 knight shows, however, were a great success. The shorter shows were much punchier, and the crowd found it much easier to understand the different characters of four knights, rather than six knights. Although the numbers for that period don't look too bad, but if you take out the 2 knight shows, they were pretty dire. In 1980, the numbers were good but a lot of the shows were 2 knight shows. However, in 1981 we did fewer shows, but they were all 4 or 6 knight shows at top class venues.

1980 seems only memorable for bad things happening. We were very excited about the forthcoming season. We had more shows than ever booked and although there were a lot of two knight shows we also had some six knight shows. In fact, our first show of the season was a 6-knight show. The show was at Macclesfield and organised by an old family friend. They understood horses and the site was exceptionally attractive. We just couldn't wait to do this show.

The show day arrived and it was pouring with rain and as the day progressed the rain just got heavier and heavier. The weather was so bad that the organisers were reluctant to let us perform, fearing the damage that the horses would do to the turf. We needed the performance fee so badly that I convinced them that the horses would do very little damage. As it turned out the only patch of green grass at the end of the day was the jousting arena. The crowds turned out in their thousands and stayed for both performances despite the torrential rain. The rain was so heavy that the water running off our jousting helms made a waterfall over our eye slits making it impossible to see our opponents. The crowd really appreciated our heroic efforts to entertain them and gave us a standing ovation all the way back to our horse box. We made a lot of friends that day and over the coming years we got a lot of other shows because of our reputation of going on in all weathers to entertain the paying public. After Macclesfield, we made a selling feature of our determination to perform whatever the weather. Since then we have performed in fog, sleet, snow, gales, dust, temperatures of 40 degrees Celsius and even at an altitude of over 8,000 feet.

A show, early in July at West Bromwich brought home the stark realities of how Britain was changing. You hear of things on the news, and you think that you understand what you are hearing, but to face it is a very different thing…

We had heard on the news briefly about some race riots in Birmingham early that week, but it had never registered on our radar. The show was a small two knight show from an agency, so the budget was very tight and a pre-show site visit was not viable. This was before the days of satellite navigation. So, we just had an address and a Great Britain map book to find our way; not easy when you are going through the centre of Birmingham. As you might expect we got a bit lost. We were quite close to the site so we were not very worried as we turned into a wide street. WOW! It was like entering a war zone; smouldering burnt out cars, debris everywhere and groups of black people on street corners staring at us. To us in the horsebox it felt frightening, even menacing, but writing this now I can see that a group of white people driving a horsebox through an all-black area just after a riot must have looked as strange as a space ship from Mars landing. We did the show which was the West Bromwich Carnival to nearly an all-black audience. We went down very well and were made very welcome but in the early 80's it was quiet a culture shock.

Our last show of 1980 was at Musselburgh, just south of Edinburgh. It was a late booking and six knights' show. We were all excited about going back to Scotland, especially as it was so close to Edinburgh. Again, because of the time factor and distance, I had not done a site visit. I had stoked up excitement with the lads who were wilting a bit after the busiest year we had for a very long time, by telling them about the lovely bars I had visited in Edinburgh, and that we were going to be jousting at a racecourse right next to the sea (if truth be told it was an estuary).

We arrived in a damp drizzle that soaked us through. Our hotel was like the one in Kirkcaldy. Very Victorian, and the local bars were like gaols with galvanised mesh over all the windows and steel reinforced doors. We were warned by the local Round Table, our hosts, not to venture into any of them if we wanted to come out in one piece. We have always prided ourselves on getting on with everyone and have had some great nights out in some very rough pubs so would normally ignore their advice. However, on this occasion the pubs looked so unwelcoming that nobody was tempted to venture into any of them.

On the morning of the show the heavy drizzle had stopped so I decided to go for an early morning stroll. I hadn't gone far when I met Scots Jimmy, another early riser like myself. As I greeted him I realised he was quite agitated and asked him what was the matter. He replied that he had just had a great shock and that he didn't realise how much things had changed since he had left Scotland. I enquired if there was anything in particular that had upset him, and he replied "Aye, av just seen a woolly head wearing a kilt". I asked for a translation and it turned out he had just seen a black man walking down the street in a kilt. I reminded him that the famous news reader called Trevor Mc Donald was black. He suddenly cheered up and smiled saying "Aye, I suppose our ancestors used to put it about quite a lot when they were away from home".

By the time, we had set up the show at the racecourse, the heavy drizzle had returned, and although about a thousand-people turned up, it was below expectations. As we did our first performance the rain turned to heavy rain dampening spirits in all quarters. Before we could do the second show, a heavy sea fog rolled in and took visibility down to a few yards. We kept delaying the second show, until everyone had left the ground and then packed up soaked to the skin and set off on our long drive home. As we did so, the sun suddenly broke through and the fog cleared. It was as if Scotland was glad to see us leaving.

1981 was, as I have already mentioned, a year top of class shows and venues. The only thing that I remember about that year was an embarrassing incident that happened to Lou and me in Penzance. The enquiry came in very late, towards the end of June. It was a Round Table fund raising event and they wanted me to visit them before committing to book us. We had just finished haymaking and we were in the middle of a heatwave. I suggested to Lou that she and Mark, our son, who was just four months old, should come down with me for a day by the sea. After all the weather was just perfect. As usual, we had loads of things to sort out before leaving the Stables, so left in a desperate rush. No need to pack - just travel down in a light pair of trousers and a smart short sleeve shirt, with swimming trunks and shorts for the beach. The meeting was scheduled for 5.30 pm so we drove down chasing the clock all the way. Luckily Mark slept all the way. We just made it and I jumped out of the car to greet the awaiting committee. I immediately realised that it was much colder and then I noticed everyone had coats and umbrellas with them. The wind was brisk and getting stronger by the minute. Did I feel a few specks of rain or was it blown form the big waves crashing onto the beach? The committee suggested we look at the proposed site just down the road first and then talk about all the other details. It was only a five-minute drive but the wind which was now almost gale force was accompanied by heavy, horizontal rain. At the proposed site, a farmer's field, the committee struggled out of their cars pulling on coats and trying to put up umbrellas. A bemused committee member enquired if I wanted to go back and get my coat from the car. It was then I had to admit that I didn't have a coat. The person then turned to the rest of the committee and shouted over the gale "He doesn't have a coat". They all stared at me and I could see them thinking how stupid I was. I thought they are never going to book me now. I quickly checked the field which was thankfully straightforward. We retired to a hotel for our meeting and I changed out of my soaking clothes into the only things I had - jeans and a tee shirt. I apologised for my lack of suitable clothing and told them about the heat wave we were experiencing up in the Midlands. Surely, I must have heard about the imminent arrival of Hurricane Bret! I explained that I had been hay making right up to the moment we left and had only been listening to the local weather forecast. Thankfully there was a local farmer on the committee who nodded and reassured me that he fully understood.

Fortunately, I got the show, made a lot of good friends, and went on to do another show the next year. The tail end of Hurricane Bret had passed over by next morning and it was a lovely sunny but breezy morning. Lou, Mark and I sat on the beach for about ten minutes admiring St Michael's Mount across the bay but it was too chilly, so after about 10 minutes we packed up and set off for home

Penzance is a close-knit community and we made many friends down there. Sadly, in December 1981, just four months after our first show down there, the Pen Lee Life boat from Penzance was lost with all hands trying to rescue the crew of

The Union Star freighter, whose engines had failed in mountainous seas. It prompted a spontaneous reaction from the troupe to raise money to help the families of the heroic crew members who lost their lives. We raised a sizeable sum by organising a German beer festival in the indoor riding school complete with an Oompah Band. It was very successful and prompted the lads to regularly raise money for different charities close to the hearts of jousters. People tend to think of the jousters as wild, hard drinking dare devils but there is a deep, quiet and caring side to them, that most people fail to notice.

On our second trip down to Penzance, we were stabled at an eventing yard right next to the sea. I asked the owner if we were permitted to ride on the beach. She said that it was not a problem. However, she added that the salt water rotted the tack so didn't recommend doing so, unless we had some old tack with us. The saddles we use for jousting are old Army saddles that date back to the early nineteen hundred's, so were too valuable to risk. We were all desperate to ride in the sea so decided to ride bareback. The yard owner also said that the sand was very soft in some places and could be very dangerous if you didn't know the beach but if we still wanted to go, she would ride with us and show us the danger areas. The Owner/ Event rider was attractive and in her early twenties, so everyone was queuing up to take the horses for a ride on the beach. The lads were out to impress and made a great show of pulling each other off the horses in the sea. After about 30 minutes everyone was soaked and exhausted so we decided to go for a canter along the beach to dry off. The gentle canter gradually turned into a gallop and finally a full-blown race with the riders hollering like a Rebel Confederate cavalry charge. As the horses started to run out of steam and slow up somebody shouted out that their backside was sore and then we all started to realise that we had all rubbed our bums sore, riding bareback in wet jeans. We all decided that it was time we should head for home. When we turned the horses around we suddenly realised just how far we had ridden whilst having fun. Our original starting point was now just a speck in the distance on the horizon. We now had to ride excited jogging horses back several miles with already very sore legs and bottoms. The ride back seemed to go on for ever and was excruciatingly painful. It proved very funny to our host who was dry and comfortably seated on an old saddle. Any street-cred that they had hoped for to impress our female host was lost as we staggered out of the stable yard with our legs wide apart to try to avoid our jeans touching the raw bits on our legs.

Orlando Florida 1982

It wasn't until early March 1982 that things were finally sorted for our change of destination. I was collected by the film crew in a van full of their kit which was joined by a box containing my suit of armour. The trip down to Heathrow was great as we could get to know each other before meeting the others on the trip.

When we arrived at Heathrow, I was amazed to find out that the workers were outnumbered by more than two to one by executives. Luckily, all the photographic equipment and my suit of armour had been cleared for customs by an agent the week before and the art director was handling the paperwork.

In those days, there were no direct flights to Orlando so we had to land at Miami and clear immigration before taking another flight up to Orlando. We nearly missed the connecting flight when my box of armour set off the metal detector alarm. The security guards soon calmed down but we were held up by them trying on the helmet and playing with the sword!

We finally arrived at our motel very tired and jet lagged. We had left the UK in a temperature of 6 degrees C and arrived in a very humid 32 degrees.

The next morning I was taken to a riding stable deep in the swampy backcountry near Orlando. It was hot, steamy and stunningly beautiful. The owner, Ed Rieg, was a great guy and he warmly welcomed us with "anything you guys want, just ask".

The priorities for that first day were for me to find a horse that would allow me to ride it in a clanky suit of armour and to find a suitable lake location for the filming. I thought that getting a horse to accept the armour would be the problem. However, the first horse I tried accepted it straight away. Finding a location, however, was proving much harder. My job was done by lunchtime so I tagged along with the crew in the afternoon driving around looking at lakes. The cameraman was studying a map when he told the driver to make a sharp left turn down a track. We slowly made our way down a dirt track towards a lake. Our guide suddenly shouted "stop now! There is a chain on the ground! Backup now". We came to an abrupt halt. The cameraman insisted we carried on. It was only an old rusty chain embedded into the soil. The guide however, was now getting very agitated and he explained that if you crossed a chain across a road you had entered private land, and the owner was allowed by law to shoot you for trespass. The cameraman still insisted we drive on. At which point, the guide got out of the car and said that if we wanted to get killed, ok, but he wasn't coming. After a brief argument, we turned back. What people don't realise is that Florida is a cattle ranching state with a shoot first, ask questions later. Ed Rieg confirmed that we were very likely to have been shot at when we returned to the stables. After this incident, I started to notice that nearly every pickup truck had a rifle rack in its back window with several rifles on display.

Ed suggested that we should take a look at a lake on his own property (why didn't we say we wanted a lake?). The cameraman went off with Ed and came back saying it was perfect except they had been forced to hack their way through 400 yards of swamp jungle to get to the lakes edge. Again, Ed came to the rescue. He had his own bulldozer and he could easily bulldoze a road to the water's edge.

Filming started early to catch the sunrise and went on late to catch the sunset. One of the first shots they wanted was of me on horseback at the water's edge. I should mention that I have great fear of water and I am a useless swimmer. The suit of armour was very heavy and my helm was bolted around my head with two locking clasps. As we set up the shot the cameraman kept saying, "A little closer to the water's edge, just a little closer please", then then bank stared to crumble and I panicked! I kicked the horse away from the water's edge. I explained to the crew my fear on falling off into the water in a suit of armour especially with the helm bolted onto my head. I asked them to unbolt the helm so I could get it off, and suggested that people stand by to rescue me if the horse and I went in. Ed Rieg and most of the stable staff had also come down to watch the filming, suddenly Ed's voice boomed out, "Hell don't worry about drowning that ole gaiter over there will have you chopped up way before you have time to drown ". We all looked to where Ed was pointing and saw two big eyes protruding out of the water not 30 yards from the water's edge. His stare was definitely, on us. Suddenly it was decided that perhaps we could manage with a shot not quite so close to the water's edge. What frightened the townie crew most was Ed announcing he had got his gun with him and he was sure he could kill the alligator before it got to any of us. All the executives decided they were not needed on set and promptly disappeared never to be seen again until we went home.

The filming was hard work in the intense heat and humidity, especially for me in a full suit of armour. I nearly passed out several times from heat exhaustion. Again, Ed to the rescue. This time he turned up with a huge icebox at least five times bigger than anything we had in the UK, filled with ice and cans of Budweiser beer. Every day we bought a two-dozen slab of Bud and a big bag of ice and slowly drank them during the day. We sweated so much we never went for a pee all day.

The other thing that freaks me out is snakes. On the last day of filming we were doing some galloping towards the camera and we had done about 20 takes, at varying speeds and angles. We reset to finish off using a new line so they had a different background. On action, I spurred the mare into a good gallop and had gone about 50 yards when she stopped dead and dived sideways hurtling me through the air. It was a heavy painful fall! That left me very dazed. I might even have been knocked out briefly. We had been filming on some grassy wasteland by the stable yard. The crew were horrified and sent someone to get help. By the time, they had managed to remove my helm I was surrounded by people. Ed asked if I was ok and I said I seemed to be able to move most bits of my body. I commented how strange it was as the mare had never put a foot wrong throughout the filming. "Snakes" Ed replied. "I didn't realise you were going to work so close to the brush - always snakes in that bit". The thought of falling off onto a snake in a suit of armour still terrifies me even today. Just writing this now has given me the shivers. I think the crew were as freaked as me and they suddenly decided that they had all the shots we needed and declared we were done filming.

The second day's filming had a very early start and went very well so the director gave us the afternoon off and treated us to a visit to Disneyland. I wasn't keen to go as I thought it would be a bit childish. Well how wrong could I have been! Everything I had been doing with stunts in the jousting to thrill the audience was here but on a massive scale. It just blew me away! A few years later I took Lou and my two children, Mark and Emma back to Disney as I so wanted them to experience what I had seen and felt.

The last day involved another early start as the still photographer wanted yet more sunrises. We then spent till mid-afternoon packing equipment ready for the flight home and then decided to celebrate at a local bar with a few beers for a job well done. All American bars seem to be quite dark, with no windows and low lighting. We were all sat at the bar in a line and I was at one end of the row. We had been there about an hour when it came to my turn to buy a round. I shouted, "same again" to the owner and reached for my handbag (a sort of oversized wallet with a wrist strap, all very fashionable in the early Eighties). It had gone. I desperately scoured the floor in case I had accidentally knocked it onto the floor. The owner was fantastic. No sooner had I said that my bag had gone, he said "I know who took it. It that was that damn druggie". In seconds, he was on the phone to the police and asking me what was in the bag. All my money, passport, and flight ticket. He came back from the phone saying the police knew who to look for. After about 30 minutes, which seemed an eternity, the owner said the police were outside and wanted to talk to him and me.

Before we got outside the owner stopped and said, "I know you didn't actually see who took your bag but I'm sure who it was. When they say is this the person who took your bag? Just say "Yes sir". He said it with such force that I knew it wasn't a request. Outside was an American squad car in all its glory just like those movies about the Deep South, complete with gun toting officers bedecked with badges, white Stetsons and sunglasses. The lad in the back of the car was in his early twenties drawn, slightly scruffy and looking very frightened. After I had identified him. the Police officers asked me to wait while they had a little talk to him. After about five minutes an office came back and said that he had admitted stealing it but had passed it on to someone else and that he was refusing to give that person's name. He asked me to confirm what was in the bag and when I was flying home. He said, "Right you need to get this bag back " and I nodded in agreement. We walked back to the car and beckoned for me to get in. He explained to the detainee that I needed my bag back urgently to get home and that I wouldn't press charges if he told us where it was. The lad stated again that he didn't know where it was, then the officer next to him quick as a flash drew his gun, put it to the lad's head and then cocked the gun saying, " look you f***king piece of s***t tell me where the bag is or I'll blow your brains out". It was straight out of a Clint Eastwood, Dirty Harry movie. I nearly passed out with fright. Needless, to say they found out where my bag was. The Police ask me to get out of the car and to have a word. They wanted to know what I was doing in this part of Orlando as it wasn't normal for a tourist to be in this area. I explained that we had just finished making a film out at Ed Rieg's stables. He seemed very impressed and apologised on behalf of Orlando for what had happened. He told me not to worry but to go back to Ed's immediately. Not to worry! I was terrified. No passport and not enough money to buy another ticket home. Lou had not been happy about me going in the first place leaving her alone with two young children. Worry! My knees were going weak and I didn't know whether to throw up or pass out.

We returned to the stables. Ed was down town at his gun shop but had phoned to say he was on his way back to help get things sorted. Even before Ed got back several huge, jacked-up pickup trucks started to arrive at the ranch. When Ed arrived, he told me the police had spoken to him and explained that although they knew where my bag was they needed a court order to search the house. The order would take at least 24 hours to get, which was too late to help me. They had given Ed the address of where my bag was supposed to be and if Ed could organise a few locals to visit the house they guaranteed that the police would not respond for 30 minutes. Ed being a responsible citizen would not be coming along, but his friends would take good care of me. Six huge pickups filled with burly ranchers set off in convoy, all carried several rifles in gun racks behind the driver's seat.

We swept into a sort of housing estate of bungalows and passed a parked police car then made a left turn and after about a quarter of a mile suddenly turned off the road and onto the lawn of a bungalow. The pickup doors flew open and men armed with baseball bats charged into the house from front and back. My driver smiled at me and said, "We'll just sit here, this shouldn't take long". True to his word in less than ten minutes one of the men came out with my bag and asked me to check the contents. My passport and tickets were both there and I was just starting to check my money when he told me it was 20 dollars short. He told me they had searched the house and they were pretty sure there was no more money in the house but if I wanted, they could beat them a bit more to try and get the extra 20 dollars. I told him I was happy to forget the 20 dollars. He said that was good because the police couldn't hold off much longer. We all drove off past the police car giving them the thumbs up. I was shaking like a leaf when we got back to the ranch. I thanked them profusely and said that I hoped they wouldn't get into trouble. They assured me it had been done with complete police backing. "It's how we get things done out here. They's just trash".

I hardly slept that night and didn't feel safe until our second plane took off from Miami. In fact, I worried for weeks after getting home that I might be recalled to Orlando because I never knew what had happened in that house or the consequences. Thankfully, I never heard anything more. Before I left Ed gave me a present of some spurs that belonged to his grandfather who had worn them herding cattle on the Chisolm trail. I still have them today.

Some years later when I took my family to Disneyland, I looked up Ed. He had sold the ranch but still had the gun shop. I took my son Mark with me to meet him. When I met him, he asked if we would like to shoot some guns on the indoor range. Mark was so excited. He was only ten or eleven. I clipped his ear when he asked if he could have a go but before I could reprimand him Ed said of course he could. He also gave us 100 rounds of ammunition each free. Ed then asked us what guns we would like to shoot. I chose a Colt 45 magnum and embarrassingly, Mark asked if they had an Uzi. I was horrified. For those who don't know, an Uzi was the fastest firing machine pistol in the world and used by Israeli special forces (Mark spent a lot of his childhood secretly watching X rated videos with his surrogate Uncle Harvey including "Clockwork Orange" "Texas Chainsaw

Massacre" and the "Dirty Harry" movies). To my amazement, Ed said; "of course. Good choice son. Very little recoil," and then winked at me saying he would set it to semi-automatic, as on automatic it fired 600 rounds per minute which meant his 100 rounds were only going to last 10 seconds. Mark and I spent an enjoyable hour shooting several 100's of bullets each, worryingly at human shaped targets. We met some very strange men, women and children at the range whose views seemed shocking to me, but quite ordinary them. I don't even want to write some of the things that were said to me, but I was left with the firm conviction that man, woman or child would shoot to kill if they felt threatened. When I think about what had happened with my wallet in Orlando a few years previously, it helped me understand that guns in the USA are a way of life.

Game for A Laugh

Just two months after returning from the states in March we did "Game for a Laugh" at Belvoir Castle.

"Game for a Laugh" was a long running, prime time television series, hosted over the years by a string of up-and-coming stars. At the time, we were involved, it was hosted by Sarah Kennedy, Jeremy Beadle and Mathew Kelly. They all went on to have very successful TV and Radio careers (I still listen to Sarah Kennedy on Radio 2 where she has a regular spot).

Belvoir Castle was approached by London Weekend Television about filming an episode with the Jousters. Jimmy Durrands immediately saw the publicity potential for the castle and gave us glowing references, so by the time LWT contacted me I didn't have to sell our services at all.

Sarah Kennedy was the damsel in distress and Tony Edwards as the Black Knight had to rescue her from the battlements of the Castle. Mathew Kelly then had to rescue her from Tony's evil clutches. It was great fun filming the show which took all day, and we got on marvellously with the two presenters.

The show went out early on Saturday evening's, prime time TV and had an audience of many millions. You just could not get better publicity. At the time of filming, Jimmy sent out press releases to all local and national newspapers getting the Castle and ourselves great publicity. The big bonus was that although we filmed it in May, the show didn't go out on TV until late September, and this was just when show organisers were deciding what to book as their main attraction for their next year's function. However, the icing on the cake was that we were invited to attend the live part of the show in London in costume. We all got to stand up, take a bow and do a short interview with Jeremy Beadle. It was a great all expenses paid trip to London with an after-show party thrown in.

When we got home it was amazing! People stopped us in the street or pub saying that they had seen us on Game for a Laugh and how great we were. Jimmy again sent out press releases boasting about the Belvoir Jousters appearing on "Game for a Laugh". The phone never stopped ringing. Everybody wanted to book us for next year. Our show bookings went from 9 in 1981, to 17 in 1982 and then 29 in 1983. Our season was May though to the end of August - 16 weeks. However, we rarely had any shows in early May due to the uncertainty of the weather. This meant we were now doing a show nearly every weekend plus quite a few back-to-back shows on Saturday and Sunday. We were even getting requests for mid-week shows. On paper this looks great, but we were not set up for the huge increase in work load. There were problems with personnel, transport, horses, and equipment. They all needed upgrading. More money was coming in but it was going out even faster…

1982-83

By 1982, my two brothers and their friends were really starting to assert themselves, both in the show and in the social side of the troupe. They were performing fast, slick fights and they were becoming confident at acting in front of large audiences. Pushing the boundaries came at a cost. Stuart ended up in hospital after being hit over the head with a sword on two occasions and ended up with multiple stitches both times. Pete Webster, who was making waves both on and off the field broke his ankle during a poleaxe fight at Sutton Park in North Yorkshire. It was a bad break. We all heard it snap at both ends of the field. After being treated by St. Johns on site he refused to go to hospital in Yorkshire as he had been told it would probably need an operation and a few days in hospital. After much argument, we agreed to take him to Nottingham Hospital instead. It was a two-hour drive back to Nottingham and we arrived there around 7 pm. As we arrived at the hospital, Pete asked how he was going to get home after treatment. We assured him it was not a problem as we were going to wait for him in our friend's pub just across the road from the hospital. Pete got awkward again saying there was no way we were going drinking without him and he wanted to go to the pub for at least one drink before going to casualty. We finally agreed to this after much argument, but just the one! We carried him into the Johnson Arms which was owned by an old friend of mine called Alan Johnson.

Pete's ankle was very badly swollen by this time and he couldn't even bear to rest it on the floor so with Alan's permission we sat Pete on top of the juke box. Every time we suggested going to A & E Pete declined and suggested another pint. When closing time came Pete had no choice but to face the music. The nurses at A & E were understandably very angry about our delay and Pete's drunken state. However, things got even worse. Keen to make amends we offered to wheel Pete down to X-Ray. Unfortunately, it turned into a race and we crashed the wheelchair! Bollocking number two!

After his X-Ray, we were told Pete had to stay in for an operation and that we should all go home. This came as great news for me as I could see us all being arrested for being drunk and disorderly. I thought that I had managed to round everyone up. Not an easy job as the troupe was now scattered all around A & E chatting up the nurses and patients alike. Then I realised we were still missing Brian. We searched high and low for him but to no avail. In the end, we decided he had probably already gone home so decided to leave without him. As we went out through the exit there was a commotion coming from the back of one of the parked-up ambulances. It was Brian! Apparently after copious pints he felt the need to sleep so had climbed into the back of an ambulance that had its back doors open and passed out on a stretcher in the back. The ambulance driver had just discovered him and was trying to find out who he was and where he had come from. I stepped forward apologising and claimed him. Bollocking number three! When we finally got home I realised that nobody had informed Pete's parents about his accident, so in the early hours of the morning I phoned them to tell them the bad news. Bollocking number four! It was the end of another great day running the Nottingham Jousting Association.

 Pete's ankle was badly broken and he was kept in hospital for several days. We made a mass visit to see him at the old General Hospital that used to be close to Nottingham Castle. We were stopped by a fearsome Matron who gave us a bollocking for allowing him to drink and not bringing him to A & E earlier. I think she called us irresponsible idiots or perhaps it was morons. We mounted two attempts to smuggle him out to the pub but both were thwarted by the ever-watchful Matron. The last plan was for us to climb the fire escape which was old very, steep and zig zagged up the side of the building. Pete's bed was right next to the Fire Escape door. He was going to open the door and then we would carry him down the metal stairs to the pub just across the road. Looking back, I'm glad Matron caught us as I feel sure we would have slipped and fallen whilst carrying him down the Fire Escape, doing even more damage.

Signs that the next generation were ready to challenge the old leaders came when Harvey Broadhead undid Tony's girth during the show at Southwell Agricultural Show in 1982. It was almost at the end of the second show the point where, the Black Knight is caught cheating and disqualified. After being disqualified, he storms back to his camp screaming at his men to mount and arm up for battle. His men array for battle and his horse is brought forward for him to mount and lead them into the fray. As he reaches his horse he is still bellowing that he is going to kill the Knight Marshal and all the good camp. A moment of high drama. On this occasion when he thrust his foot into the stirrup to mount he suddenly found himself flat on his back with his huge jousting saddle on top of him. The crowd roared with laughter and so did the whole Jousting Troupe. Except Tony! Tony went ballistic. The crowd thought it was all part of the show and cheered Harvey as he fled the arena like a scalded rabbit. Tony finally recomposed himself and finished the show, but he was so angry we had to hide Harvey until after Tony had gone home.

At the post show debrief we all thought it was great and should become part of the show. However, Tony took the view that it made him look ridiculous and vetoed the whole idea. This would not be the last time a Black Knight would oppose the rest of the troupe when called upon to make a fool of himself for the sake of the show. It highlighted a problem that still exists within the Troupe today and was a problem throughout my time running the Jousting Troupe.

Some people join the Association to develop new skills in riding and combat. Their focus is to thrill and amaze the audience with those skills. They are vital to the show, and we could not be successful without them.

The other group are actors who see themselves as part of the cast of a theatrical production. They are quite happy to demean themselves in front of the audience if it helps the overall production. They understand that playing a part of someone who is incompetent can be vital to the show and if done well may steal the show from the naturally skilful stars. Good examples of this are Baldrick in Black Adder, Basil Fawlty in Fawlty Towers and the great Alan Rickman playing the Sheriff of Nottingham in Robin Hood Prince of Thieves.

What made our shows so good was that we always managed to have a good blend of both types within the cast.

1982 was a record year for shows performed by the whole troupe on tour since we started in 1970. The statistics show we did one more show in 1980, but 7 of those shows were just 2 knight shows, and only involved less than half the troupe so we could rest people on a regular rota, giving wounds time to mend and take the pressure off work and family commitments. Our season in 1982 was 14 weeks long and we performed 17 shows. It was hard. Lots of travelling, and being away virtually every weekend, often for the whole of the weekend. This put a lot of strain on personal relationships and we were very glad when the winter break came.

1983 saw our season stretch from 14 weeks to 19 weeks and our shows leap to 29. The strains of last season became cracks. Our season started early at the beginning of May with Leicester County Show. The show is always held on the first Monday and Tuesday of May so all the lads had to use their holiday entitlement to take time off from work. We had also crammed in an evening show the Friday before as a warm-up, in our indoor school and to raise some money for charity.

By the beginning of June, we had already performed eight full shows. Two years before, that would have been the total for the whole year. Our first show in June was at Flint Rugby Club for Deeside Round Table. We performed on the rugby pitch which over looked the beach and the Dee Estuary. It was a stunning location and the show went down a storm, but we nearly didn't make the show. The AA route map that we used for planning journeys, estimated it would take about approximately 3 hours. But it didn't consider holiday traffic, and mountains that required first gear to grind our way up. It took us over four hours to get there, but luckily our pledge to arrive two hours prior to the first show gave us about 45minutes to set up and get into costume for the first show.

As we raced to get ready for the show my biggest worry was that Tony and several key members of the cast still had not arrived. Tony was a fast driver and always thought he could make a journey in less than time than I allowed. This time, however, he was running late just like us. We were all getting changed when a cloud of dust boiled towards us as Tony and co. arrived down the dirt road like a rally driver. He jumped out of the car grinning like a Cheshire cat. I hit the roof. All the stress of trying to get to the shows on time, and Tony always just arriving in the nick of time, had just built up to boiling point.

I was particularly stressed that day because in our efforts to arrive on time I had decided to take a short cut using" B" roads. The route saved us quite a few miles but as I was starting to learn there is a reason "A" roads follow the route they do. Our shortcut brought us straight down Flint Mountain into the town. It looked fine on the map. However, it was a nightmare. The road was very narrow with a few passing places, extremely steep and full of sharp bends. Definitely a place to avoid in a TK Bedford full of horses. Once committed there was no turning back. At first, everything had been ok - low gear and plenty of brake. For the first half of the descent, we were able to hold our speed, but after that we started to gain speed as the brakes began to heat up and fade. The engine was screaming and I was praying that it didn't jump out of gear. As we took the last few bends I was standing up in the cab pulling up on the steering wheel trying to put all my weight and muscular strength on the brake pedal. We nearly didn't make the last bend but thankfully we arrived at the bottom safely. Brian who was in the cab with me just turned and quietly said; "Well done Bro." I don't think I would have made it down without him quietly insisting that I take my foot off the brake after each bend to allow the brakes to cool a little before the next bend.

My rantings were shrugged off by Tony who just gave me a big grin and said " well I'm here now. Let's give them a, f***ing good show" and so off we went and gave them two f***ing good shows. This show was very rare as we had a changing room and showers for after the show, courtesy of the Rugby Club. Normally we would change at the side of the horsebox with hundreds of people gawping at us, and stay hot and sweaty after the show.

The rugby lads opened their bar for us after the show, treating us to free drinks and when suitably refreshed, we played rugby against them on the beach. It was 7 pm when we all piled back into the Club House for more drinks. At this point I announced it was time we should be heading home to be greeted by jeers and groans and being told by Tony that I was a miserable bastard who didn't appreciate the great shows they had performed. What was the point of doing these shows if they couldn't reap the benefits of being famous after the shows? The point was that I had to drive a lorry load of tired horses back home which was a four-hour trip.

This was a typical day jousting and it repeated its self virtually every weekend often on Saturday and Sunday for the whole 1983 season. Writing this now I can see this was the beginning of the rift between Tony and me. In fact, I think it was "Game for a Laugh" that changed Tony, especially the television coverage. He revelled in his notoriety and felt that he should have special privileges over the rest of troupe. I saw the whole troupe as a team, some would always get more adulation than others, but everyone was an equal, vital piece of the jigsaw. Our paths were slowly diverging! The next weekend we had back to back shows in the London area.

First was St. Albans followed by a regular yearly show for Ford Motor Co. in Romford, Essex. The plan was to stable over night after the St. Albans show, close to City, so that we could all have a night out there. The younger members of the troupe elected to sleep in the horsebox and coach, which were parked at the stables and use their hotel allowance for partying on the town. The geriatrics, as we were known, Brian, Tony and I would stay in comfier accommodation. Tony wanted the whole troupe to go out for a meal together. Something the younger generation were not keen on, until I offered to pay the drinks bill for the meal in recognition of the great show we had done that day. After much wandering around St Albans, we finally found a Greek restaurant that that could accommodate our numbers and was also in the right price bracket for the younger crew. It was a night to be remembered!

It started with Tony ordering beer and wine as if was going out of fashion. As the night progressed I gave up on worrying about blowing the overnight allowance budget, and went with the flow. Brian had managed to pick up a girl at the show and had brought her along for the meal. After about two hours we were all very drunk and noisy. Brian to our amusement, was turning on the charm to his latest conquest, when he suddenly froze and went very pale. I got up and moved around to where he was sitting to ask if he was ok. He told me he had just noticed the people at the table across the room staring at us. So, what? "We are making a lot of noise. What's the problem" I asked. The problem was it was his next-door neighbour and his family. They were his wife's best friends. It was another nail in the coffin of his already failing marriage.

When we finally settled the bill the food was one third and the drink was two thirds. Brian and I had booked into a local pub.

Tony chose to stay elsewhere! Tony gave us a lift to our pub along with Brian's partner and we finished the night off in the pub bar with a few shorts. Brian's plan was to sneak his girlfriend up to his room for the night, but the landlady was well ahead of him. As soon as she called time she came over and told Brian his guest had to leave. Not to be thwarted he tried to pay the landlady extra for her to stay if she had a double room available. The landlady was having none of it. She obviously kept a very respectable house. However, she did have a single room the young lady could have, but there was to be, definitely no hanky panky. Brain agreed and paid up with obviously no intention of keeping the agreement. So, off everyone went to bed very worse for wear. Next morning, I awoke to an almighty hangover and a bursting bladder. No ensuite in those days so down the corridor to the bathroom. I was confronted by a several people already waiting. I passed a comment about it being very popular this morning only to be told that someone was hogging the bathroom and they had all been awaiting ages. I certainly couldn't wait so went down to use the toilet in the bar and then have breakfast, during which there was much commotion. There was no sign of Brian or his girlfriend, and time was getting on so I decided to see if he was in his room and try to wake him. After much banging on his door, he finally opened up, and on peeping in was glad to see no sign of his girlfriend. I had been expecting to face the wrath of the landlady at any minute for whatever Brian had got up to during the night. Great! I thought, he must have passed out as soon as he got into his room last night no need to worry. Then I saw it. His bed was surrounded by pots of geraniums. In fact, the whole room was full of pots of geraniums. Brian seemed to have only noticed them at the same time as I did and asked me if I had put them there. When I explained to him quite forcibly that it could only have been him as nobody else had a key to the room, I also asked him if he had been to his girlfriend's room. After a short delay while his brain got working, he gradually remembered he had tried twice to get to her room but been arrested by the ever-watchful landlady and sent back to his room. On the second occasion, he had gone to the bathroom and climbed out of the bathroom window and shinned down the drain pipe with the intention of doing the same back up to her bedroom window, but again he was caught and escorted back to his room. Then it struck me and I asked him if by any chance, he might have locked the bathroom door before he climbed out of the window. Brian's brain was not working well but eventually he decided that he did lock the door. I told him very forcibly to get dressed, pack, put the geranium's back from where ever they came from and meet me outside the pub before the landlady put two and two together. I could see the gravity of the situation was finally seeping into his alcohol fuddled brain.

Thankfully there was a stranger checking people out. I paid our bills and checked there was nothing extra to pay for Brian's girlfriend. I asked the receptionist to explain that Brian had a busy schedule and had to leave very early. Tony was picking us up from the from the pub but we dared not wait outside in case the landlady saw us. We also didn't know which way Tony would be coming from (no mobile phones) so we hid up the road at a place where we could see the road past the pub from both ways. It was a very long wait and Tony was late as usual but we escaped and never heard anything more from the pub thankfully!

When we arrived at the stables the younger generation had fed, watered and loaded the horses ready to move onto our next show at Romford. Romford was a great success as usual, and after a pub stop on the way home, we arrived back at base about 12.30 am, absolutely exhausted.

The pace of shows in June continued with yet another double weekend. This time Saturday in Ponteland, north of Newcastle, Sunday at Belvoir Castle and then straight down to London to appear on TV.AM.

Ponteland was a five hour drive each way in the horsebox and coach. Our second show was the last event of the day so by the time we had derigged and packed up the bar had closed on site and everyone gone home. We had, however, been invited down to the Diamond Inn by the organisers for a thank you drink. Always happy to agree to the organisers´ wishes, we naturally agreed and as it happened it was also on our way home. It was a beautiful old coaching inn set next to the river Pont and heaving with post carnival revellers, some of whom had already made it into the river. It took an age to fight your way to the bar and even longer to get served. After two drinks, it was about 7 pm and I started to round up the troops ready to hit the road as our E.T.A. home was already midnight and we would have to have another pub stop just before closing time. Tony once again objected saying we were all miseries and that the party was just getting started. Tony and a couple of mates stayed on as Tony had come up in his car. We arrived back at the yard past midnight but for some of us the day was not finished. There were horses to put to bed and the costumes to be sorted for washing overnight. I crawled into bed about 2 am. Some of the lads didn't even bother going home. They just slept on the bus because we had an early start to mend the broken weapons before leaving for a show at Belvoir Castle.

I have laboured on about these shows, not because they were particularly important, but to demonstrate what it was like that year of 1983. This was the norm week in week out throughout the season. In fact, for some of us, this weekend was even harder because four of us travelled down to London after the Belvoir show to appear on the new, early morning television show called "TV.AM". It wasn't a paid job but the prestige and publicity was priceless. I took the younger generation with me because they had fewer commitments and were easily wooed by the offer of a top-class hotel in London along with appearing on Breakfast Telly. As it turned out it was another hard slog with no reward. We didn't arrive at the hotel till after midnight so no out on the town. The hotel bar and restaurant were also closed. After much argument with the night porter we managed to get 4 warm bottles of lager at an exorbitant cost. We also discovered we were being collected by taxis at 4.30 am to be taken to the studios. So, no breakfasts either. I assured the lads that I was sure TV.AM would be doing a slap-up breakfast as soon as we got to the studios. We got breakfast! A glass of orange juice and a croissant! I had a very pissed off group of jousters. The day was saved in the Green Room (a small sound proof room for people waiting to go onto live television). As we sat in this room nervously waiting, Kenneth Williams (Carry On star) came in and chatted to us for about 15 minutes. He was fantastic. Talking to us as if we were theatrical equals. It made all the hardship worthwhile. Then suddenly we were on. Two quick fights, a 30 second interview, thanked for a great show, ushered back to our dressing room then straight to waiting taxis. We were home just after lunch. We never saw anything of London and we were starving hungry. That's fame for you!

Two weeks later we were involved in an experimental show at the Sherwood Forest Visitor Centre involving various Robin Hood groups. The idea was to create a re-enactment of the Sheriff of Nottingham chasing Robin Hood, and Robin hiding in the Major Oak to avoid capture. It was all very chaotic, with the archers getting over enthusiastic and shooting us and our horses. It ended up with us and the Sheriff's men seeking refuge inside the Major Oak along with a group of Minstrels who were just as terrified as us, of the crazy archers.

The minstrels were called Robin Hood's Minstrels, also known as Kick and Rush. They immediately became our close lifelong friends, joined the show and travelled the world with us. Without that chance meeting, I don't think the Jousting Troupe would have survived the stresses of the next decade.

Robin Hoods Minstrels

They were three guys from Mansfield. Dave Clay, Steve Haig and Pete Tom. They dressed in classic Errol Flynn style Robin Hood costumes. Short green tunics, tights and pointed hats. They sang a short repertoire of Robin Hood based songs which they happily repeated as they strolled around playing mandolin, penny whistle and wash board. I was looking for an extra dimension to the show because, performing on a regular basis at Belvoir and Bosworth, meant that a lot of people were coming five or six times a year to watch us and seeing the same show.

Jimmy Durrands and I were of a like mind, so when I met the lads at the Major Oak, I rang Jimmy the next day and persuaded him to book them to open our show, entertain the crowds during the interval and again sing up in the castle court yard after the show. In the early days, we used to have a falconer to perform a similar role but sometimes the birds would just fly off and sit in a tree. He was also very expensive in terms of entertainment value so he became a casualty of the tight years in the late seventies.

Robin Hood's Minstrels were never an intrinsic part of our show but an optional extra that I strongly recommended to clients. They soon became regular features at Belvoir Castle and Bosworth Battlefield, plus many of our touring shows.

The three of them also performed as a skiffle band playing a mixture of folk and rock n' roll songs interspaced with monologues, ditties and ribald jokes. Like everyone else in the troupe, they were soon known by nick names. Dave's was Pidge, Steve's was Hippy and Pete's was Geordie Pete or just plain Geordie.

We didn't know about the skiffle band when we first started working with them but very shortly afterwards at the after-Belvoir show party in the Windmill Pub in Redmile, they offered to play a few numbers. They disappeared and returned with a variety of instruments including an old tea chest. This had a pole tied to it with old fashioned washing line and a large hole in one side of the chest. We all gawped at their strange instruments and attire. It was not only us gawping, it was the whole pub!

They struck up with "My Old Man's a Dustman" (not the best-known pop song in the Eighties) but within minutes they had the whole pub rocking and singing along. We stayed until closing time, plied with free beer from the locals and the Landlady to stop us leaving earlier as planned. As we left everyone wanted to know when we were coming back. It was the best night they had had in years.

At first, they only played at the Windmill in Redmile after the Belvoir shows and when on tour with us. The fame of these after show sing-song parties soon spread throughout the Vale of Belvoir and we started to get offers of food and free drinks if we would condescend to stop at their pub. It was said that a landlord could pay for his annual holiday in Spain with one night's takings on the bar if they were lucky enough to get a visit from the Jousters when Kick and Rush were with them!

Unfortunately, the success of these nights over several years led to their end. Kick and Rush were becoming much sought after and were playing virtually every night, so the last thing they wanted was to do a free concert after a day of Minstreling. They still did a few party sessions with us when we were away for a few days on tour and if possible I would try and get them a gig as part of their contract so that they were not always playing for free. In many cases, they got regular bookings on their own after performing at a jousting show. Belgium, Ireland and Inverness in Scotland were but a few of these.

We had so many crazy, wild nights with the lads. Pidge and Hippy were always there but over the years the third member has changed several times. Geordie Pete also played with an electric rock band which made him unavailable at times.

The drinking and raucous singing seemed to be the perfect salve for the pain and adrenaline of a jousting show. We stopped at a pub north of Wakefield one night. It was a small isolated country pub and after buying a round of drinks we asked the landlord if we could set up the band for a singsong. The landlord cautiously asked what sort of music the band played to which I replied "skiffle". He told me with a smile "weed best hav um im then". As usual it turned into fabulous night. The crowning glory was when someone appeared with two chickens under his arm just before closing time. He threw them up in the air over the band and they continued playing as the chickens squawked, fluttering all over the place and depositing feathers over all un sundry.

Another time we did a two day show at Grimsthorpe Castle near Bourne and camped overnight in the park. We had a great sing song around a camp fire with the stallholders who were also camping on site. The party went on until sunrise which was about 4 am at that time in the summer. As the sun rose over the park Steve the Hippy was suddenly overcome by a mystic moment and announced that he was going to swim naked in the lily covered lake as the sun rose to its full glory. We watched in awe as he strode down the hill discarding his clothes and then diving headlong into the lake. Moments later we were howling with laughter when he staggered out of the lake covered from head to toe in black, stinking mud. Although the lake looked ideal for swimming it was only 6 inches deep and Steve's spectacular dive had ended up as a mud belly-flop!

On another occasion in Ireland when we were working in Kilkenny we had a day off so decided to go out for the day. The locals suggested we visit Thomastown. A quaint little town by a picturesque river and with lots of pubs. It was a perfect place for the jousters to see some local culture. The plan was to wander around and drink in as many pubs that we could find. There were 19 of us all together including my son Mark and Tom Arris, who were in their mid-teens, but not old enough to drink legally.

After visiting the first pub we meandered up the street looking for the next pub. Pidge was quite overcome by the fact we had brought the band over to Ireland and decided he would show his appreciation by moving quickly onto the next pub and getting a round in. So off he went on his own to the next pub and ordered 10 pints of Guinness, 7 pints of Smethwick's and 2 bottles of coke. As Pidge was the only customer at this early hour the barman looked a little bemused. After 15 minutes or so, Pidge had finished his pint so popped his head out of the pub door to hurry the lads up. To his amazement and horror, the street was empty. He returned to the bar and started to drink his way through his very large bar order whilst receiving some strange looks from the barman. We finally arrived at Pidge's bar about 45 minutes later having been in the pub on the other side of the road wondering what had happened to Pidge. It was so funny to see Pidge sitting on his own at a table surrounded by drinks. We all laughed for about ten minutes, and then set to drinking…

The Band was so popular in Ireland and Belgium that they were asked to go back every time we went over and sometimes on their own. One of my favourite recollections is Kick and Rush playing in the small courtyard of Horst Castle in Belgium. It was a lovely warm summer's evening and they played on a small stage lit only by a string of coloured lights that gave the courtyard a lovely warm glow. The courtyard was full of jousters and Belgians associated with the show. We were all sitting at improvised tables drinking the strong Belgian beer and singing our hearts out. There were no language barriers that night. Just the beginning of a great friendship between two Nationalities made possible by three lads from Mansfield, a small mining town in north Nottinghamshire. It was because of this great ability of simple music to forge relationships with different cultures that some of the jousters formed their own band years later when working in America and Canada, but more about that later.

There was also a fourth member of the band when they played after our shows, and his name was Raymonde. His real name was Tim Badder. A long serving member of the jousting troupe who was one of the senior men at arms. Tim was a beer monster with a roly-poly character and body to match. He loved winding people up and playing practical jokes. I can't remember how it all started but his character just kept on growing.

The band just stopped playing halfway through a set one night and announced that there was a guest singer going to do a number. Everyone in the bar gave a great cheer for this unknown singer. I think Tim had convinced even Kick and Rush that he could play the guitar and sing. He asked if he could borrow Geordie Pete's beloved, twelve-string guitar and proceeded to re-tune it and making a comment to Pete about how it was a bit out of tune and he was surprised that they managed to sound so good with a guitar so out of tune.

The audience was becoming electrified with anticipation. He settled himself down on a bar stool, wriggling a bit to get comfy. He then cleared his throat twice, drew the guitar into his body, carefully positioned his fingers on the frets and took a huge breath. The audience fell silent, and then gasped in amazement. Tim wildly strummed the strings producing the most awful incoherent noise, out of tune and out of time. His rendition of Elvis Presley's, "From a Jack to a Queen" was even worse. His hoarse monotone voice shouted the words, with inter-spaced screeches for the higher notes which ended as a silent hiss of air at the top end of the scale. The audience just didn't know how to react, and then suddenly it was over. Tim gave a sweeping bow and as he came up there was a massive, mischievous grin across his face. The audience suddenly realised that they had been well and truly had with one of Tim's practical jokes. They went wild cheering and clapping for a good five minutes.

Raymonde was born!

After this whenever Kick and Rush played there would be chants for Raymonde about half way through the set. This would build until everyone in the room was chanting, "Raymonde! Raymonde!" It was typical of the jousters' sense of humour. They loved to trick people who had not seen the Raymonde act into believing that he was a truly great guest singer and guitar player.

Tim, whose nick name was Slim, developed his act so that he played two songs. The second being "Blanket on the Ground" another Country and Western classic but with ruder words that were blocked out by Hippy slapping his hand over Slim's mouth just a little bit too late so the audience understood the word. It was a real class comedy sketch up there with Morecambe and Wise. In later years, Slim ended his act strutting around the stage naked with a set of jousting plumes (three coloured ostrich feathers) protruding from his backside. With his large beer belly and an arched back, he looked like giant, plucked rooster strutting around the stage. I really can't remember how or why this came about. It was extremely bizarre but with a drunken audience, it brought the house down and never seemed to offend anyone.

Stresses and Strains the rest of 1983

We were but half way through the season when we met Robin Hood's Minstrels, yet already we were tired and battered and although we were not doing the number of shows that we did at Gwrych, the pressures were probably worse. In Gwrych we had a static professional troupe. We just had to walk out the door and perform. The lads worked about 4-5 hours per day. Now we had a semi-professional troupe doing 12-18 hour days with the travelling. We were now working virtually every weekend from May to September plus a few midweek shows that ate into the lads' annual holidays. This was not good for anyone who was married or had a steady relationship or, for that matter anyone who was trying to move ahead with their career.

If someone has a raging meltdown, the lads still describe it as having a "Panda Pop". It was me who created the Panda Pop, and the lads still tease me to this day about the incident. It happened at The Stratford on Avon Festival on the 23rd of

July. The weekend before we had done back to back shows at the Robin Hood Centre in Sherwood Forest and then Ashby Agricultural Show. Both shows had been disappointing by our standards. What kept us going was the cheers and standing ovations of the crowds at the end of the shows. Tony, in particular, judged his performance, by the volume of boos that he got as he left the arena. Later we would come to understand the difference between the types of audiences we were playing to and the way they reacted to our show. Sherwood Forest was our first attempt at diversifying the jousting theme into the "Robin Hood Myth" and working with other medieval groups. To us it felt fragmented. Tony hated his new role. He was playing the Sheriff of Nottingham, which in my view was basically the same character as the Black knight, but he just didn't get it! The show we did that day was not our normal tight, character based stage show and was never meant to be. The idea was to paint a broad canvas of Robin Hood characters to fire the imagination of the visitors. At the end of the performance we received a warm applause as we all took a bow together. Tony was furious and said we should never attempt anything like this again. His view was that people only came to watch the jousting - to see him as The Black Knight.

Nottinghamshire County Council however was delighted with the outcome and the Robin Hood festival is still going strong, thirty years on.

The next day we did Ashby Agricultural Show. We had done many Agricultural shows in the past; they were very prestigious to do but we found the audiences very hard to perform to. There were three major problems with these shows. First, the arenas were massive making it impossible to use dialogue and create audience participation. Second was that most other arena events were parades of winners or displays of skill so the audiences just didn't get a theatrical show. Third was that most people hadn't come to see a jousting show. They were there for their own niche hobby - cows, sheep, vintage tractors, etc.

The show we did at Ashby was good and solid. At any other venue, we would had brought the house down. At Ashby, we got a round of applause, the same as all the other events, but no cheering for the main characters. Tony blamed everyone, while I stuck up for everyone. Tony left in a foul mood straight after the second show.

Next weekend we did Stratford-upon-Avon Festival; a huge event in an equally huge park along the banks of the River Avon. As usual I had requested a quiet place for us to park the bus and horses. The organisers did a great job putting us right next to the river almost opposite the Royal Shakespeare Theatre. Unfortunately, it was at the opposite end of the site to the Festival control centre and a long way from the arena.

This meant carrying all the props several hundred yards to the arena and back again after the show. I also had to make several trips to the control centre during the day. A half mile round trip each time. We were in the middle of a heatwave, and temperatures were hovering around 30 sweltering degrees. We performed two great shows to massive crowds but the heat totally exhausted us. After the show, we had to lug all the kit back to our parking area. When everything was finally loaded we, all flopped down on the grass by the river watching people glide by in rowing boats and canoes. As we dozed in the heat a canoe swung in close to the bank and started to splash us and call us names. When we jumped up in anger they paddled off calling us names and laughing. Quick as a flash, Gordon Hall, who had swum as a junior for

England dived into the river and chased after the boat like a human torpedo. The lads in the canoe just couldn't believe someone could swim faster than they could paddle. Within 25 metres he had caught the canoe and tipped the canoeists into the water. Several of the lads decided to join Gordon in the river for a cool off swim. It was at that moment we nearly had a serious accident. One of the lads was about to dive in, when another passing boat shouted a warning not to dive in at the particular place. On closer inspection, about a foot under the surface was a concrete structure with bits of sharp rusty metal sticking out of it. The consequences of what might have happened if the person in the boat had not shouted a warning do not bear thinking about.

At this point our food arrived. A baker's tray of by now rather dried up sandwiches along with some small bottles of lemonade called Panda Pops. The person delivering the food also brought a message that our money was ready for collection so I grabbed my briefcase and trudged off through the crowds to the control centre. It was slow going and when I finally arrived there was a queue. Ten minutes later I finally reached the front of the queue and announced that I had come to collect the money for the jousting display only to be told that I needed to go to the secretary's office that was on the other side of the festival ground. Thirty minutes later very hot and tired I arrived back at the bus to be met by moans and groans about me keeping them waiting as they were desperate to leave and find a pub as there was no bar on site. I grumpily told them they could just damn well wait till I had had my sandwiches and a drink. They had eaten all the sandwiches and drunk all the Panda Pops. It was the final straw. I ranted and raved at them telling them how ungrateful and selfish they were. That all they could think about was getting to the pub whilst I was walking miles in the heat to collect their money. I finished my rant by saying that they didn't even save me a Panda Pop. Someone piped up "Why would you want us to save one of those bloody horrible warm Panda Pops" and we all dissolved into laughter. Even to this day I get presented with a Panda Pop if any of the old boys see them on sale. From that day on whenever I furious about something they would try and calm me down by saying, "Calm down, don't go having another Panda Pop!"

We were all tired and the slightest little thing could and did set off almost violent arguments even between good friends. It was a powder keg waiting to explode. Three weeks later it exploded!

As I mentioned earlier when writing about Tony this week end was supposed to be the highlight of the season; four days in Southport, and then a big day at Bosworth Battlefield, with me also fitting in filming an interview for the BBC Schools Programmes about the role of castles in medieval times. Stuart and I were particularly excited about going to Southport because of its connections with the Grand National and the famous Red Rum who was trained on Southport Sands. Southport was also famous for its saunas and steam rooms that helped the Aintree jockey's sweat weight off, and also, repair their battered bodies, just what we needed for our long jousting weekend. Most of us travelled up to Southport on the Wednesday evening with the horses, and the rest of the lads who couldn't get time off work, came up on the Friday morning. The idea was that the lads could have a bit of a break by the seaside as a thank you from me before this mega weekend, and hopefully get rid of some the tension that had been building over the last months. When the advanced party arrived on Wednesday evening we were ready for a night on the town and so off we went, all fired up to paint the town red. After about an hour of trudging from pub to pub trying to find somewhere that had a bit of life we began to realise that Southport was not like the seaside towns we were used to. In fact, it was rather up market, parochial and, seemingly to be still stuck in the Fifties. All the bars had a quiet hush to them and certainly no juke boxes. We still managed to consume a fair bit of beer and luckily for us the hotel bar had closed by the time we returned because we were greeted by some disapproving looks on our return by guests and management alike. We did, however, discover that there was a sauna just around the corner from the hotel and that the main municipal steam rooms and baths were at the far end of town near the famous sands used for training racehorses.

The sauna just around the corner became the place where we sweated off our hangovers in the mornings and the municipal baths were used after the shows with their many dry heat and steam rooms to melt away our aches and pains. Friday morning saw the rest of the troops arrive, except for Tony, who arrived mid-afternoon arriving about an hour before the show. With the benefit of a day in town the "recon party" had located some slightly livelier bars for the Friday night, and that's when it all started to go wrong.

Next morning, we came down to breakfast very hung over and faced disgusted looks from both the management and the guests. We were very definitely in the wrong hotel; all married couple's late fifties to sixties, very middle class. We felt like aliens that had just landed.

We did our two shows at the Southport Flower show, which in reality, was a county show by the seaside with international show jumping and many other "country" things going on. Both shows were an enormous success! A good steaming and then an ice-cold plunge at the baths and we were ready for another night on the town. The younger generation went off in search of the elusive lively bar whilst Brian and I decided to find a high-quality restaurant. We had expected Tony to join us but he declined. After our meal, Brian and I bumped into Tom Hudson, the Television Equestrian Commentator who lived close to Belvoir Castle and was also Secretary of the Belvoir Hunt. Tom was also working at the Flower Show commentating on the show jumping. Tom was renowned for his love of food and drink so we spent the rest of the evening swapping tales of traveling around the show circuit and drinking far too much Armagnac Brandy. By the end of the night I had the beginning of a mega hangover and Bri had an extra job next day helping Tom do the Main Ring commentary.

Always an early riser I staggered down first for breakfast to be greeted by a hush in the dining room broken only by gentle tapping of cutlery on plates. I think everyone else must have been going to church as the men all wore suits and ties whilst the women were all in smart dresses. They all stopped and stared at me as I entered in jeans and a tee shirt. Worse was to come! The lads slowly filtered down in various states of disrepair, noisily chatting about what stupid things they had got up to the previous evening. Very soon, the manager was asking to keep the noise down. Almost as soon as he turned his back, Pete Webster entered giving his trade mark lion roar and shouting something like "did you see that bird with the big tits and short skirt in the such and such bar last night ". The Manager was back this time furious. He thought Pete had deliberately flouted his warning, although Pete had not been in the room at the time. We all apologised again, and I could sort of see his point as his genteel other customers were looking either annoyed or very uncomfortable. Just as he turned his back there was a huge crash, and a table with all its food went flying. My brother Phil was having an epileptic fit; quite a common occurrence in those days if Phil had a late night and had been drinking. Phil had suffered from fits after being hit over the head with an iron bar during an altercation outside the Durham Ox night club on the A46 near to where we live. We knew what to do and set about making him safe until the fit passed, and asked for an ambulance to be called. It was all too much for the manager who I think thought that we were staging it to embarrass him. So, while we were trying to deal with a genuine medical emergency, he was trying to throw us out of the hotel. As soon as Phil was in the ambulance we checked out of the hotel before someone punched the now obnoxious, manager and went off to the sauna to sweat away the previous night's alcohol.

Thankfully Phil got the all clear at hospital and met us back at the show ground. When Tony arrived at the show ground he announced that he was fed up with playing the Black Knight and wanted to be the good knight for a change. This was not too much of a problem as it only involved changing the endings on a couple of fights. As Tony and I had only ever played the Black Knight, I decided to take over his part. People have often asked me why I agreed to such a major last-minute change to the show. The simple fact was that Tony had been problematic for most of the season and after what had happened at the hotel earlier, I just didn't want any more trouble that day.

We pulled off the show with Brian's commentary covering up any mishaps caused by the change in the line-up. At the end of the show Tony, as the Good Knight, cut me down with double-headed axe which was the usual ending. However, he didn't pull the blow. The blow across my chest severely winded me and felled me like a tree! I didn't have to do any acting! As I lay on the ground gasping like a fish out of water, he bent over me and said with cold menace "fucking hurts, doesn't it?" and then walked away to take his acclaim. Although Tony was a far better Black Knight than I was, the applause for each of the characters was about the same as the day before. I think Tony hoped that the show would be a flop and prove what he believed, which was that without him we had no show.

Tony left straight after the show, and I never had time to talk to him about what happened at the end of the show.

The next day we were at Bosworth Battle Field, which next to Belvoir was our biggest crowd pulling venue. I had agreed to do an interview for the BBC Schools Service about Knights and Medieval Castles. It didn't involve anyone else as nobody in the troupe except me had any interest in medieval history. Perhaps with hindsight I should have explained to Tony why nobody else was involved. After we had set up, I did the BBC thing which was only supposed to take 30 minutes but ended up being one and a half hours. I soon realised that it was going to take longer than planned so I sent the lads off to the pub for lunch.

Tony still had not arrived, not unusual at this point as he seemed to think it was the job of the younger members to set up. He had been asking for a separate road crew to be employed, so none of the troupe had to set up, just like the top pop bands. He also asked me to amend our contract so that he could have a separate changing room or tent with a bottle of whiskey and other drinks such as Bacardi, wine and beer, so he could entertain his fans' post show. He was very serious about this so I mentioned this to our agent and Jimmy Durrands. They both laughed and said "No way!"

The filming dragged on until it was almost time to start the first show and I had to say that's it we have run out of time. The lads were already preparing to mount as I rushed to change into my costume with the help of the men at arms. Gilbert Harvey, one of the men at arms whispered in my ear as he helped me into my kit "Watch out for "The Captain" he's in a really funny mood and has drunk a lot more Scotch than usual." ("The Captain" was the lads nickname for Tony).

The show went as normal until my Joust as the Drunk with Tony as the Black Knight. Tony knocked me off on the third joust as usual; he remained mounted and knocked the sword out of my hand, all going to plan. The next bit I have no recollection of, but according to Brian, who was commentating, instead of circling me and tapping me on top of the helm which had extra padding there for this stunt, Tony rode past me, wheeled and cut me down at the gallop, striking me on the back of the helm. I was knocked out cold and they had trouble getting the helm off my head it was so dinted. I vaguely remember being in an ambulance and someone continually asking me what my name was. By the time, I reached Glenfield Hospital I was starting to come around but was very not really compos-mentis. It took several hours for my skull to be x-rayed and the doctors to decide if I was fit to go home. I was eventually released but have no idea how I got back to the Red Lion at Costock.

When I arrived, the lads were well into their post-show party and I received loud cheers as I entered the bar. Noise was the last thing I wanted to hear as I was still very concussed and remained that way for most of the week. I did manage one pint of bitter (against Doctor's orders) but then went gingerly home, glad to get away from the noise of the juke box. I still don't know to this day why it happened, and like all incidents people's recollections vary so much. Whether it was an accident or deliberate I will never know, but I did know that injuries to other members of the troupe by Tony were far higher than by anyone else. He had cut my brother Stuart's head open twice with a sword, put a duelling sword right through my other brother Phil's thigh causing a massive loss of blood, plus many other injuries to other lads.

What to do about Tony? My parents thought him to be a dangerous liability. The troupe was split but most people thought he should be stood down for the next weekend to give him time to sort himself out. This suited me because it was heart-rending for me; Tony had been a close friend for many years, our families had holidayed together, our children had grown up together but I knew in the end, I had to make a decision. He was a great showman; could we continue without him? Or, if he stayed would something even more terrible happen?

The next weekend was the August Bank holiday. We were booked as usual for shows Sunday and Monday at Belvoir Castle, plus we had a parade from Nottingham Castle with the Lord Mayor and the Sheriff of Nottingham down to the Council House in the Market Square to open the Annual Medieval Market.

I decided to ask my brother Phil to take on the role as Black Knight. He had played Richard of Gloucester, the Black Knight's loyal henchman for many years, and I would move Pete Webster up from a temporary knight for six knight shows into Phil's old role as Richard of Gloucester. Despite a lot of nerves and trepidation the whole weekend was a remarkable success; all the lads rose to the occasion and Brian's excellent commentary as the Knight Marshal settled everyone down and gave confidence where needed.

I had spoken to Jimmy Durrand's a couple of days before the weekend explaining what I intended to do regarding the shows for the Bank Holiday. To my surprise, he was most supportive, citing great West End shows that constantly changed their leading actors during the run of a show. He emphasised that no one person is bigger than the show. He also pointed out that injuries during a show are not liked by the audience, although they could get us rather good publicity post show. I also spoke to Michael Harrison at Bosworth, our other regular venue, who also said thrilling action was good but serious injuries at a County Council site were very much frowned upon. He was well aware of what had happened the previous weekend and that Tony had been drinking heavily before the show. He also commented that he was concerned about our pre-show visits to the local pub for lunch. I do believe it was the first time I ever heard the words "health and safety" mentioned. Again, he did not see a problem with changing who played the Black Knight.

Tony came to both Bank Holiday shows that weekend and helped with the shows. I think he thought the shows would fail and that after the Bank Holiday I would reinstate him. The troupe was divided and so was I about Tony's future in the Troupe, but after the Bank Holiday shows I was confident we could move forward without Tony. The major deciding factor for me was, that what we did was highly dangerous, and you had to trust your fight partner with your life and I had lost that trust with Tony.

Tony left the N.J.A. Monday 29th August 1983

The Rise of the Young Bloods

Our next show was the following Saturday in Gloucester for the City's 500year Charter celebrations. It felt a bit like a Football team playing its first match after its star player had just left the club. The lads all worked very hard, and the show was another success. On our way home, we stopped off at a lovely Coaching Inn on the edge of the Cotswolds for a drink and something to eat. We didn't stay very long as it was a slow drive up through the Cotswolds to Leicester and we had a mega day the next day. We were booked to perform at Nottingham City Show which was held at Wollaton Park where we had done our first-ever Joust. The city show was a scaled down version of the now defunct Nottingham Festival but still attracted huge crowds of 10,000 plus.

 Leaving a pub with twenty odd semi-drunk lads was always chaotic some were keen to get home; others hung back, trying to have another one last drink. My routine was to clear them out of the Bar, then check the Gents was clear before leaving to do a head count. It was not unusual for the odd lad to swap to the horse box if he was tired so that he could have a quiet uninterrupted sleep in the Luton over the lorry cab because the Bus was always full of noise and mischief.

When I came out of the Inn it was dark; the bus was already pulling out of the car park and the Horse Box ticking over ready to leave, so I jumped in and drove off after the Bus. We had no Mobile phones in those days, so it was not until we reached home that we realised Pete Webster was missing. The lads on the bus thought he was with us, but later we found out that he had decided to phone his girlfriend before leaving the Inn. In those days, hotels used to have public phone booths for clients to use and they were often tucked away in a quiet corner or under the stairs just off from reception. They were often quite plush, with oak panelling, a matching door for privacy and just a small window so you didn't accidentally disturb the caller. Unfortunately, Pete forgot to tell anyone what he was going to do, and he was so engrossed talking to the current love of his life he never saw everybody leaving. He hadn't phoned the Stables and two hours had passed so we had no idea where he was, so it seemed pointless to go back and try and find him.

He finally made it back home in the early hours of the morning having walked until he managed to thumb a lift to Leicester and then taken a Taxi from there to home. The next day at Nottingham City show there was a Tannoy announcement saying that Mr & Mrs Webster had lost their little boy and that his name is Peter, "if anyone finds him could they please bring him to the commentary box where his Mummy and Daddy are waiting to collect him"!

The sometimes cruel and heartless humour of the new generation had started!

During the latter part of the season I was offered a part in the BBC costume drama "By the Sword Divided" that was being filmed in and around Rockingham Castle. It was as a riding extra for the military scenes which meant that horses were provided. The initial job was for just two days filming but as is often the case with Films if you do a decent job more days get offered to you. As most of the extras were not professional rider's I was soon being asked by the Assistant Director if anymore of the jousters were available to come and take some riding parts. Although most of the lads were tied up Dad, Stu and Brent were available. We also met up with Bill Hammond who we already knew, and a friend of his Mike Lane.

Probably 90% of one's time on a film set is hanging around drinking coffee and talking. It turned out that Mike was a Comedian and he supplemented his income by doing film and television extra work. To work in television, you had to be a member of Equity, the actors and entertainers Trade Union. There was, however a dispensation to allow non-Equity members to be employed if they had specific skills that Equity members didn't have, which is how the BBC got around employing us. Mike Lane was much more in the know about TV and Films than us. He suggested that with all our recent TV appearances and our work on this production we could probably qualify for Equity membership. An Equity card in the 80s was like gold and very hard to get, but Mike was confident he could get us in. His grand design was to set up an elite group of Equity riders for television productions. Mike was true to his word; Dad, Stu, Brent, Bill Hammond and I all got Equity cards and signed up with a theatrical agent specialising in TV work.

The Perfect Storm 1984-85

1984 started early with a Television appearance on the Saturday Show a live fast moving children's show hosted by Jimmy Greaves, the retired famous England football player. It was a great morale boost for the new young team and good for boosting their street "cred". We appeared with the Nolan sisters and an up and coming pop group called Deacon Blue who were playing their latest release. It was all very chaotic and I think Jimmy Greaves could sense we were a little nervous. In those days "Greavesy" was like David Beckham is today, with a worldwide fan base. He quietly sauntered over to us shook our hands and said "Don't worry about these stupid fuckers I know you are good at what you do or else you wouldn't be here, just go out there when it's your turn and be yourselves". We did and it all went very smoothly! They were Great words from a Great Man.

For weeks after doing the Saturday Show we were stopped in the street by people who had seen us on the show and they told us how good we had been. For a few weeks, we were famous and it was a massive boost to the younger generation's confidence and a terrific way to start the new season.

It was a busier season than the previous one, but we seemed to take it in our stride, there was a youthful vibrancy about the Troop and with Robin Hood's Minstrels often travelling with us, we had some great after-show parties with music and communal singing. Looking back, we were very much like a touring Rugby Club.

The old coach died early in the season, as already mentioned earlier in the book. It was replaced by a more modern and faster one with more beds. Again, the year was mostly endless traveling up and down the length and breadth of the country but there were some high points, new challenges and of course, some amusing moments. We did two shows in the North East, one at Alnwick Castle and another at Cramlington which is on the outskirts of Newcastle. I must say I think the North East is my favourite area for performing. There was always an exceedingly warm welcome in that neck of the woods. During our shows the audience was always very loud and vocal. We already had a massive fan base in the region and in it continued to grow for the next 20 years. People always came to talk to us after the shows, wanting to shake our hands, always thanked us for travelling so far to entertain them and left us with comments like, "Bloody fine show. You done a right good job" After performing at Cramlington we had to refuse the offer of post-show hospitality to dash home for an early start next day to perform at the National Exhibition Centre, in Birmingham. We were going to take part in the Olympic Gala that was being held there. We didn't take any horses as it was on stage and we were part of the opening sequence spectacular that was a collage of the history of Great Britain. It was one of the most stressful things that we had ever done….

The show was massive Neil Diamond was the headline act Prince Charles and Princess Diana were the guests of honour, and a capacity crowd of 15,000 plus attended. We arrived in total chaos; there were hundreds of performers all queuing to get signed in. When we were finally signed in we were escorted to a passageway full of people and told to wait and not move. It was stifling hot, with nothing available to eat or drink. We waited for over two hours before someone came to fetch us. A man with a clip board shouted '' Knights of Nottingham!'' and when we responded, were brusquely told "Follow me". I enquired where we could get something to eat and drink as we had left home very early. I was told again very brusquely that we should have brought our own food and drink; there was no catering for performers and we were to get changed quickly as we were rehearsing in ten minutes. Before I could explain it took more than ten minutes for us to get kitted out the clip board had disappeared up the corridor. Another clip board summoned us to back stage where yet another clip board outlined what we had to do.

We could not believe what we were being told.

 We had to split into two groups and told to enter from stage left and right waving banners, have a quick fight until one knight was left standing; he was then to wave the banner victoriously and then quickly leave the stage as the next act came on. We would also be required for the Finale´ when all the acts came on and sang the National Anthem whilst waving enthusiastically to the Audience. Time allowed for the Battle 1 minute 30 secs! Although it was a long boring day with the lads threatening mutiny most of the time, I loved the sheer magnificence of this opening sequence and I acquired new knowledge that I would use in later years. It was the first time I had seen computerised lighting and special effects like thunder, lightning and smoke-flashes. It was like Danny Boyle's Opening ceremony for the London Olympics condensed and put onto a stage.

The whole show was run to the second. As we waited to go on stage it was like a war film of paratroopers about to leap out of a plane. We had a ten second count down and were then pushed onto the stage by another clipboard shouting in our ears "GO, GO, GO!" Ninety seconds of pure adrenaline and then we were shuffled off down a corridor to await the end of the opening sequence. This turned out to be the hardest part we had to dance and sway our arms in time with several hundred other performers. At the rehearsals, the very gay choreographer tried his best to teach us the few dance steps we had to do in time with everyone else. I can still hear his words today, 'No, no, dears! its side step right, side step left, then back step," he tried in vain for the allotted rehearsal time to get these few simple steps into our heads to no avail. Finally, he sighed and waved effeminately to a clipboard at the edge of the stage and said, " David, be a dear and put this lot on last at the back where no-one will be able to see them". He then shouted in a contrite voice " NEXT " ...

Two weeks later we did our first show at Lincoln Castle which was an immense success, so much so that it became an annual event. It was a very atmospheric venue, and the people were delightful to deal with both those in the office and the site staff on the day of the show.

We were now doing eight shows at three major tourist attractions within a 30-mile radius of our base each year, and we had a huge regular fan base, some coming to all eight shows every year. Autograph signing after the shows became the norm and could go on for a long time. This caused resentment with the footmen who were always left to pack up most of the gear after the show, whilst we signed the autographs. The knights always tried to get away as soon as possible to help and gradually the foot lads accepted it was part of our job to do the signings. We had always asked for Favours from the ladies in the audience as in Medieval times, a scarf or some other token which the knights would tie onto their arms or lances. Now, with our young line-up we were attracting more teenagers as fans, and the favours were changing from scarves and handkerchiefs to bras and knickers! The knights and even the men at arms were being showered with them, so much so that we had to have a man at each tent responsible for returning the favours after the show. This soon became a prized job as they got to meet the owners of the double D bra or the black lace knickers! Many favours were never collected but we would keep them on the coach for the rest of the season as people often wrote in asking for their return or came up at another show and asked if we still had whatever they had given. Wives and girlfriends were not happy about finding piles of sexy underwear stuffed on the luggage racks along with the lad's kit bags!

In late May Dad, Louise, Brother Stu, Brent and I all got our Equity Cards just as Central TV's new Lenton Lane Studios came fully online. They were just six miles from Bunny and would become a major source of work for us over the coming years. However, this was early days and we threw ourselves into doing Television Extra work all over the country. It paid off; we made a lot of new contacts and gained a name for reliability. In June Mike Lane and I were recalled for some more filming on "By the Sword Divided" and we were able to seal the deal we had been working on the previous year, which was to provide a crack troop of horses and riders for the cavalry scenes in the second series that was due to start filming at the end of September.

There was a strange interlude at the beginning of August when we received an invitation from Max Diamond to take part in a Jousting Competition against the French at Chilham Castle in Kent. It was a five-day Tournament starting on the Wednesday and finishing on the Sunday. There was not much interest amongst the lads in taking part for two reasons; it required, including traveling, a full week's holiday at a time when two weeks per year was the norm, and we had agreed a two week break of no shows at the beginning of August which everyone's battered bodies were looking forward to. I personally didn't like Max; he was all bonhomie if he wanted something but blank you the next minute. Every time we worked with him we came away with a bad taste in our mouths. In the end, Dad, my Brother Phil and Brent went down with a few others. England won but Brent said that he wished he had never gone as the cheating by judges in favour of the English was so blatant that even the spectators were booing. He said that the French team were nice people and very skilful; he felt embarrassed to be English.

It was a very long season and we continued working right through September and into early October. One of the last shows of the season was at Burgess Park Walworth which is a suburb of Southwark in London and at the time quite a deprived area. Part of our contract was for us to lead a parade through the local streets. To our shock, we were not greeted by cheers and clapping but jeers and sullen looks. As we came to a narrow section of road bordered on either side by high tenements. Suddenly we came under attack from above; at first, we didn't understand what was happening and then we realised that we were being pelted with eggs from the tenements and the crowds were now cheering. We were well pissed off! We all hated parades and this just rubbed salt into the wound. When we returned, I leapt off my horse and stormed into the Organisers Tent. I didn't mince my words I screamed at the people in the tent " What the fuck is going on? Why are the people we are here to entertain attacking us?" There was a deathly silence for a moment and then someone stood up and apologised profusely. He then explained that there had been a lot of social unrest in the area and the whole idea of the Festival was to try and heal some of the wounds. There had been running battles between the Police and residents, and that Police horses had been deployed to break up the protesters. He explained that people in this area had never seen a horse before except for the Mounted Police. "They must have thought you were Police dressed up as Knights". Like the West Bromwich Riots in 1980 we were so naive about the social unrest that was going on in our Cities.

Our last show of the season was for IBM Computers and heralded a new line of work that would become very popular for the next decade - that of corporate entertainment.

Straight after this show we started filming "By the Sword" with our own troop of horses. It sounds great, but it was very hard work; the days were exhaustingly long now that we had to bring the horses every day. A typical day would start at 4am. We'd prepare the horses for travel and then drive to Rockingham for a call time of 6 am, work until 6 pm, then go back through costume and make-up, which usually took 30 to 45 minutes, then bring the horses home, finishing work about 8.30 pm, if we were lucky. This was the start of a period in my life when I did a lot of repetitive travelling, and when I think back now I remember each job by a song that always being played on the Radio at that time. The song for "By the Sword" was "Tainted Love" by "Soft Cell"

It was while working on "By the Sword" that I learnt two new tricks we could do with horses. The first was carrying flaming torches on horseback and the second was to fire a volley of muskets whilst mounted.

Ledbury, on the Welsh Border, was the first location for filming with our own horses. The scene concerned a man hunt in the narrow alleyways of a 17-century town. We were the mounted soldiers, scouring the town at night led by foot soldiers, who were lighting the way with flaming torches. The scene was shot in daylight using a special night filter to make it appear dark. After the first take the Director asked if it was possible for some of the riders to carry flaming torches on horseback as the shot was not looking right with just the foot soldiers carrying them. Eager to please, we said we would give it a try but that we would need some time to rehearse to make sure the horses were ok with the flames. That was fine with him as he had other scenes without horses to shoot. He left us with the Assistant Director and the Special Effects crew to see what we could come up with and to our amazement we had very few problems. We had soon completed several successful rehearsals and were ready for a take. The only big problem we did have was to avoid setting fire to the thatched cottages either side of the twisting, narrow alley way we were galloping up, as the flaming torches were now at the same height as the eves of the cottages. The Director got his shot and was delighted. It was the best possible start to our filming; the Director trusted us and we had his ear, which became invaluable as the "dirty tricks brigade" started to try to stop our new troop of horse before it even got off the ground.

The Horsemaster, Dave Goody, was very, annoyed about us being employed as it robbed him of a lot of money and threatened his position within the BBC. He had just brought himself a second-hand Rolls Royce after landing several contracts as Horsemaster which had not gone down well with BBC executives who were now wondering if they were getting value for their money. We were doing it for less and doing a much better job.

Nearly every day on set, I would be approached by the Assistant Director and asked if our men and horses were capable of performing the next scene, because some of the "other people" working on the set (i.e. Dave Goody) were worried we might make a mess of it. I kept reassuring them, and the troop kept doing things better than expected. One of the last scenes we worked on was also the most lavish. It was the scene where King Charles II is restored as King and involved a Royal coach (provided by Dave Goody) and a guard of flamboyantly-dressed mounted Cavaliers (us). Again, I was approached, by a by-now embarrassed Assistant Director because doubts had been raised about our ability to provide the right type of saddles and bridles for a royal parade. This was a problem as we didn't have a huge stock of historical saddlery such as the film lads had. I was worried. I thought they had really got us this time but Dad came to the rescue. Dad had close contacts with the Army Remount Depot at Melton Mowbray and a call to the Commandant secured us the loan of, as many sets of ceremonial saddlery as we needed, in exchange for a generous donation to the Army Benevolent Fund. I had to smile when I saw Mr Goody's face as we rode up on horse attired in highly polished glittering tack. Best of all the Army requested that we didn't clean the tack before we returned it as they had their own unique way of doing it.

The firing of a volley of muskets from horseback was also one of the last scenes we shot. Not only did we fire the volley, but the horses had to gallop through smoke and fire and endure a huge explosion when a cart loaded with gunpowder was blown-up during the battle. The crew were ecstatic with the results, and it was one of the most exciting scenes of the whole series. We had rehearsed the firing of the volley at home with shotguns and using live ammunition. On the day, the horses all stood in line and never moved a muscle as the muskets were all fired together on the Officer's command. I was so proud of both horses and riders.

It was a lovely warm autumn, and the filming was all new and exciting but things were just starting it was the beginning of the Perfect Storm.

After finishing filming "By the Sword" if was only a matter of weeks before we were back in action, this time working for Central TV on a series called "Shine on Harvey Moon" set in the late forties and early fifties. This time we were a troop of Royal Canadian Mounted Police taking part in the Coronation of Queen Elizabeth II. The scene was shot at some playing fields close to the studios in Lenton which is a suburb on the southern edge of Nottingham. We were still very excited about filming, and I remember us all slipping of at lunchtime still in our RCMP costumes to have a pint in the Johnson Arms owned by my old mate Alan Johnson. It was the same pub we took Pete to when he broke his ankle. The weather was now cold and drizzling and the work not quite as glamorous as "By the Sword," but we did get some more extra work on the series, but not riding horses. However, we did meet and become friends with the floor manager, David McDonald. David lived in the village of Rempstone, only 2 miles from Bunny Hill and I often met him in the local village pub. David was a rising star at Central TV and we worked with him on many different programmes including 5 series of "Boon" and 2 series of "Peak Practice" before it went to being filmed entirely in the studio.

Early in December I got a call from the BBC who wanted a knight dressed in black, on a white horse, for a sequence in a new series called the "Golden Oldies Picture Show", presented by Dave Lee Travis. The idea behind the show was to create music videos for hit songs that were made before the age of video. The video that I was to do, was for Twinkle's song "Terry". This happened to be a favourite song of mine from my motorcycle days in the 1960s. We filmed it at Sutton Park which is a wild, rough area close to Sutton Coldfield. I had never heard of the area before and I was astounded that somewhere so wild could be so close to Birmingham. It reminded me of the open areas of the New forest, gorse, bracken and the odd copse of silver birch trees. Although it was a cold and misty day, they shot some very atmospheric footage. The horse I used was my regular jousting horse, Jontie! He was very quiet which was a good thing as I had to scoop up a woman dressed in a long, white wedding dress across the front of my horse, and carry her off into a fog of smoke. I had only just finished filming at Sutton Park when we got a call about filming some scenes on a proper feature film in and around Chatsworth House in Derbyshire.

The film was called "Lady Jane Grey". Lady Jane had been crowned Queen of England following the death of King Edward VI in a bid to stop Henry VIII's daughter Mary, who was a Catholic ascending to the throne. Jane reigned for nine days before being deposed and beheaded by Mary. We were originally just booked for a hunting scene in Chatsworth Estate Park, but again riding skills, good horses and availability got us a lot more work on the film. We had great fun and a lot of laughs on this film. The Horse Master, Jimmy Lodge was a great guy; easy-going and always mindful of the hardships that both horse and rider were enduring. I remember one bitterly cold day filming on a ridge above Chatsworth House in over a foot of snow. The Director had already brought ski clothing for the crew and we had rugs for the horses when not filming but the riders had only their costumes which were not winter wear by any stretch of the imagination. By early afternoon we were all about to mutiny when Jimmy the Horse Master appeared with urns of hot chocolate and several bottles of whisky and brandy just for the riders. During the last weeks of filming it was bitterly cold, we had to leave the stables at 4.30 in the morning to get to Chatsworth for the 6 am call time. It was so cold one morning that the lorry brakes froze and we had to tow the lorry with our tractor to free them off. Dad was the lorry driver and one morning he did one of his classics. We had been travelling up to Chatsworth for about ten days, and this particular morning we were running late. The traffic was building at the A610 / M1 traffic island that has several lanes; Dad was not concentrating and ended up in the wrong lane; upon realising his mistake Dad cut straight across two lanes of traffic without indicating, causing much squealing of brakes and honking of horns. Dad's comment was, "stupid bastards they should have known where I was going by now, we have been coming this way for over a week now! "

On our first day on set we all had to go and get our costumes sorted out. Most of us were selected to be members of the Royal Hunt, but Dad and Mike Lane were pulled to one side. They had been selected to be the Kings Guard and when they joined us later they were dressed in very grand, black leather costumes with slashed sleeves and shiny metal helmets. They were both swaggering around like the cats that got the cream and making fun of us lowly huntsmen. However, we had the last laugh because their skin-tight costumes were freezing cold to wear, whereas we were all clothed in thick wool and fur jackets! Poor devils - they never stopped shivering and we never stopped laughing!

All the scenes that we were shooting were supposed to take place in deep snow, and although the snow was forecast it never came. We spent over a week sitting in costume in a heated marquee eating and drinking, just waiting for the snow to arrive. Eventually they gave up waiting and decided to lay artificial snow at the cost of tens of thousands of pounds. It took a day and a half to lay the artificial snow. Next morning, of course it snowed, and the artificial snow turned purple making it impossible to shoot the scene yet again. Luckily, we then got more snow which buried all the purple snow - so then everything finally went ahead.

It was a new location after the Christmas break to nearby Haddon Hall and by now we had a good covering of snow. I had never been to Haddon Hall before but instantly fell in love with it and it is still one of my all-time favourite places. Haddon Hall is unique in that it is a fortified medieval manor house that dates from the 12th Century but was left dormant from 17th Century when the owners inherited and moved to Belvoir Castle. There is a special tranquillity to the place both inside and outside, untouched by modern times. As part of the continuity of the film, some of us had to be present for the interior shots with the stars and it was during these sessions that I saw and started to appreciate the skill of lighting a scene to produce a fantastic atmosphere.

One of the scenes near Haddon Hall required about thirty of us to gallop down a very steep hill. Bill Hammond was riding one of our horses, Sovereign. Every time we did the scene, Sovereign would start to "bronc" and slowly but surely, Bill would be thrown further and further up the horse's neck until he fell off. This appealed greatly to the jousters' sense of humour and we would position ourselves so we could get an unobstructed view of this slow-motion falling act. Unfortunately for Bill, the Director insisted on us repeating the scene about eight times, by which time we were all in hysterics and poor old Bill battered and bruised.

At the same location, another strange thing happened to us. The location was situated up a long narrow lane so the horseboxes had to drop us off the horses and riders at beginning of the lane. We then had to hack the last half mile. Luckily for us we were stabled at Caroline Dale's, a friend of ours who specialised in driving horses and had an amazing collection of horse-drawn vehicles. Her stables were only about a mile from the location so we rode from the stables along an old disused railway line to the location. The scene was the end of the Stag Hunt and was long and drawn out. This was because it involved sedating a stag so that it appeared to collapse and die. The Director knew he had only one "take" for this scene so everything had to be set perfectly. He had just shot the dying scene and was adding some further shots around the sleeping stag. It was bitterly cold, and the horses were starting to shiver. As we stood on the hillside hoping the Director would hurry up we noticed a white cloud further up the valley illuminated by the pale winter sun. We were all intrigued by the phenomena until we realised it was rapidly approaching us. Within less than a minute the whiteout blizzard hit us and chilled us to the bone in seconds. The days filming was immediately abandoned, and the crew tried to radio for the horseboxes to come and collect the horses and riders. The horses were getting distressed and we could hardly move for the cold. Rather than wait half an hour or more for the lorries to arrive, we decided to make a run for it back to the Stables. The first part of our journey home was slow because the road was slippery, but as soon as got onto the old railway track through the woods it was full gallop; we knew things were getting critical. The snow was now about two inches deep and the sound of the horses´ hooves were muffled by the soft, new snow. We raced silently through the snow-covered wood; we could only see a few feet in front of us. Suddenly out of the snow loomed two joggers running towards us, also caught in the unexpected blizzard. The look on their faces was of sheer horror; they stopped frozen to the spot and still hadn't moved when they disappeared behind us into the swirling snow. It was only later that we realised how we must have appeared to them. Six horsemen dressed from head to toe in white medieval costumes, galloping silently through a wood, appearing and disappearing in a matter of seconds. They must have truly believed we were a ghostly apparition and are probably still telling the story at dinner parties to this day!

We started the 1985 season with hardly any winter break. We finished filming Lady Jane Grey mid-January and did our first show at Bosworth on March 3rd. We had completed our first season without Tony.

Things had been going far better than I had hoped since Tony had parted company with us, but as the number of shows and other events grew, I couldn't help wondering if we had peaked. We were all exhausted and there were rumblings from partners and employers about the time spent away jousting. We were also moving into Film, Television and Corporate entertainment. These were a whole new ball game; there was a lot of hanging around, and no adrenalin rush from a cheering crowd, in fact most of the time we had no idea whether we'd had done a decent job or not. A big problem was the way we were paid; our usual way of working was 10% on booking and then cash or bank draught on the day of the show. The lads were all paid at the next practice.

Television was very slow paying. If you were an extra, then you were paid through your agent who deducted his commission before paying out, which sometimes stretched into months. However, if I supplied horses or properties then I had to invoice these and usually wait 6 – 8 weeks for payment.

Films were totally different; extras were paid on the day with a large deduction for a day membership fee to the Film Actors Association, but they had a separate way of paying for a horse and rider. Each person signed a form every day when they arrived which stated how much they were being paid. Unfortunately, the form didn't mention the horse. Sometimes people were paid daily or at the end of the week and sometimes I had to collect all the chits and send them off for payment. The transport and any grooms we brought along to look after the horses were paid on invoice by a different department. This system caused a lot of problems in the early days as the lads thought they should be paid the fee stated on their chit as it made no mention of the horse. To complicate things further if you rode as an extra on a horse supplied by the film company, then you got the full fee stated on your chit, although this was considerably less. When we supplied a horse and rider we were sub-contracting through the Horsemaster who took his cut a bit like an agent. The lads just didn't "get it" and it was something that caused a lot of bad feeling.

We soon found out that all was not so rosy in the corporate entertainment world. Although we were doing shows for big multinational companies we were being paid by an agency or even a sub-agency. Being a bit naïve we got our fingers burned a couple of times and so did Belvoir Castle. As a small family business, we were not used to the way these big organisations worked. Our ethos of pay and be paid just didn't work with our new customers.

We started the New Year with a healthy number of shows already signed up, but this was mainly down to the regular 6 shows at Belvoir and, because it was the 500-year anniversary of the Battle of Bosworth, we had 8 shows at the Battlefield. Then early in the New Year my old mate Terry Goulden from Art & Archery called and offered us a job at Pinewood Studios, to make an advert for Carling Black Label Lager! It was made by a lake in a forest close to the Studios, and was shown on Television and at Cinemas for several months. We were very excited about doing the advert and imagined that there would be loads of drinking and partying, but it was cold, clinical arduous work and we never even saw a can of lager! It was a super advert and one in a whole series of, "I bet he drinks Carling Black Label" adverts. Although it didn't come out before the start of the season, it gave me a great sales pitch to drop the name of such a famous brand!

The next thing that came out of the blue was a summons to Leicestershire County Hall for a meeting with the Assistant Director of Property and Land Agent, Michael Harrison. Mr Harrison ran his Department like a Medieval Fiefdom. Everyone who worked for him referred to him as Mr Harrison, and he ran his department with military precision. I had only dealt with him once when I met him at Bosworth Battlefield, for a meeting prior to our first booking, and since then had only dealt with his assistants. I did, however, speak to him at every show we did at Bosworth. He was always there checking that everything was running smoothly, and dressed immaculately in a tweed suit carrying a brass tipped walking stick of military style. He would use his stick like a Brigadier directing his troops - pointing it here and there. After a long wait, I was summoned into his office and was given an effusive welcome. Even an offer a chair in front of his rather grand desk! He seated himself and pressed the intercom on his desk and ordered his secretary to ensure that there be absolutely no interruptions until this meeting was concluded. I felt worried. Who had the lads upset this time? Mr Harrison then spent the next ten minutes instilling me with the need for absolute secrecy in the matter we were going to discuss. Nothing was to be spoken of the forthcoming event until he gave his explicit permission, and I must create a cover story for the things he was going to ask me to do. "Gosh are we going to invade Europe?" I thought.

It turned out to be a lot less sinister. A Royal visit by HRH Prince Charles and HRH Princess Diana of Wales most probably, but not yet, fully confirmed!

As it turned out we had two Royal visits- first the Duke and Duchess of Gloucester and then the Prince and Princess of Wales. The first was low key and relaxed; the second much more formal. For the Prince and Princess's visit there were just a handful of chosen council dignitaries who jealously hogged the limelight throughout the visit. After a tour of the new visitor centre they were driven across the Battlefield to watch us perform a short jousting show after which we all lined up and were presented to the Prince. As Prince Charles walked along the line he had a quick word with each of us, when he got to my brother Phil, he asked about what protection we had under our costumes. To the absolute horror of the council entourage, Phil hoiked up his costume to show the Prince his leather breast plate. There was a gasp of horror from the entourage, and several rushed forwards to intervene at the perceived insult, but to our great amusement, they were stopped in their tracks by the Prince laughing at Phil and saying "I know you. You're the farrier I chat to when hunting with the Quorn". It was so funny to watch all the faces of these councillors, who were so stiff and formal, as they looked on as the Prince chatted with familiarity to Phil. This visit was another great boost to our credibility as a top-class entertainment and along with the Carling Advert made us a very desirable show to book.

The first part of the season went off without a hitch until we got towards the end of June when we had two shows in the north of England. We were doing Malton Agricultural show on the Saturday staying overnight in Malton and then moving up to Darlington for a Round Table event on the Sunday. This was our first away weekend of the season, and most of us were looking forward to it except for a couple of the lads who were getting grief from their girlfriends. The first thing to go wrong was during the show at Malton; Phil was playing BK and riding his horse Step, who was like a missile when jousting. Phil lined up for his first joust and Step suddenly reared up and plunged forward with such ferocity, that Phil did a backflip off the horse knocking himself out cold. He was taken by ambulance to hospital and missed the rest of the show. We were all very worried about Phil and to try and perform a show without the main character was well-nigh impossible. Brian was marvellous! He re-rigged the show and we followed his lead, but all we could do was an old-fashioned display rather than our slick theatrical production. Thankfully Phil was ok and discharged later that day in time for the pub crawl! Lou had very thoughtfully booked us into a B&B with its own bar but it was not our cup of tea - very quiet, prim and proper so we set out to look for some livelier pubs. We drowned our sorrows caused by the poor show we had done and then headed back the B&B for a few more after hours in their bar. As we approached the Town Square we could hear a lot of noise and assumed it was post agricultural show revels. Perhaps we were missing a good party so we quickened our pace. We had nearly reached the Square when we were ambushed by a squad of Riot Police complete with shields who then surrounded us, demanding to know where we thought we were going to. "To the Square" we innocently announced only to be told. "No way - just turn around and go home or else you'll all be arrested". We didn't take kindly to this threat especially with about eight pints of beer inside us. We tried to explain about our B&B but the Police were not listening until one of them finally noticed our accent and realised we were visitors, not locals. Their attitude changed and they said they would escort us to our digs. As we got to the Square there was a full-scale battle taking place with plastic tables and chairs flying everywhere. We asked the Police what it was all about and they told it was the usual Saturday night in Malton and it always ended in a mass brawl.

At the B&B the barman seemed happy to serve us into the small hours, so the lads settled in for a session. Personally, the day's events had drained me so I just had one nightcap and then retired to bed. As usual I was sharing with Brian and remember him staggering in sometime much later. Next morning everyone was hungover but in good spirits at breakfast, although we did notice certain a frostiness from the landlady. After breakfast, I hurried the lads to pack and get on the bus whilst I paid the bill. I explained that I was settling the bill for everyone and said how much we had enjoyed our stay, adding that I hoped the lads hadn't been too noisy in the bar after I had gone to bed. It was at that moment the landlady exploded: "Was I trying to be funny! She had never been so insulted". I stood at the desk dumbfounded, apologising for something I knew nothing about. When she had calmed down she explained what had happened. Someone had entered her bedroom totally naked, walked over the top of her and her husband in bed, thrown open their bedroom window, stood on the windowsill and urinated; he then turned around walked back over the top of their bed, and left the room. Although I was sure I knew who had done this I asked them if they had spoken to the offender, but they were so shocked and frightened, that they were rendered speechless. After endless apologies, whilst the credit card payment was being completed I ran to the waiting bus, jumped in the driving seat and sped off. Although Brian claimed no recollection of the incident he did admit it most probably him and after the flower pot incident, I was positive.

My mind was still churning over the Brian incident as we sped along a clear A64 in the bright early morning sunlight, when I glanced in the wing mirror and to my horror saw something large floating through the air behind the bus. Then I realised what it was. It was one of the tilt sections we used to create the barrier between the two horses when jousting, twelve feet long, four feet high and a heavy wooden frame covered in canvas. Luckily, there was a hard shoulder, so I hit the brakes and pulled over as quickly as possible, just in time to stop another section taking off. The lads were marvellous; although heavily hungover and engrossed in a game of three card brag, they dropped everything, leapt off the bus and were running back down the dual carriageway to retrieve the section in a matter of seconds. It was like one of those WWII Battle of

Britain films where the Spitfire pilots are reading and dozing one moment, and then in the next moment they are sprinting across the airfield to their Spitfires. As we were retrieving the section, a car stopped and told us that there were two more sections about a quarter of a mile back down the road! Some of the lads ran off back down the road to get them out of the way of traffic, whilst the rest of us reloaded this section. Luckily there was no traffic on the road at this early hour, so with a lookout in the back window for any approaching vehicles, we reversed down the hard shoulder to retrieve the other two sections. The lads had just lifted the last section back onto the roof and were in the process of securing the ratchet straps when we heard a siren in the distance, and almost immediately a traffic police squad car with blue light flashing appeared; my heart sank we had so nearly got away with it, and I was also wondering if I was still over the alcohol limit after last night's session. There were deflated sighs of defeat from the assembled crew, and then to our amazement the police car flashed past us and disappeared as fast as it had appeared. Now it was sighs of relief and whoops of jubilation. Nobody owned up forgetting to secure the tilt sections but after that we always double checked that the ratchet straps were secure before leaving.

We all needed a good show to make up for the disappointment of the previous day's show and by god we gave Darlington one of the best shows we had ever done, earning a nice bonus along the way!

After the first show, a man was brought to me by one of the lads who explained that the man was one of the show's main sponsors and had asked to speak to the man in charge. He introduced himself and he asked if he could have a private word with me. He had a strange proposition for me; he wanted to know who was the best knight and the knight most likely to win the Tournament. That was not a problem, as it was a scripted show, but I didn't have the heart to make him look a fool for thinking it was a real competition. He then went on to ask me to tell this best knight that if he won the tournament he would give him £100. He explained that he was about to have a bet with his arch rival and co-sponsor about which Knight would win the tournament. So, I primed the lads not to let on it was a scripted show, and asked Phil and Stu to make the last fight extra good. True to his word he came and gave Stu the £100 adding that he thought he had lost his bet and that it looked like the Black Knight was going to win until the final blow (Thank heavens for good choreography!). The sponsor had won a substantial sum off his mate and not only did he pay his £100, but he invited us all back to the Sponsors Tent for food and drink. We had an extra-long stop on the way home to drink all the bribe money. The end to another mundane Jousting weekend away!

The following weekend we performed at Britannia Park, a new highly publicised Theme Park north of Nottingham. Attendance was poor, and the cheque bounced. I took the cheque to our solicitor, who was also a friend, to find out our options for trying to get our money. Her advice was disappointing, suggesting a long legal procedure, but word had it that they were in financial trouble and although we were in the right legally, getting the money was another matter. It was whilst giving her advice that she noticed something about the cheque that was very wrong. The cheque bore a stamp duty crest and stamp duty had been abolished several years previously. Technically it was an illegal cheque, so she suggested I contact them and say my solicitor has suggested I go to the Police as this was cheque fraud. I rang the director who had booked us and repeated what our Solicitor had advised, but added that we were a well-known local celebrity act with very good contacts at both the BBC and Central TV News Departments, and unless I was paid immediately I would be making a press-release the following morning. He thanked me for my discretion and said he would be back in touch later that day. About an hour later he phoned and said if I brought the cheque immediately to their head office I would be paid in cash, provided I was willing to not to take the matter further. It was a surreal affair like something in a spy novel. I was shown into an office with two gentlemen present, the Secretary was dismissed and told, "no interruptions;" I was asked to confirm that I had the cheque and that I was prepared not to say anything to the press about this unfortunate matter. I replied to both in the affirmative. They then opened a large safe that was behind their desk and produced a huge pile of small denomination banknotes. They then counted out what I was owed, which appeared to be nearly the whole contents of the safe. We shook hands and I left with a briefcase stuffed full of cash! Three days later they went bankrupt for millions of pounds, thereby also bankrupting many other local businesses that had done work for them. We found out later that they were trying to put a rescue deal together when I contacted them and could not afford the bad publicity. A lucky break!

The season ground on relentlessly, but our next weekend away did not come until late in July. Both shows were reasonably close together, very much like Malton and Darlington. This time we were at a small village near Ross on Wye, which is on the border with South Wales, and the other at a small village on the Gower Peninsular called Gowerton and near Swansea. It was not until I wrote this book that I realised that the North East was rivalled by the southwest around Bristol and South Wales as a Nottingham Jousting Association fan base.

Dymock still rates as one of my favourite shows ever, not because we did a fantastic show or that it was on a grand scale, but because it was personal.

The village of Dymock is mentioned in the Doomsday Book and they were celebrating some multi-centennial anniversary. There is also a quite rare surname of Dymock, which has its own society, and members of the Dymock Society would often come and visit Dymock. For their special day, they decided to invite all the Dymocks in the world to a Jousting tournament at Dymock. Dymocks responded from all over the World. Over one thousand came, and it was like a big family reunion, but the special thing was that so many came to talk to us and thank us for making their day so wonderful. The show was a six-horse show but our next one at Gowerton involved only four horses so we borrowed another horsebox so that Dad could take two home whilst we travelled on to South Wales. Martin Brown took a heavy fall during the Dymock Show and was badly concussed so we decided to send him home with Dad. Dad told us Martin kept repeating, *"I think I am feeling better now"* every two minutes all the way home for the whole two-and-a-half-hour trip - driving Dad crazy.

The lads were quick off the mark after the last show at Dymock, and we were soon packed and the horses loaded ready for the trip down to Gowerton, which was about one hour forty-five minutes' drive. I remember stopping for fuel on the way; it was a beautiful evening and the scenery was stunning. I thought life couldn't get much better than this! Gowerton, like Dymock, was not an ordinary show in that we were there to promote the opening of a Riding School, so we had good stabling on site and we were staying in local B&B's.

Our hosts were marvellous. They took us down to see the famous coast of the Gower Peninsular, which at sunset was stunning, and afterwards they treated us to a raucous night in the pub. The licensing laws were strict down there so it was an early night for everyone.

Next morning everyone was bright and breezy; not a hangover in sight. There was a good crowd and we were keen to put on a good show for our generous hosts. The show started well and was going great until my joust against Phil. I was riding a new horse called Molly, and although she had gone well the day before, I think it must have frightened her a bit, as she was swerving away from the super-fast horse, Step. We had done three of the four tilts without a strike and Phil as Black Knight was supposed to win 3 strikes to one. I knew I had to make an extreme effort to keep the mare in close to the tilt so Phil could get a strike to win the joust. When I made my turn at the end of the lists, the mare veered away from the lists, instead of spinning around on her back legs. As I turned I saw Phil's horse, Step, rear and then plunge forward at full gallop and I knew I had only seconds to get her close enough for Phil to hit me. I was kicking frantically with my outside leg to push the mare closer to the lists. There was a huge crash - I felt pain and saw sky, earth, sky, earth…. Then a blur of sky, surrounded by a ring of faces peering down at me. A voice said, "Don't worry the ambulance is here". The only words I could croak out were "how is Phil?" I found out later that my horse had jumped the 4-foot barrier head on into Phil's charging horse. Remarkably neither of the horses were injured. Phil was very battered, but the only injury he suffered was that a large nail had stuck in his backside when he landed on the broken barrier.

There followed a most bizarre incident. As part of our contract we had an ambulance on site during the shows. This was usually a St. John's Ambulance who were   part- time first aiders and this was the case on this occasion. Because of the horrific nature of the accident, someone had called 999 and an NHS Ambulance had been dispatched. The St John's crew were just loading me up into their ambulance when the NHS one arrived. They demanded that the St John's crew hand me over to them to which they, St John's, refused to do, saying that they got me first so I was theirs. I was drifting in and out consciousness, but I was told later that after about five minutes someone stepped in and stopped the stupid bickering. I still don't know to this day which ambulance took me to hospital!

I was very lucky considering and had only broken my collar bone, sprung some ribs on my sternum and had concussion. The hospital wanted to keep me in but I discharged myself, as I would have been stuck on my own in South Wales. The coach home was a nightmare. I felt every bump in the road, especially on the M50 which was a concrete road with joints every 30 yards. Just writing about it turns my stomach. Despite strong painkillers, I still nearly passed out on several occasions. The lads dropped me off right outside my house. Lou knew nothing of my accident (no mobile phones in those days) and was a little shocked as I hobbled through the door with my arm in a sling. Our dog "Meg" came bounding up towards me and I screamed at her to go away before she jumped up at me. Lou shouted at me saying " don't be so miserable! Pat the dog - she is only pleased to see you". It was a fitting end to an awful day….

Two weeks later we sailed to Guernsey. Our first trip away from England and our first ferry trip with the horses. The trip had been a long time in the planning. In the 1980's we had no mobile phones or internet so all information had to come from the library, or by phoning the company or relevant government department. Just finding the right Ministry and then the right department could take days. Lou and I worked for months on the project constantly phoning and waiting for information to arrive by post. My contact in Guernsey was Roy Burton, who was a member of the show committee, and he and I were in almost daily contact. During the eighties, the TV series "Bergerac" about the Channel Isles was extremely popular, and portrayed a wealthy, glamorous life style. Every time I phoned Roy, his wife would say, "I'm sorry he is still out driving his horses and carriage". I had visions of a retired, wealthy gentleman with a large house with estate roads that he drove his horse and carriage around, a bit like Prince Philip.

When we had finally sorted out costings and regulations for the trip, I decided I needed to go over there to check on several things, such as accommodation and stabling, before signing the contract. One of the problems we had to overcome was that the maximum permitted width of vehicles allowed onto the Island, this was considerably smaller than both our coach and horsebox, so we needed Government approval, plus a police escort. Luckily there was a flight from East Midlands to Guernsey, so I flew over and stayed overnight to tie up the loose ends and sign the contract. Roy had told me that everyone was very excited about my coming over and that he would be picking me up personally. The organising committee would be hosting a dinner in my honour at a hotel. I felt like a visiting celebrity! So, dressed in my best business suit and clutching a briefcase, I arrived at Guernsey Airport, which was tiny. The flight had been full and it was quite chaotic at the airport. I looked in vain for a wealthy, country gentleman waiting to greet me. Gradually, the Arrivals Hall emptied until only a farmer in an old, tweed jacket and a tattered cap, that hung on the side of his head, was left. He was accompanied by a collie sheepdog at his heel, as he ambled towards me with a huge grin saying "you must be Sam! I'm Roy Burton. Come on let's get going! Brenda is desperate to meet you". He ushered me towards an old, rusting Morris Minor that had empty feed sacks on the back seat for the dog to lie on, but judging by the amount of collie hair on the passenger seat, I think the dog spent most of her time up front with her master. By the time, I reached their farm, my dark business suit was covered with white collie hair.

Roy and Benda were true Guerns, the original inhabitants of Guernsey, who for hundreds of years had eked a hard living off their small farms before the island became a tax haven for the wealthy. They were so welcoming and nothing was ever too much trouble for them. We became instant friends and we keep in touch to this day, thirty years on. Roy was amazing! Despite being a small farmer, he seemed to know everyone, including members of the government, or the States as it is called. Within hours, we had permission to bring our oversized vehicles onto the Island, and a Police escort arranged from the Port to the show ground, and all the documentation sorted for importing our horses into Guernsey. I was even measured up for a Guernsey sweater that Brenda would hand knit for me and which would be ready and waiting for me when I returned to do the show!

We were sailing from Weymouth. It was a blistering, sweltering day when we drove down and we were all very excited about our trip abroad, even if it was only to the Channel Isles. Luckily, we arrived early at the docks and as there were so many regulations to deal with, I thought it best to check in early. Then we received a bombshell! It might be a heatwave in Weymouth, but it was too windy in the Channel for the ferry to be allowed to carry horses. They told us to come back and try again tomorrow! Thankfully, they had a livery yard on standby for such eventualities, so we were easily able to arrange overnight stabling for the horses. Stabling for the lads proved much harder, as it was the height of the holiday season, and most B&B's were fully booked. After an hour of trying to find somewhere to get all the lads in together, I split them into pairs to try and find an odd room here and there. It took nearly four hours for the lads to get fixed up, and cost me a fortune. One of the annoying problems was that there were loads of double bedded rooms available and the lads were quite happy to bunk up together, but the homosexuality laws of that period, forbade hoteliers to let a double-bedded room to two males. Thankfully, the winds died down in the Channel overnight, and we sailed the next day. As we left the harbour in Weymouth, Scots Jim asked this famous question. "Hey Sam, are they the White Cliffs of Dover." Robin Hoods Minstrels had also travelled with us and Hippy Steve, the washboard player, commented that I sounded like a tired mother talking to a child when I replied " No Jimmy they are the white cliffs of Weymouth, Dover is 200miles away". As Hippy Steve and I stood on the stern of the ferry, the shoreline fading away and we were watching some hovering sea gulls, when Steve sighed and started to say "Ah Jonathan" and I finished the sentence "Livingstone sea gull". We burst into laughter. We had both read the same poem and were having the same thoughts.

Our stay in Weymouth was not without incident. We were lazing in the sun on a jetty next to the beach, and a little further along kids were jumping off into the sea. Andrew Ducker was always impulsive and seeing the kids, leapt up shouting at everyone to jump into the sea. Before we could stop him, he had leapt off the jetty. It was about twelve feet down to water and unfortunately, he had failed to notice that we were only about three yards from the beach. Instead of landing in ten feet of water like the kids further out, he landed in six inches of water. He let out a terrible scream of pain and was rolling around in agony. We all thought he had broken his leg or ankle, but thankfully, he had only badly jarred and bruised his feet. Having said that, he couldn't walk and two lads had to carry him everywhere. Great! A man down and we hadn't even left England.

The ferry crossing took several hours so it was a boozy trip and this time it was Harvey Broadhead who provided the amusement. Harvey was very sea sick so the lads took him to the bar, as their logic was beer cured everything. Harvey often "necked" a pint in one, which was what he preceded to do on this occasion, slamming his glass on the bar and ordering another, before running outside to be sick over the side into the sea. He then returned, paid for his drink and repeated the same operation again. In fact, he did it about eight times until his money ran out. The barman and several other customers in the bar were amazed that he could drink eight pints of beer in about 30 minutes, and all downed in one gulp. It also seemed to have had no effect on Harvey. This, of course, amused the lads greatly and so they funded Harvey for several more pints. As on the coach, there was a marathon card game from cast off until docking, with fortunes being won and lost.

When we finally docked at St Peter Port, we were treated like royalty. Everyone seemed to know who we were and formalities kept to a minimum. Even the Police escort was waiting for us, complete with blue lights flashing. Next morning, it was an early start as we had lost our rest day, stuck in Weymouth. The coach and horsebox were not allowed to move until we left the Island, so all our costumes and equipment had to be ferried to the site by tractor and trailer. Our first show was at midday, so it was quite a rush. To make matters worse the weather was turning bad again and by the time we started our first show, the rain was lashing down. I was commentating as Brian could not get the time off work. It was only two weeks after my accident and my collarbone was a long way from healing, as was the rest of my battered body. The rain was so heavy I could hardly see the lists in the centre of the arena. As the show progressed I started to get more and more pain from my collarbone; so much so, that I was struggling to speak by the end of the show. It was not until I was trying to get out of my costume that I realised that my chainmail had shrunk in the heavy rain and was pulling my broken collarbone apart. Whilst the lads were trying to extract me from my shrunken costume, the show chairman, Larry Ozanne, popped his head into our changing tent to thank us for performing in such terrible conditions. He was very concerned to see me writhing in agony and after it had been explained to him the cause of my pain, he just said leave it to me and left. Ten minutes later he was back to say a car was outside ready to take me to a 5-star spa hotel. He had arranged for me to use the steam room and sauna, followed by a massage, all free of charge. An hour and a half late, I returned a rejuvenated man, ready for the second show. Whist I was away, the lads had discovered a new gambling game called Crown and Anchor. It was very addictive and kept them occupied for the whole of their stay. The game was in fact illegal in Guernsey, but was so popular that it was still allowed to be played on show days. The rest of the shows were performed in glorious sunshine, we were front page news in all the newspapers and super stars all over the Island.

When we sailed home, there was a crowd at the docks to wave us of. It was just incredible. Thirty years on, myself and Martin Brown, still keep in touch, with Roy and Brenda Burton. They are in their ninety's now. Roy broke his back in an accident driving his horse and carriage some years ago, but still manages to get around. The trip home was uneventful but the whole trip was exhausting and full of unexpected incidents, despite all our meticulous planning. However, it was great preparation for far more arduous trips to come.

The next show on our calendar was the 500th anniversary of the Battle of Bosworth, which attracted huge crowds and press attention. After Guernsey, we had a welcome weekend off, so everyone was fully fit and raring to go. We were spurred on by being informed that Peter Woodward, the fight arranger, son of actor Edward Woodward, and the Assistant Curator of The Tower of London, would be amongst the special guests coming to watch us. We performed one of our very best shows that day. Peter Woodward praised us for the quality of our fight arrangements and the use of so many different weapons. I was also visited by the Curator from the Tower, who was similarly impressed. In fact, he invited me to visit the Tower and view all weapons that were not on public show. The visit was incredible. There was room after room stuffed with thousands of matching weapons that were never seen. I commented that it was such a shame that all this this stuff was hidden away from public view. He told me, in confidence, that there were already advanced plans to build a special place to display all this hidden treasure. It opened eleven years later, as the Royal Armouries Museum in Leeds. It is mind blowing the stuff they have on display there, even my wife Lou was impressed and that takes some doing, especially if it has anything remotely associated with jousting. They do demonstration jousts there as well and I have always wondered if that visit to Bosworth was where the idea came from. We were asked to quote for doing the jousting, but it was a six day a week contract running for about nine months of the year. After our experiences at Gwrych Castle, I had no interest in doing something like that ever again.

Cyprus

Towards the end of the season, I got a call from Terry Goulden, our chainmail supplier. He had had an inquiry about doing some jousting as part of a new hotel opening in Cyprus, were we interested? I said yes straight away, but after I had put the phone down thought, "oh shit what have I agreed to". After talking it through with Lou, I realised it was going to be much more complicated than I first thought. The major problem was horses. Road transport was out of the question, and when we finally tracked down an airline that flew horses, the quote was £40,000 each way. I rang Terry and told him, the bad news, but that if they wanted any foot fights then we were still on board. I didn't hear anything for several weeks, and then out of the blue, Terry rang to say the organisers had found some polo ponies at an English army base. The base was called Happy Valley and was a rest and recuperation Base, not far from Paphos, where the new hotel was being opened. My reply was that was good news, but I didn't think the British Army were going to lend their prize horses to a load of Jousters. Then he dropped the bombshell; the officer in charge knew us well and had no qualms in letting us train and ride their horses, because he knew us. and he had nothing but praise for our riding ability. The Officer's comments had impressed the Organisers very much and they now wanted us more than ever. I had no idea who the mystery Officer was and asked Terry to get in touch with Cyprus to find out who we were dealing with. It turned out to be Captain Tim Hercock, his father was Master of the Quorn Hunt and we had hunted regularly with Tim and his sister for many seasons. Years later, Tim himself became a very successful and long serving Master of the Quorn when he finally left the Army.

The preparations for the trip were long and hard, and not helped by the fact that we still had bookings in October and November. Besides repainting and repairing everything after our longest season ever we also had to modify several things for air freight. All our kit had to fit into a box 8ft x 4ft x 2ft 6 ins. This was jousting super light, but would help us secure several other trips out of own horse travelling range.

Finally, on Wednesday 20th of November, we set off in the middle of the night for an 8 am check in at Heathrow. Alan lane drove us all down in the coach, and I still remember the immense sense of pride pulling up at the British Airways V.I.P. Departures area, and alighting from our sign written coach. British Airways had part sponsored our flights, so there were photographers and press everywhere. When we finally boarded, after much razzamatazz, we were delayed for nearly an hour, because they had problems loading our very large, heavy kit box.

We had to fly wearing our costumes, as part of the British Airways, "deal". Four hours on a plane, dressed in chainmail, certainly gave us a reality check about being VIP'S. However, we were allocated our own stewardess and had free drink all the way We were all invited up into the cockpit to meet the pilots. Most of the lads were too busy playing cards and drinking, but I did go into the cockpit and talk to the pilots. It really shocked me how small the cockpit was. The pilots were virtually shoehorned into their seats and I could barely squeeze in behind them. I felt slightly embarrassed to be disturbing their work, but they immediately put me at ease, saying that they were glad of the company. It was not at all like you see in films; they were not flying the plane, but just sitting there keeping an eye on the instruments. Unlike the passenger windows you couldn't look down, so all they had to look at through their windows, was a never changing pale blue. Just before I left, a little buzzer sounded, and they told me they were changing course in 2 minutes. The co-pilot read out the new heading, and the Captain turned a little knob, that changed the numbers displayed on a dial. The co-pilot confirmed the numbers. A button was pressed and the plane changed course. The pilot then told me that was all they had do until the next course change, in one and a half hours' time. I really don't know how they managed to stay awake.

Meanwhile back in the passenger cabin, the lads were in full party mode, making the most of BA's free booze. Unbeknown to me, Mark Lacey was terrified of flying, and to calm his nerves had consumed copious port and brandies. Just before landing he staggered off to the toilet and still had not returned when the announcement to fasten seat-belts for landing was made. The stewardess went off to get him out of the toilet, but there was no response, and so after circling the airport several times, the pilot decided he must land without Mark fastened in his seat. We were very worried for Mark's safety, but we need not have worried, as he appeared shortly after landing, smiling, and wobbling back to his seat, blissfully unaware of the drama he had caused. He had passed out on the toilet, but when the plane landed he had shot off the seat and head butted the toilet door, which brought him sharply out of his drunken slumber.

As the plane taxied in a stewardess came and told us we had to wait in our seats until all the other passengers had left the plane. We all went very quiet. For most of the lads, this was their first ever flight or trip abroad, and we all thought it had to be something to do with the Mark Lacey incident; but it proved to be much worse.

We were celebrities and there were about thirty journalists, photographers and dignitaries waiting for us on the tarmac at the bottom of the plane's steps, ready to greet us and interview us, and we were all rolling drunk. Luckily, Terry Goulden and his crew had flown with us, although they were in a similar state. We persuaded Terry that they should have the honour of leaving the plane first to meet the delegation and be photographed. Terry always liked to be the centre of attention so fell for the ruse immediately. Our next big problem was how to get Mark Lacey off the plane, as his legs were not working very well. We got two of the big lads to hold him up, and the rest of us walked slowly down the steps, pausing regularly to wave to the photographers, whilst the lads manhandled Mark down the steps one step at a time. It took us about 5 minutes to get down those steps, and all the time I was saying to the lads, keep waving, keep smiling, have you got him down the next step yet. The press wanted a group photo of all the people in costume and I still have a copy. Mark is being held up by his sword belt from behind. It's a great photo; we just look happy to be in Cyprus. Nobody would suspect we are all drunk as Lords. We soon sobered up because the temperature was in the high eighties at Larnica Airport and we had had to wait nearly two hours for our box to be unloaded and processed by customs. The facilities at the airport were very basic, as until recently it had been a military airport and had not really changed since the Second World War. As always, the downfall with drinking alcohol is dehydration, and sitting around sweating in a tin roofed shed made it ten times worse. We had been warned very strongly not to drink the tap water, but this was sorely tested, as our mouths and throats turned to sandpaper and our heads started pounding. There were no facilities in the shed, not even a toilet. I still feel ill writing about it now. Eventually, everything was cleared, and our transport arrived to take us to the hotel. Part of our group had been lucky enough to go to the hotel straightaway, and we imagined them all sipping cold beers by the pool. We were much cheered up by our mode of transport, which was two stretched limousines, with chauffeurs who bowed, and opened the doors for us. Our first thought was that they might have a bar in the back, like the James Bond movies, but no such luck. So, we stretched out in the back of our limo, enjoying the cool night breeze, looking forward to a lovely, cool drink at our hotel. We had no idea about the geography of Cyprus at all, and only knew the name of the hotel, which was called the Cypria Maris, and it was in the town of Paphos. After about half an hour, our elation about our mode of transport faded, and our raging thirst took over again, so I tapped on the privacy window to enquire how much further it was to the hotel. Luckily, our chauffeur spoke good English and cheerfully told us about another two and a half hours. We were dumbstruck, almost suicidal; another two and a half hours without water. How could I have been so naïve not to think about transfer times and water? I was so angry with myself. We asked if he had any water in the limo, but the answer was no, but he offered to find a bar and stop if we wanted to, but they were few a far between on this mountain road. Unfortunately, we had to decline his offer as none of us had any Cypriot money as it was not available to change in the UK. After another hour of purgatory, the limo swung into a town square and parked up. The driver announced, "we stop have drink". I explained yes, we would love a drink, but didn't have any money. To our amazement, he threw his hands up in the air grinned broadly and said "no problem, I pay. No problem, no problem". We loved that guy; we would have given every penny we had for just one drink of water at that moment. He brought us a large glass of water and a pint of ice cold beer each, and more bottles of water for the rest of the trip. The man was just a saint. We felt so humbled by his generosity.

When we finally arrived, we were rejuvenated and ready to party again. The hotel was magnificent, and was decorated with Arms and Armour from the Crusader era, that Terry Goulden had obviously supplied; hence his connection with this project. After showering and changing, we met in the bar before going off to explore the rest of the hotel. Terry explained that we had an allowance of one bottle of wine each at lunch and another at dinner; all drinks were free at social occasions that we had to attend, and all food, including snacks was also free. Terry also had a generous entertaining allowance, so if we saw him in the bar, he would buy us drinks. Anything else, we signed for and got a 20% discount, that we paid on leaving. Then he warned not to use the mini bar, as they were very expensive and no discount would be given; a half bottle of champagne was about £80, which was a week's wages to most of the lads. To add icing onto the cake, we had a fleet of stretched limos at our disposal, day or night, free of charge. We thought we had just died and gone to Heaven. Then he added, we had to be at Happy Valley Army Base at 10 am tomorrow morning and that it was about 1½ hours' drive from the hotel, so breakfast at 7 am; "damn, we had to work as well".

Next day we were up bright and early. Dad and the riders went off to Happy Valley whilst the rest of us unpacked our kit and I started to put a show together which included Terry's group performing with us as one show. Terry was renowned for being sparing with the details when making an agreement and now he dropped his bombshell. I had agreed that we would do our jousting for a set duration and provide a guard of Honour for the opening ceremony. However, he failed to mention that he was bringing over other medieval performers, and that we were all performing as an integrated show, so we were in the arena for three times longer than expected. He also announced that I was to be the commentator for the whole event. Most evenings, there was something happening, so we were in our chainmail for several hours every night; not pleasant when the temperature was 80°. Of course, it was it was "Muggins Me" who had to break the news to the lads, and it did not go down well; coupled with this, several of the younger members were feeling out of their depth and homesick. It was one thing to go to the Channel Isles where everyone spoke English, but to be in a country that spoke a different language, had different food and customs, was a leap from their comfort zone. Being in a 5-star hotel, surrounded by celebrities and even the President of Cyprus, put even more pressure on them. The lads seemed happier down at Happy Valley than in the hotel. They had made friends with the soldiers who looked after the horses, and enjoyed a beer with them in the NAAFI, after training.

I was very jealous of them, as I was stuck at the hotel, trying to sort out a heap of problems. The biggest of these was that we had no arena; the plan had been to select the horses we were going to use, and then have a couple of dress rehearsals with the horses at the hotel, but all we had was a beach covered with sand dunes. The other main problem was the performers; each group thought they were the most important and wanted to be the stars of the show, and this included

Terry, who thought he was Robin Hood reincarnated. He dressed and had his hair curled like Richard Greene, who played Robin Hood in the TV Series during the early Sixties. He even signed his hotel chits, *(Robin Hood, followed by a Bow and Arrow),* a quirk that would cost him dear over duration of our stay, but that's another story for later. My biggest problem, was a man who had come over as part of Terry's party. Back in England, he rode his own horse around in the arena at shows, dressed in a suit of armour, whilst the commentator talked about the horse and armour. My problem was, his show was not a show; his armour was 400 years later than our costumes; it had nothing to do with the Crusades, which was the theme of everything happening at the hotel. Worst of all, he was a very weak rider, in his late fifties, who was terrified of the army polo ponies. To top this off, he was under the allusion that he had been brought over as star of the show and as such, should have a special, top billing and all the privileges that went with it. He was the reason I got to go to Happy Valley, because he was driving the lads mad with his demands, and the only horse that he could manage to ride, was the one Dad had already selected for himself. Unfortunately, Terry was very much on this Guy's side. I think Terry had made his armour for him and charged him an absolute fortune for it, but promised him he would get him loads of work, so he could recoup his investment.

But every cloud has a silver lining, and I was able to solve another problem whilst I was at the base. Pete Webster was usually the life and soul of the party but not on this trip. On this occasion, he was very down in the dumps and I must say, the only time ever in over forty years of knowing Pete, that he has been this way. I had taken him aside in the hotel and had a heart- to -heart with him, managing to jolly him along with, only a few more days before we go home and everything will be more relaxed after we did our main show. The one problem I couldn't solve was that he didn't like the food; most of us thought it was the best food we had ever eaten, with sumptuous banquets every night. Pete however just wanted baked beans on toast. I had asked the hotel if they could help, but they had no idea what I was talking about. So, I was sitting in the NAAFI having a beer with the army lads, telling them about Pete not liking our hotel food and his craving for baked beans. The Corporal started to laugh and said "baked bloody beans. If he wants baked beans, we've got tons of the bloody things. He can have as many as he wants, any time he wants". Pete and the rest of the lads joined us shortly afterwards and I ceremoniously presented him with a huge catering tin of baked beans, that held about 10 normal tins of beans. He sat in the corner with a spoon and scoffed the lot cold. We had a happy Pete who now dined regularly with the Army.

I solved the other problem of our man in a suit of armour by pandering to his wishes. I put him on first as a separate act which gave us time to redress the horse for Dad to ride later. It was a ploy I used with other prima-donna groups we had to work with in later years. They all thought it a great honour to go on first; little did they realise they were acting as our warm up act.

We settled into a routine of work in the morning until about 11 am and then play until about 6 pm, when we were, more often than not, performing or wandering around in costume. Most days we used our chauffeurs to take us down to the bars in the old town; they knew all the best bars and even changed our money for us, giving us far better rates than the hotel. There is nothing like turning up in a stretched limo to get very best service in a bar or restaurant. One day however we all decided to hire scooters and go exploring ourselves. There was a hire company based at the hotel so we booked them to our rooms, "as you do when you are celebrities". We were in trouble even before we left the hotel; Pete was pulling wheelies around the car park, whilst the rest of us were still being given our scooters. I remember the very annoyed manager saying in broken English to Pete, "no! no! it not a 'orse", and mimicking a horse rearing with his body. We finally roared off as a pack swerving all over the road like a scene from the movie, "Quadrophenia". That was just the start, as we hit Paphos there were loads of restaurants with raised wooden boardwalks in front of them. In a flash, there were scooters driving along the boardwalks, like a car chase from a James Bond movie. Luckily the Greeks tend to eat late, so there were not too many diners to upset. I fully expected the Police to arrive at any moment and arrest us all. I needed to get them out of Paphos as quick as possible, so I suggested that we go out along the coast and do some exploring. Bad move. We were now using the scooters as moto-cross bikes, weaving our way through scrub and volcanic rock. Little did I realise that things were about to get even worse. They had discovered a huge, cave complex and were now driving in and out of these caves, filling them with smelly fumes and smoke. I don't know whether they had missed the sign, or just ignored it, stating that the caves were an ancient monument linked to Greek Mythology. Again, I had visions of us all in jail for desecrating a Cypriot ancient monument, so against my better judgment, I suggested we find a Taverna and have a beer. Thankfully it did the trick we drove back to Paphos and settled into several pints of Keo Beer the strong Cypriot beer that's guaranteed to give you a thumping head later. Several beers later we wove our scooters back to the Hotel miraculously all undamaged.

As always, on every tour there had to be a silly game, and on this tour, it was to steal the very expensive champagne from the mini bar in someone else's room, and drink it, so that they had to pay £80. I think only one got drunk, but it set off endless raids on each other's room to steal a bottle, to replace a missing bottle. I got raided early one morning whilst in the shower. When I realised what was happening, I leapt out the shower and gave chase. They slammed my room door closed so that when I got into the corridor, they were back in their room a couple of doors further down. I knew who it was, so ran down and hammered on their door. screaming "let me in you bastards - I want my champagne back ". After a short delay, the door opened and I faced a huge, very irate German, with a big black moustache, who drew himself up to his full height and bellowed "vas machen sie" (roughly translated - what do you want or what are you doing). It was at this point, that I realised several things. I had got the wrong room. It was 7am in the morning. And I was stark naked and dripping wet. I ran as fast as I could back to my room constantly shouting, "I'm sorry, I'm sorry". This incident ended the room raiding, as the lads found that my incident with the German much funnier, and it turned out nobody had drunk the champagne in the first place. They had just hidden the bottle that had started the whole crazy game.

When we first arrived at the hotel, the "Clebs" were very aloof, and kept themselves to themselves in a tight little group. We tried to talk to them but only got short polite answers. The worst was Samantha Fox - a Sun, page three girl, famous for displaying her large "boobs". She was about the same age as the lads, but didn't even reply when spoken to, and was always ushered away by her Mother, who would always look down her nose at the offending person, as if she was a medieval Duchess being approached by lowly serf. When we were not working, the lads spent a lot of time swimming in the indoor pool. The pool was the social hub of the hotel with its own bar and snack restaurant. It even had live bands playing in the evenings. One evening, the lads were in the pool, when Samantha decided to have a swim. Aware that photographers were watching her, she swam over and splashed the lads who were sitting on the edge of the pool, creating a good photo opportunity for the waiting press. Unfortunately, it backfired and the lads took it as a gesture that she wanted to play, and jumped into the pool, bombing her from all angles; she now looked like a drowned rat rather than a sexy celebrity and was not amused, neither was her mother. There was a bit of a scene and Terry was called to keep his unruly jousters under control, but the lads stood their ground, stating she started it and as far as they were concerned, she was just another girl and would have done the same to anyone who deliberately splashed them. They didn't think she deserved any special treatment, as like her, they were here working doing the same job. After that, she was fine and spoke regularly to the lads. I think it came as a breath of fresh air that they treated her as a normal young person, instead of a sex goddess.

Finally, the afternoon before our performance, a bulldozer with a crew of workers arrived, and created our arena. It was finished literally an hour before the start of our show; talk about cutting it fine. Before the show got underway, there was a procession of all the celebrities around the arena, before they took their seats, and it was my job to introduce and give a short biography for each one of them. This meant I had to interview them all, to get the information they wanted me to read out about themselves. Some had brought a biography typed out, but they tended to be a bit too detailed. It was during this process that I really got to know them, and they realised that I held their reputation in my hands. After we had performed our show on the beach and I had introduced them all, they realised we were professional performers and became very friendly and chatty. When we returned home, there was a lot of "nudge-nudge, wink-wink" about us working with Sam Fox. I think most people thought that she ran around exposing herself at the drop of a hat, and was a nymphomaniac. In fact, she was just the opposite and seemed totally disinterested with male company. This attitude became abundantly clear some years later when she came out declaring she that she was in a long-term lesbian relationship.

After the big beach show on the Sunday, we had only some sword fights and an archery display to do on the Monday. It was a small, thirty-minute display and was no stress at all. We now had two and a half days to relax and enjoy ourselves. The only problem now was that we were spending a lot more of our own money. Everyone was stressing about how much their room drinks bill was going to be. Then someone had this great idea! Let's try and forge Terry's bow and arrow signature. With great trepidation, we ordered a round of drinks, gave Terry's room number and signed the chit with a little bow and arrow. It worked a treat, and we were all able to live like the VIPS we were supposed to be. Poor Terry got a hell of a shock when he checked out, and a hell of a bollocking from the manager for being so lavish with his entertaining allowance. He strenuously denied spending over £800 pounds on drinks, but the manager pointed out all the chits were signed with a bow and arrow. "Robin Hood's personal signature." The last couple of days were all sun, sea and hangovers; except for Pete, who never returned from the Army base. By the second day, we were getting quite worried about him, but thankfully, he returned the night before we checked out. Typical Pete - he had stopped back to get his baked bean fix, and was going to join us later when the army lads came to the hotel for a drink. He then decided to join the base farrier on a shoeing trip up into the Troodos Mountains. Unfortunately, the farrier never said, and Pete never asked, how long the trip was going to take going to take. I think he had the best idea - he got to see rural Cyprus, snow on top of the mountains, and miss out on some serious hangovers.

On our flight home, not one of us could face an alcoholic drink, and as if to reinforce the rule that for every high a low will follow, it had snowed when we arrived back in the UK. To make matters worse, the heaters were not working on the jousting coach and we had no warm clothes. A sad end to the best jousting season we had ever had!

1986 -87

1986 was another busy year, with just as many shows as 1985, but without any foreign trips or filming. We were still attracting huge audiences and for some reason I recorded all the attendance figures for that season, which you can see on the 1986 dates list, in the Appendix at the end of the book. It was a long scorching summer with constant traveling; I think I should have recorded the mileage we did rather than the attendance figures. There was no carrot of a film or foreign trip to spur the lads on, just a long hard grind. We did however have a few amusing moments and some not so amusing during the season.

1985 had worn me out and setting up 38 shows for the coming season, meant I didn't get a break at all, and so for the first time in my jousting career, I had no enthusiasm for the coming season. Dad had turned 60 in February, and more and more of the Riding School business, was falling on Lou and me. However, my youngest brother, Stu, was keen to get involved with running the jousting side of the business, so I decided to let him take charge of the first show of the season. The show was at a hotel right at the side of the A1M, at Washington Services near to Newcastle on Tyne. I was like a new mother about to send her child off to school for the first time, fretting over every minute detail and driving everyone mad! I had made Brian second in command, with twenty-three years' experience, and all lads were battle hardened veterans of several years. What could possibly go wrong.

What went wrong, was that the horses escaped out of the arena and galloped down the Western Highway into Washington. Stuart got a lift on the back of a motor cycle and chased after them. He finally found them grazing on a traffic roundabout. Thankfully, there were no injuries or repercussions. I think the lads realised that being in charge, was not as glamorous as it had appeared.

Not long after the Washington incident, we had another disaster at Filey, a lovely little seaside town just north of Hull. The show was held in the Town Park, which was an excellent and pretty venue. The show was well organised, and everything we asked for in the contract had been provided. An official was waiting at the entrance to direct us to our special parking space, surrounded the lovely shady trees. The bus arrived first and as it drove into our parking space, promptly sank up to its axles on what appeared to be solid hard ground; luckily, we managed to stop the horsebox before it too sank. I thought we were going to be in trouble for wrecking, what was undoubtedly, a very beautiful part of the park. I was just about to apologise, when the Council official beat me to it. We found out later, we were parked on what had, until recently, been an ornamental lake that had been filled in the previous year for Health and Safety reasons. Although beautifully turfed, the ground underneath was not compacted and it was still a natural collecting point for drainage water. The Council were most apologetic, and arranged for a tow truck to pull us out after the show. Crisis over!

It was a lovely sunny day and the crowds were huge. We set up wearing just shorts, as it was so hot and the last job was for me to do, was a sound check, which was just fine. I was commentating that day, because Brian was away visiting the new love of his life; he had met her whilst doing the fateful show in Washington. As I left the arena, a huge police mobile command centre arrived, and parked about 50 yards from our arena, and put up a 30-metre telescopic aerial. I gave it no thought except it looked a bit over-the-top for the size of the show. The crowd was large and I was looking forward to a great show; I tapped the microphone just before stepping out into the arena to make sure it was working properly; it was dead! I hurriedly checked the plugs, connections and battery. Everything seemed to be in perfect, order but still no sound. The crowd were waiting and so were the lads. I had no option but to start the show and commentate without a microphone. Brian has a strong booming voice that carries extremely well but sadly I am not blessed with such a voice. Not everyone in the audience could hear what I was saying, but with a lot of help from the knights, we could communicate what was happening to most of the audience.

After the show, whilst the lads were packing up, Alan Lane helped me try to find the PA fault. I powered up the system and to our utter surprise, everything was working perfectly. We were bemused; what had caused the fault? We had not touched anything. The only thing we could see that was different was that the Police transmitter had gone; could that have had something to do with blocking our radio mic system? It was not until 4 years later at the first Robin Hood pageant, that I found out that my suspicions were well founded, but more about that later.

It was in 1986 that we first started to visit the American Early Warning Base at Menwith Hill, high up on the Yorkshire Moors to help them celebrate the 4th of July. We made many visits up there over the next decade. Security was very tight and I had to submit all the lads' names and addresses for prior, security screening. It was a real ball- ache to get into the base, being stopped at several layers of security, being checked and double checked. For several years, we also had to run the gauntlet of the women's peace camp which was a squalid affair, muddy with loads of multi coloured bits of chiffon tied to the trees and onto the outer fence. The hecklers looked very grubby, but we couldn't help having some sympathy with their cause, as I think most sane people would like to see a world at peace. Sadly, we are never short of a few mad people wanting to start a war.

The Americans were great hosts, and really appreciated us coming up to help them celebrate their Independence Day. We got to eat real American hamburgers and drink real American beer, not the insipid rubbish that is sold over here in the UK purporting to be genuine American food and drink. On our first trip to the base, we stayed over at a pub in a village close by, as we were performing at Alnwick castle that weekend in Northumberland. We could not get the horsebox or coach into the small car park, so parked on the road, just up the road from the pub. It was quite an up-market village and Dad got a phone call back at Bunny, just as he was going to bed. It was from a very angry, well-spoken man, demanding to know when he was going to move his horsebox, as it had been parked outside his house for several hours, and was spoiling his view. It was still pre-mobile phone era, so Dad had no way of contacting us. He told the man very bluntly, that it was legally parked on a public highway, and as it was dark now, it could not be spoiling his view, and it would no-doubt be gone first thing in the morning, so he should go to bed, like Dad was trying to do. The down side to having your name and telephone number on your cab door!

We drove onto Alnwick the next morning, in a leisurely manner as we were already halfway there, arriving mid-afternoon. The Alnwick show was very special to us as we had done it in 1981 and had a fun time, but had not been able to give our best show as we had a stand-in commentator. They asked us to quote again in 1984, but Tony had set up a rival Jousting group and undercut our price, so to get it back meant a lot to us.

When we arrived all the organisers, were rolling drunk! The reason for this was it was the last two days of the week-long Alnwick Fair. I discovered later that it was traditional for the town inhabitants to party all week. It was also normal for husbands and wives never to see each other, for the whole week, or to enquire where they had been to, or what they had been up to! In this jovial mayhem, it took some time to find the person I had been dealing with. We had already stabled the horses, as Lou had sorted that out from our end. We had been asked to bring sleeping bags, as all the hotels were already full when they booked us, but they had been found somewhere for us to sleep. The accommodation they had sorted out, was below even our flexible standards; we were to sleep on the floor of a small restaurant, in the centre of the town. Most of the lads decided to sleep on the coach; it happened to be parked outside in a small square, but unfortunately there was not enough room for us all to sleep there, so the rest of us were stuck with the restaurant floor. I can't remember how, but somehow, we managed to get the use of a shower in someone's hotel room. Despite our sub-standard accommodation, which I quite rightly got the blame for; we had a great night out. The whole town was in full party mood. We ended up in a cellar bar that was a private club, and had an extra late licence. I don't know how we manged to get in, but it was a great bar! We were having a wonderful time with the locals who all wanted to buy us drinks. The younger lads were not allowed into the Club so had gone back to sleep on the coach. Suddenly, there was some pushing and shoving, and I thought someone was starting a fight, but it was someone trying to get through the crammed bar to tell us that our bus was being attacked! We ran out, backed up by most of the bar, and soon routed the attackers, who were hurling anything they could find at the coach and our besieged younger lads. The locals captured a couple of the attackers, and demanded to know why they were attacking our coach. It turned out that they came from an estate on the edge of town, renowned for thieving and fighting. They were all fanatical Newcastle United Football Club fans and saw Nottingham on the side of our coach. Nottingham Forest were their arch rivals at that time, so anybody or anything from Nottingham needed to receive severe damage. We just couldn't understand their warped mentality. Oddly it happened to us again later in London. We had just finished a show in inner London and were stuck in a queue at some traffic lights, when the coach was attacked by a gang of Crystal Palace supporters, who threw anything and everything at our coach including their own bodies. Thankfully the lights quickly changed, and we could escape.

Thankfully, no serious damage was done to the coach or the lads on board, during the Alnwick incident. It was a sad end to a splendid night, which had included attending a reception at Alnwick Castle held by the local Round Table, and being presented personally to the Duke and Duchess of Northumberland. The show was an enormous success but it was a long and weary trip home. We didn't arrive back to Bunny until the early hours of the morning.

The highlight of the year came in the middle of August, when we had two of the biggest shows we have ever done, within a few miles of each other, on consecutive days. The first was two days at the Bristol Balloon Festival followed by Gatcome International Horse Trials. We did a very early show for Breakfast Television on the Friday morning, and our full show on the Saturday when the attendance was 25,000 people. We then moved on to Gatcome Park, which was less than an hour away, nestled on the edge of the Cotswolds and overlooking Cheltenham where a crowd of 80,000 awaited us.

We drove down to Bristol through the night, to arrive at the Festival site for 6 am. This was because we had to perform live for the TV Show, "Breakfast." It was a very big and tightly-run affair, with Sir Richard Branson in the Virgin Balloon being one of the many celebrities attending. Security passes were issued together with Sky blue bomber jackets with, "Entertainer", printed in large letters across the back. We were also being put up, in a very nice hotel. The only problem was that the horses were stabled out of town, so the logistics were very complicated and boring due to the heavy traffic. The show was good and tight, but it lacked atmosphere because there were so many other things happening all around. We were learning that big, is not always the best. The second night, we stayed in a different hotel, which I paid for. It was even nicer than the first, and had its own large, indoor swimming pool. The lads hadn't been out on the Friday night, as there was a reception at the hotel for all the participants of the Balloon Festival, so they were more than ready to sample the delights of Bristol's night life. Worried about our huge day at Gatcome the next day, I made a stupid speech to them before they went out. I reminded them that it was a huge day tomorrow and that we would probably be performing in front of Royalty. "So please don't get hammered, and make sure you all get back to the hotel early". They didn't let me down! Why, oh why did I say those stupid words? They arrived back at the hotel early alright, but at 7 am and still drunk. I was having a swim when they arrived back; I had thought they were all safely tucked up in bed, but no. Worst was to come, as they all decided to join me for a swim. They just stripped off to their underpants and dived in. A man I had spoken to in the bar the previous evening passed through the pool area, and commented that I was a hard task master, making my lads have a fitness swim, at this time, on a Sunday Morning. When I went to pay the bill, the manageress looked very worried. She asked if something was wrong with their rooms, as the maids had just reported that only two out of the sixteen beds had been slept in. She also commented that she had never seen the pool so busy so early on a Sunday Morning.

When we arrived at Gatcome Park, we hit our first problem. Although we had passes for the lorry and the coach, they hadn't sent us any individual passes, so Security would not let the coach in. Eventually I managed to persuade them to radio down the secretary's office, who gave them permission to let us in. Once in, I then went off to get the passes sorted out and arrange the show times. Again, I was stopped by security. This time it was "catch 22". I couldn't get to the secretary's office to get our passes, because I needed a pass to get into that area! After much name dropping, I finally got our passes but had lost a very valuable hour. I met with a man of military appearance in a bowler hat to confirm the times of our shows. His first statement was you are 45 minutes late. I tried to apologise and explain, but he just carried on talking as if nothing was coming out of my mouth. He told me very forcefully that the arena had to be run to the second, and that our 45-minute show had to include setting up and having the arena completely cleared. I tried to explain that our show was 45 minutes long and that we needed extra time to set up and derig, but to no avail. We had been allotted 45 minutes and that was our lot; the quality of the show was just not on his radar at all.

I fought my way back through the crowds and stifling heat to the coach, and broke the bad news. The lads were marvellous despite having no sleep and serious hangovers. Everyone to a man said they were up for it; no-way were they going to cock up at one of the biggest equestrian events of the year. Brian was at his best, and promised us he would speed up the show so we would have 5 minutes to clear the arena. He pointed out that this was quite achievable, as we also had an Army arena party at our disposal. We rattled through the show at double time. As Brian left the arena after double checking that everything was perfect, he marched up to the bowler hatted Chief Steward, saluted and said, "Arena completely cleared 30 seconds ahead of schedule, SIR!" The Steward had the good grace to reply, "that was bloody marvellous; you lads really do know what you are up to. Well done!" He was much nicer for the second show, and members of the Royal Family were watching! We did however, have one minor mishap halfway through the second show, when one of our men at arms collapsed unconscious in front of the Black Knight's Tent. The lads quickly dragged him into the tent and discreetly fetched a paramedic to the tent, he was diagnosed to be suffering from dehydration due to the extreme heat. We didn't like to mention he had been drinking all night and had no sleep. As we drove out of the car park, only the drivers were awake; everyone else was sound asleep. It was slow going driving home, and we were still in the Cotswolds when I started to feel drowsy at the wheel. I suddenly came awake with a jolt as I thought I was hallucinating. The sun was setting and I was surrounded by balloons silently falling from the sky. They were landing all over in the surrounding fields. It was quite mystical but real. It was the end of the Bristol Balloon race. What a surreal end to one hell of a weekend!

1986 was the pinnacle of our UK touring. At Belvoir Castle, we did seven major show days with daily attendances all over 4,000 per day and with some hovering around the 5,000 mark. Many other shows were major UK events of the highest calibre. I don't know why I asked for all the attendance numbers for that year, but I did and it added up to a whopping 718,000 people. I'm not saying that they all came to watch us, but it gives an understanding of the world we were now moving in. However, we never got big headed about it and still performed at a lot of small private shows with attendances of less than 200 people. After 1986, I felt we were treading water on the UK touring front. But unknown to me, there were still several unexpected, exciting projects ahead that would keep me enthralled for many more years.

The first of these happened in early 1987. Belvoir Estate office phoned to say they had received a call from NATO Headquarters in Brussels, from a man who wanted to contact The Belvoir Castle Jousters. Apparently, he shared a desk with someone whose family lived in Woolsthorpe, the village which is just below the Castle and that was how he came to know about us. I phoned him back and fortunately he spoke good English. The enquiry was on behalf of his cousin, who had a castle in Flanders, and was interested in having a jousting tournament. I thought it was a crazy idea and totally undoable. I had no idea where this Castle was and knew nothing about Belgium, the people or the language. When I made that call to NATO, it was more out of politeness, than a desire a to do a show in Belgium. Little did anyone realise that this was just the start of an incredible 20 years of International tours, together with Film and TV work. To detail these events year by year, would be too drawn out, so I intend to deal with tours to different countries as individual chapters shortly, but first 1987.

1987 was another incredibly busy year of touring in the UK, performing the same number of shows in the UK as the previous year. However, we didn't have the high profile shows of the previous year. The biggest event was the closing ceremony for the Junior European games held at Alexandria Palace, Birmingham, but probably the most important work we did, was a day's filming on the film "Willow". For those that haven't seen the film, it is a fantasy film, like Lord of the Rings. It was on that day that we renewed our contacts with the stunt men, who we had worked with during the early seventies. We spent the day filming a huge battle scene and our expertise didn't go unnoticed.

We also did another morning TV show and provided a dramatic end to one of the "Treasure Hunt" programmes with Anneka Rice. Anneka arrived by helicopter in the middle of a jousting show at Belvoir Castle, to claim a favour from one of our knights. Both shows were Jimmy Durrand's work and had massive audiences, and so enhanced our UK profile enormously.

I also received our only ever complaint about the show. The complaint came from a consultant paediatrician at Nottingham Hospital, and concerned a show that he had seen at Belvoir

Castle. It was about the Black Knight's violent treatment to his squire, "Filth". Filth was virtually the same character as Baldric in Rowan Atkinson's Blackadder series. The only difference being was that we had Filth long before the Blackadder series was created. The paediatrician complained about the rough treatment metered out by the Black Knight to his squire, and that we were encouraging violence towards children. As both films and TV programmes in medieval period dramas, showed violence towards children, I could not understand the consultant's point of view. We decided to take his letter as the ultimate compliment in that he thought what he witnessed could be construed as real, and not acting. We always had a waiting list for squires to play the part of Filth, as it was the first acting part on the way up to playing a knight.

Belgium

Although Lou and I decided that Belgium was beyond our capabilities, we decided it would be interesting and only polite to meet with the man who wanted to hire us. This may seem a rather expensive whim, but we had discovered that the Castle was very close to the town of Leuven, and we had stopped overnight there a couple of times when driving to Germany to visit Lou's brother Nick, who lived and worked over there as a Golf pro. It just so happened that we were taking our family on our annual skiing holiday and visit Uncle Nick in just a few weeks' time, so we arranged to meet at the Leuven services on the E40 motorway. The E40 is the main route to Germany and is roughly halfway to Fulda where Nick lives, so it was not really an inconvenience to stop and take a break at this point in the journey. Our biggest worry was that we had our children Mark and Emma with us who were aged 8 and 7years. I felt very awkward about turning up for my first International meeting with my two young children, who were always arguing, and often fighting like cat and dog. Between Calais and Leuven, we must have threatened them a thousand times with the terrible punishments that would be metered out to them if they were naughty at this very important meeting. The plan was that after initial introductions, Lou would take the kids off to eat in the services, whilst I had the meeting with the Belgians.

Frank Claes was my NATO contact and Ashcile Claes was the man who wanted to hold the jousting. Frank spoke good English, but Ashcile spoke very little, so for much of the time he spoke to me through Frank. We made our introductions and I apologised for turning up for a meeting with my whole family, but explained that we were on our way to a skiing holiday, and that they would wait at the services while I had my meeting with them. To my surprise Ashcile said he was delighted that I had brought my family to the meeting. It turned out that he had two children of similar ages; only his daughter was the eldest, they were called Bart and Inga, and his wife was called Miriam. Ashcile insisted that Lou and the children join us for lunch at a restaurant he had already reserved, and then also visit the Castle. Before I could think of a way to politely decline, the kids start jumping up and down with excitement and thanking Ashcile. So, a business lunch with the family it was.

Our first culture shock was that there was horse meat on the menu, but thankfully Frank, who was translating tactfully whispered that bit in my ear. It was very different from England in that all the meat was displayed raw, and you chose the piece that you wanted and then a chef cooked it in full view of the restaurant customers. Over lunch I explained all the costs involved in getting us to Belgium along with accommodation, stabling and meals for fifteen people and that for a two day show we would have to be in Belgium for five days. After lunch, Ashcile took us to view the Castle and the proposed show site. Belgium was in the grip of arctic weather at that time, and was blanketed in about two feet of snow, with temperatures well below freezing. Frank had had to go back to his duties at NATO HQ, so communication became more fraught but the most difficult thing was keeping up with Ashcile as he sped down narrow high banked country lanes in his Porsche Carrera. A fully laden diesel Vauxhall Cavalier was not my first choice of car to try and keep up with a Porsche, driven by a wanna-be racing driver. There were several occasions when I completely lost sight of the Porsche and I had visons of driving around un-signposted Belgium lanes for hours trying to find the E40 so we could continue our journey to Germany. Thankfully, just when I thought we were lost, his car would appear parked in a pull-in waiting for us. The Castle was called Horst, after the hamlet close by, and sat in the middle of a lake which was frozen and snow-covered, so it looked like a flat field. We accessed the Castle over a small bridge into a snow-covered courtyard; it reminded me of the set for a Dracula horror film. Inside was even worse; bitterly cold, damp and with plaster falling off walls that didn't seem to have been painted since the 16th century. The Castle was, in fact, very small and our tour lasted no more than about 10 minutes, after which I was shown a snow-covered field near to the Castle, which was to be the show site, and some derelict cowsheds that were our proposed stabling, but totally unsuitable for horses! My main concern was access for our lorry, coach and the cars of the spectators. The roads were single-track in many places and the high banks either side made it impossible for large vehicles to turn into the gateways, and I just couldn't see thousands of cars all getting down such a narrow road. We concluded our meeting and Ashcile escorted us back to the E40 at racing speed. As we drove away from the Castle, I said to Lou "well that was a lovely meal and journey break, but a total waste of time as far as a jousting show is concerned. The man's mad if he thinks he can stage a jousting show here. He will never manage to cover costs - let alone make a profit", and we continued our long drive to Germany, and then onto Austria for our skiing holiday.

How wrong could I have been! Not long after I returned from holiday, Frank phoned me to say that Ashcile wanted to go ahead with a two-day show, and asked if I could provide detailed costings so that we could move forward to a formal contract. I was astounded and very worried. The costs involved were enormous, far beyond anything we had ever done before. If things went wrong and the show was a failure, it could bankrupt the whole family business. Not only that, both my parents and Lou and I could even lose our homes as they were held as guarantees by the Bank for our company overdraft. Lou and I agonised over the dilemma for many a day and night. Had my desire for success taken us back to the days of Gwrych Castle? We had been totally out of our depth then and we were still paying off the cost of that adventure. Finally, we put together a strategy that would minimise our risk exposure. We would ask for all the travel fees to be paid upfront three months before departure, together with all the vets and customs fees (*this was of course before all customs and travel restrictions were abolished in the EU.*) Also, we would ask for a 20% deposit on the signing of a contract, which was twice that of our normal contract. This would go some way to covering all the pre-show, travelling and fuel costs. As I was not convinced that the show would succeed, I was happy to make it a "Take It or Leave It" offer. I was convinced that the enormous amount of money required up front, would make the show a non-starter. Again, how wrong could I have been! All our terms were accepted and Ashcile asked for the contracts to be sent over for signing. I think it was at that moment I realised we had a top-class product, and we didn't need to do deals to secure shows in future. That contract became our standard terms for all future

International shows. Before I sent the contract, I had a meeting with the whole crew and told them my concerns and explained that if the show went bust, I would not be able to pay them. They all agreed that as all food and hotel accommodation was provided, they would treat it as a cheap holiday if things went tits up.

We took the overnight ferry from Calais to Ostend; the trip was uneventful but I was not impressed by Ostend, which was a typical drab, dirty, port town and driving the lorry on the other side of road was not easy. However, when we got onto the Belgium motorways, they were far better than those in England and we were soon eating up the miles. We arrived at the Castle just before 10 am, tired and hungry, but it was a beautiful day and the Castle looked very different from my last visit. The trees were green, the lake sparkled, the courtyard was sunny and welcoming.

We had arrived ahead of schedule, and although we received a warm welcome, it was noticeable that there was some panic as we had spoiled their planned reception. The horses were stabled with a family close to the Castle. The stables were great, and so were the family. Even as we were unloading the horses, the family were pressing bottles of beer into our hands. We became great friends and still see their daughter, Pasquale, to this day. Sadly, her mother and father passed away a few years ago. I still have two, beautiful liqueur glasses her father gave to me and I treasure them very much. We also shared a love of blues music; he gave me some rare tapes of old blues artists and told me about a small blues bar in Leuven, called the Blue Cat, which became my sanctuary during subsequent tours to Belgium.

When we arrived back at the Castle, after seeing to the horses, I was greeted by the rest of the Troupe, who were seated around a long table. They were all grinning and smiling, everyone had a beer in their hand and a massive amount of food was being brought out of a small door in the castle wall for us. I can honestly say I have never seen the Troupe so happy! Much later, we went to our hotel in Leuven. I have no idea how we got there *(hopefully we didn't drive but possibly we did)*. The hotel was called the Binnenhof, and was located close to the centre of this stunningly, beautiful town. It really must be seen to be believed. Although only 100 yards from one of the main squares, our view from our bedroom windows was somewhat bizarre. Directly opposite was the prison, which had a castle-like entrance and guards outside, whilst next door was a brothel. The brothel intrigued the lads as they had never seen one before and didn't realise they still existed. One day, I was in my room when I was disturbed by a commotion in the street below. When I looked out of my window, Harvey Broadhead and Martin Brown were being chased down the street by some of the prostitutes. Harvey and Martin were only about sixteen at the time and were always up to mischief. I discovered later they had gone into the brothel to enquire about prices and services. The Madam was very uncomfortable about them even being there, as there were strict age limits for using a brothel, but after extracting the price of services from her, they then had the cheek to ask if she would do a bulk discount if they got some of their mates to come along as well. That was the final straw for the Madame, who proceeded to throw them out and chase them down the street, much to the amusement of the Prison guards.

We did seven tours of Belgium, often performing six shows in three days. They were all huge and nearly every one of them was a sell-out. They were on a grand scale that we had never encountered before. The sound systems and lighting were of a quality that you would expect at a major pop concert. The entrance into the arenas was always a castle façade with a proper back stage. We had an Artistic director, sound engineer and a costume and makeup area. We even had our own beer pump back stage! We performed four shows at Horst Castle, two in Leuven, one in Knokke- Heist and one in the centre of Bruges. The two shows in Leuven were staged in the town's biggest Square known as the Ladeuzeplien (library square), which had the stunning back drop of the very ornate Gothic Library, that dated back to the Middle Ages. The special effects got grander each tour. On our last two tours the night shows were lit by huge gas flames from a specially laid, six-inch steel gas main, that ran around the perimeter of the whole arena.

I could write a whole book about things that happened in Belgium so here are just a few highlights.

Public toilets in Belgium are different to those at home, in that ladies must walk through the Gents to get to their toilets, and that means walking past the men using the urinals. On our first visit, I was taking a pee, when Ashcile's wife, Miriam, tapped me on the shoulder whilst I was peeing, and said *"Ah there you are Sam, I've been looking for you everywhere, Ashcile wants me to clarify the following points with you"* and proceeded to hold a business meeting with me as I continued to relieve myself. I suppose you could call that multi-tasking.

The weather was extremely hot on our first visit, and I asked if we could have some drink put in the jousting tents, as we quickly get dehydrated in our armour. When we opened the tent doors at the start of the show, we found to our astonishment, that the whole floor was covered with glasses of beer. There must have been 80 in each tent. The Belgian's love their beer, and when I proposed two 45 minute shows with a ten-minute break between act one and two, I was told that we must have more breaks in the show, as the audience could not possibly sit for 45 minutes without a beer break. On one occasion in Bruges, we were on a pre-show visit and I left the rest of the group in a pub, whilst I went to look at some potential stabling. On my return about an hour later, I found them so drunk they could hardly speak or stand. After I had left they had ordered a round of Stella Artois, but the attractive bar maid had enquired as to why the British always drank girl's beer. They of course rose to the challenge, and she duly sold them several rounds of strong, Belgium beer with 8.5 % alcohol!

One of the most marvellous things about Belgium, was that you could eat and drink twenty-four hours a day. This was unheard of in the UK as, at that period in time, everything finished at 2 am prompt. We discovered bars and restaurants that didn't open until three or four in the morning. This was marvellous when doing night shows, as we would not be finished until well after midnight. The lads often came in at about 9.30 in the morning, had breakfast, and then went to bed for a few hours before the afternoon show. I remember once, in Knokke-Heist, when I had gone to bed in the early hours well inebriated but having to be up early for a press conference the following morning. I suddenly woke up to the sound of music and much jovial chatter. It was broad daylight and the bar outside the hotel was packed with people eating and drinking. My heart missed a beat in panic; had I over slept and missed the press conference?! It was only when I looked at my watch, that I discovered it was only 6 am, and the party was still in full swing.

It was on this same trip that I had I lucky escape from serious injury. I was jousting and we were doing a stunt using a breaking lance. For some reason the lance, didn't break as easily as usual, and the impact knocked my shield back, exposing my unprotected body. The remainder of the lance then followed though and stuck me in the neck. Luckily my neck was bound with a thick scarf and it was only a glancing blow, but it was still enough to unhorse me and knock me out. Thankfully I was not unconscious for very long, and was able to remount to finish the show. As I left the arena, the enormity of what had happened hit me; I collapsed from my horse shaking and sobbing uncontrollably. I could not understand what was wrong; the lads fed me beer but that didn't work, so they wrapped me up in a horse rug because, although I was dripping in sweat, I was freezing cold. Most of the troupe thought I had just lost the plot, but someone thought it might be shock; any way they decided to take me back to the hotel and put me to bed. I slept solidly for six hours, woke up feeling fine and joined everyone for the evening meal. Everyone looked very nervous as I think most still thought I had had a nervous breakdown, and it was not until someone gave me a large glass of brandy, which I downed in two large glugs, did everyone relax. I'm sure we broke every medical rule regarding severe shock, but hay-hoe - I'm still here!

The Castle at Horst became a very special place for all of us, and we had some magical summer evenings with Kick and Rush playing in the courtyard, and everyone just sitting around drinking and singing along. It was on our second trip that I took my son, Mark, who was about the same age as Ashcile's son, Bart. Ashcile had invited Mark and I to stay with him in his house, as Mark was too young to stay with the troupe. One evening in the courtyard, I suddenly noticed that Mark was not with Bart. Both were about 10 years old, and had been inseparable all weekend. Alarm bells started to ring in my head and I dashed over to ask Bart where Mark was. As with most kids of that age, he couldn't remember when they had parted company. Within a few moments, we had the whole jousting troupe searching for him, and after fifteen minutes we still had not found him. I was really starting to panic, cursing myself for allowing him to come on this trip when he was so young. The most terrifying thought concerned the huge lake that surrounded the Castle and I was starting to feel physically sick. Thankfully, at that moment Bart's older sister, Inga, came running up to say they had found him. The relief was immense; he was curled up fast asleep on top of one of the refrigerators in the Castle kitchen which was in the basement of the Castle; how he had managed to climb up there we had no idea. Bart's mother, Miriam, who was working in the kitchen agreed to keep an eye on him, so we left him sleeping soundly, curled up on top of the fridge. Even to this day, Mark can happily sleep anywhere especially when he has been drinking, which was exactly what he and Bart had been doing that day. I later found out that they had pinched some bottles of beer that were stored in the Castle kitchen.

There was always huge publicity for the shows in Belgium; there were pictures and features in every newspaper, and we were often on National Belgian TV. People were so friendly, they invited us into their homes for meals, and took us out to bars and clubs. It was not unusual for lads to end up miles away from our hotel, having no idea how to get back to base. On one occasion Paul Cooling, aka Wicksey, had no idea where he was, but managed to hail a taxi. He couldn't remember the name of the hotel so told the driver to take him to the prison, and then promptly fell asleep. When the driver woke him to say they were at the prison, he couldn't recognise where he was in fact, he was not in the City at all. Unbeknown to Wicksey, there were two prisons in Leuven, one in the City centre and the other seven miles out of town, and it was to the one seven miles out of town that he had been taken. It proved to be a very expensive taxi ride!

One morning, a group of us were sitting outside a bar near our hotel having a medicinal breakfast beer, when Wicksey and Gilbert Harvey arrived, clinging onto to back of a dustbin lorry. The Hotel Manager also witnessed their arrival and was not amused at his guests arriving on the back of a bin wagon. Within a few hours, it seemed that everyone in Leuven knew about this unusual mode of transport, and they became cult heroes!

Mischief was what fuelled the Troupe, and one of the most audacious pranks ever was carried out in Belgium. Mark Lacey was renowned for charming the ladies and was given the dubious nickname of "Golden Bollocks" by the lads. On one trip, he had found a particularly pretty girl, who he promptly disappeared with; he only returned briefly to perform in the shows. He had become a bit of a recluse, so the Minstrels and a group of lads decided enough was enough. Incredibly they found out this girl's address, which was a first-floor apartment, that had a balcony. Somehow, they managed to acquire a long ladder and then climb up onto the balcony, along with the band's instruments, and sit on the balcony edge. This was all done at 6 am in the morning. When all was ready, they knocked on the bedroom window, and after some persistent knocking, Mark opened the curtains to be serenaded by the lads singing the Banana Song which starts *"One Banana, Two Banana, Three Banana, four."* The moral of this story is that there are no secrets within the Jousting Brotherhood.

When I took over the commentary from Brian, I decided to try and recite the opening speech in Flemish. It went down very well, and I got a standing ovation from the crowd before the end of my first sentence, but also some laughs when I fell afoul of the complex Flemish accent. When I called for a Flemish knight called Van Sasken to enter, there was great uproar. After the Show I asked Chris the show director what was so funny. He explained that I had mispronounced, the name Sasken and my version, meant "Scrotum"! After that, I decided to do a dual commentary with an English-speaking local, who then translated it into Flemish.

We were very lucky not to have any serious accidents during the shows we performed in Belgium, because we pushed the boundaries. Our night shows used smoke as an entrance curtain, fire, strobe lighting and pyrotechnics. We did, however, have a very serious accident on site during rehearsals. I was not on site when it happened, but some of the knights were practicing the entrance through the wall of smoke, as a couple of the horses were a bit nervous. They were waiting back stage on horseback whilst something in the arena was made safe. Suddenly, there was a great Whoosh! Smoke from a concealed smoke cannon, suddenly fired smoke underneath the bellies of the horses. Edward Kopel's horse, Declan, was a lightweight thoroughbred; he spun around so violently, that Edward was thrown off, causing a spiral fracture of his lower leg, even before he left the saddle. Hitting the deck, with an already broken leg, caused the bone to come out through the side of his leg. It was a very serious fracture and he had to stay in the hospital in Leuven for several weeks after we had gone home. Although he was stranded on his own in a foreign country, Ed said he had a regular stream of visitors, many of whom he had never met before. They came bearing gifts and sat talking to him, wishing him well, and thanking him for coming to their city to entertain them. They were such marvellous people.

The politics of Belgium are not dissimilar to those of Ireland, consisting of two communities that loathe each other. In Belgium's case, it is the French and the Flemish, but add in the fact that they have been ruled at some time by most of their neighbour's, plus Burgundy and Spain, then you have the recipe for long held, political grudges going back centuries. We worked for the Flemish, and all our shows had a theme of Flemish defiance against their unjust overlords. The Flemish are fanatical about their heraldry, and the costumes that we made for their shows, had to be made with exacting heraldic correctness. Although, I argued many times with Ashcile about the scripts he presented us with, he was always adamant we did it his way. We knew just how delicate a successful script was. Just changing the winner of a simple foot-fight and you could go from a standing ovation, to a muted round of applause! The only way to work with Ashcile was to let him have his own way for the first show, and then when the show went flat, rewrite the show for the next day. Our show in the Main Square of Bruges was the worst. Bruges is much closer to France than the rest of our venues, and so about 30% of the audience were French speaking. It was the most biased show we had ever been asked to perform; we pleaded with Chris, the Show Director. to make some changes, but he was adamant that Ashcile would not allow changes. The result was that halfway through the show, most of the French walked out, and the show was slated by the French speaking Press. Next morning, I had a very difficult meeting with Ashcile, and eventually, he agreed a complete rewrite of the script. By the end of that morning, I had rewritten the script and fine-tuned it with all the major characters. Thankfully, the show was a great success, but we did not play to a full house until the final day, when word had got around how good the show was, and counteracted the initial bad press.

Bruges was also the smallest arena we have ever performed in and we nearly refused to perform in it at all. When we arrived to do the show, our arena had shrunk massively from the agreed size. Unfortunately, Chris the Show Director had been seriously ill and was in a coma for several weeks just before the show so was due to open, and so things were changed without his knowledge. The arena was only 15m wide by 30m long, and surrounded by huge gas flames, that were 2m high, and moreover at one end, there was a huge, stone statue that the knights had to swerve to miss at the end of each jousting run. At the other end, the knights were galloping straight at the audience, and had to whip their lances up into the vertical position, to avoid spearing a member of the audience! I have no idea how the arena, or the show, was ever approved by Health and Safety. It was only my belief in the brilliant capabilities of our horses and the skill of their riders, that led me to reluctantly allow the show to take place. I was so relieved when the final show ended without any mishaps.

On the plus side, there were many professional riders who came to watch the shows, and they queued up after the shows to congratulate us on the fantastic feats of horsemanship they had just witnessed. This took place in June 2006. I had originally planned to retire from the jousting in 2005, after 35years at the helm, but decided to do another year, when Ashcile proposed Bruges.

A Year to Remember 1988

1988 should be described as a unique year because it had repercussions that changed the Jousting Association, and still affects it today in 2016, as I write this book. They were not dramatic, but this was the year the seeds were sown, and it was our last really, big year. Things were changing on many fronts, and it's easy to look back and say this, or that happened, because of this or that, but at the time, was much too busy to think of the implications of events. If things had not started to change, I don't think the jousting could have survived, and I think many friendships would have been broken. From 1983-88 we had been away for over forty days every season, and as our season was basically sixteen weeks long, we were therefore away two to three days every week. Add in rehearsals every week, you can understand why the lads were under pressure from both home and work. I think the fact that we managed to sustain it for five years was remarkable.

Early in 1988, Dad went on a tour with the Association of British Riding Schools to Portugal, to visit some of the classical riding schools near Lisbon. Whilst on this tour he met John Perestrello, who was a descendent of Christopher

Columbus! John's house had been the family home of Christopher Columbus's wife; I say "house" but it would be better described as a Chateau. In Portuguese, a house like this is called a Quinta. In fact, John's was called Quinta Do Hespanhol. It came with acres of vineyards, a wine press and a winery capable of storing thousands of gallons of wine. Unfortunately, for John, most of his family wealth had been confiscated by the Communist Government that came to power after the Revolution of 1974-75. John had been a merchant banker in London, his wife was English and all his children had been educated in England. The Quinta had simply been a summer holiday home, but in 1988, with all his foreign assets confiscated, he was living at the Quinta full time, trying to make it into a money-earner through tourism. The Quinta had been used briefly by the Duke of Wellington as his headquarters during the Peninsular Campaign, which lasted from 1807 until 1813, and John was already focusing on events about this period in the Quinta's history. He was keen to stage an event that would give the Quinta lots of publicity to put it firmly on the map as a tourist and a corporate event destination. John saw the jousting as just that event. John was Dad's contact and Dad was determined that he was going to set the show up for us himself. In fact, he was very excited about the whole project, so against my better judgement I told him to get on with it. I had already got another full season of big shows and two international tours on my plate and neither myself or the lads, were keen on doing a third tour. So, I left Dad to see if John was serious. I honestly thought it was just an excuse for Dad to go and have another "jolly" in Portugal.

By 1988 Belvoir Castle, Bosworth Battlefield, Lincoln and Spalding Flower Parade were regular bookings, together with some biannual shows. At Belvoir, we performed nine days that year so I didn't need many more shows to fill the season. Our first big one-off show was at Lyme Park near Stockport, and it was arranged for the weekend after the Spring Bank Holiday. We had performed for two days over the Bank Holiday at Belvoir and had picked up quite a few injuries. To make matters worse, Lyme Park was a six-knight show, something we rarely did in those days, so we were short of both horses and riders. To solve the problem, we pulled Dad out of retirement. Dad was 62 years old by then and had not ridden in a show for many years; he wasn't going to joust or do anything dangerous, just make up the numbers. He was so pleased to have a weekend away with us and be in the show again! Dad was always very vain and liked to think he was very trendy, even in his sixties. On this trip, he had brought some boxer shorts that were the latest rage for men's underwear, and he never shut up telling us he had some, even strutting around the changing room showing everyone. The problem was that they were cheap ones, bought from the market, and had an open fronted fly, as did the chainmail trousers we wore. At the beginning of the show, I brought the knights forward to salute the audience. I detected a titter of laughter from behind me, and as I scanned the line-up of knights, I saw the reason for the amusement; Dad was proudly displaying his private parts to the whole Grandstand! I started to get the giggles and had to turn away and take a couple of deep breaths to compose myself, before I could continue the commentary. For the second show, he solved the problem by wearing his boxers back-to-front!

Later that evening there was more fun at Dad's expense. Gilbert Harvey, one of our long serving knights, had a new trick that he claimed, made a person the centre of attention, and of course this was just up Dad's street. The trick involved Gilbert muttering mumbo jumbo and touching Dad's face.

Unbeknown to Dad, he had a burnt cork hidden in his hand, so that every time he touched his face, he left a black mark. By the end of the performance, Dad looked like a Red Indian who had over-done his war paint, and everyone in the bar was staring at him. It was taking all our acting skills to keep solemn straight faces, but the icing on the cake was when Dad turned to one of the lads and said, "you see, I still haven't lost the touch. Those two pretty girls at the bar can't take their eyes off me, and look, they are smiling at me now! I think I'm in there". That was our cue to burst out laughing; we told him to go to the toilets and look in the mirror. He was not amused.

The season continued at a hectic rate; we had some great and varied venues that kept us going. I returned home from playing to a record crowd at Lincoln Castle, to be given the terrible news that Jimmy Durrands had died suddenly earlier that day. I have said everything about Jimmy in his own chapter, but I reiterate, that day I lost one of my best friends. All the jousters loved him and we lost our greatest supporter. Jimmy sang our praises everywhere he went; without him things were never the same again. He was to us what Brian Epstein was to the Beatles.

At the beginning of August, we set out on our most ambitious project ever, and I'm confident it will never be beaten. It had taken months of planning and even today I can't believe we managed to do it without mobile phones or the internet. We were about to embark on an eight-day tour with six horses, eighteen men, in a coach and a horsebox. The coach and horsebox were both over twenty years old. The trip included eight shows, four ferry trips and travelling nearly one thousand miles. We had two days of shows in Guernsey and then 48 hours to get to Leuven, which is half an hour beyond Brussels.

Our planned itinerary looked fine on paper; exhausting for both humans and horses, but nevertheless achievable.

Our itinerary was to leave on Monday 8th August drive to Weymouth, and catch the ferry to Guernsey (after our previous problems, with bad weather we allowed an extra day for bad weather) arrive in Guernsey, and relax with a rest day before our two days of two shows per day, leave next morning, sailing this time to Portsmouth, drive to Dover, catch the ferry to Calais, drive to Leuven, perform two double shows at Horst Castle, and return next day to Bunny via Calais! Except for one blowout, our trip to Guernsey was uneventful, the shows were, an enormous success and the weather beautiful. The organisers threw a party for us to celebrate record crowd numbers. I recall meandering back to our B&B that night down high-banked lanes; it was a beautiful, still, warm night and the night air was filled with the scents of flowers growing on the banks. We had done two days of very successful shows and had a nice party full of rich compliments, I was very proud of the lads; I thought life doesn't get much better than this!

I was sharing a room with Andy Buttery, in a very high class B&B, as the hotel couldn't accommodate all of us; it was a lovely retreat from the hustle and bustle of the rest of the troupe. I vaguely recall Andy coming in much later and him getting up to use the bathroom, but other than that, I slept very soundly that night. It was an early start next day and when the alarm woke me, I was surprised to see Andy was not in his bed, as he was usual a very heavy sleeper. I quickly finished packing and went down to join him at breakfast. This is when things started to go wrong.

I cheerily greeted the owner with a "Good morning" but he replied, "Not for you I think" shocked, I asked why. He suggested I look out the window; I did and wave of nausea ran through my body. The palm tree outside the kitchen window was having its leaves ripped off by a howling gale. The owner smiled smugly and said, "think you will be staying with us for a bit longer ". As I was explaining to him that we had to be in Belgium the following day, his wife appeared with my breakfast, and enquired if I knew what time Andy would be coming down for his breakfast. I explained that he was already up and must have gone for an early walk. The owner was fantastic. He called the Harbour Master and explained our problem. The Harbour Master said he would talk to the ferry captain, study the weather reports and report back to us. I had just finished my breakfast when the landlady popped her head into the dining room to ask if Andy was back yet. I was getting a bit worried about Andy - he had come home, his bed had been slept in, he always overslept and I had never known him go for an early walk

A few minutes later there was a scream from upstairs and the owner rushed off to see what the problem was. The chamber maid had checked the empty room opposite our room to make sure it was all in good order for guests arriving later that day, and found a man fast asleep in the bed. We had found Andy! I vaguely remember Andy getting up during the night to go to the toilet. Somehow, he had gone through the wrong door, crossed the corridor, used the toilet in the other room and then got into the new bed. The poor chamber maid was really shaken and I offered to pay for re-cleaning of the room, but thankfully after a few minutes, everyone saw the funny side of the whole incident. Meanwhile, I was anxiously awaiting the call from the Harbour Master. We were still in the pre-mobile era, so I had to communicate with the lads via the pay phone at the B&B and the hotel reception. Fortunately, I had the room numbers of the key members who kept everyone updated as news came in. When it finally came, it was good and bad; the storm had delayed the ferry by over one hour, but the wind and sea were starting to ease out in the Channel. The ferry captain was hopeful that by the time he reached Guernsey in three hours' time, things might be calm enough to load the horses; we were to come to the docks ready to go. I had already made the decision to load the bus with all the lads and equipment, so at least they would be able to set up in Belgium, even if the horses were delayed. It wasn't until the ferry was entering the harbour that we finally got the green light to load the horses. It had been a nerve racking morning, we were behind schedule but, thank god, we were on that ferry as there was only one ferry per day.

I was now able to relax with a much-needed beer, and work out the consequences of our now three-hour delay. We landed in Portsmouth late afternoon/early evening; the docks were huge, nothing like peaceful Weymouth; it was all hustle and bustle. It took me ages to find the right customs office, and I had to wait nearly an hour before I could present my papers. We were now over four hours behind schedule, so reluctantly, I sent the coach off on its' own to Dover. After another hour and a half, I was called back to the desk and told my export stamp from Weymouth was missing; there was no proof of me bringing these horses from the UK, and as far as they were concerned, I was trying to smuggle six horses into the UK from Guernsey; my lorry and the horses were to be impounded. I tried desperately to explain that people could vouch for me in both Weymouth and Guernsey, but their response was to tell me this was a proper port, not a little, tin pot ferry port like Weymouth. We were directed to a high sided compound and told that if we moved the lorry again, both Brent and I would be arrested. I was sick, distraught and it was stiflingly hot; luckily, I had Brent with me who was Mr

Calm. He suggested we go through the paperwork again; there was a lot of it! Eventually, we came across a crease in one of the sheets. When we smoothed it out, there was a Weymouth stamp! I had to queue for ages again to get to the customs officer but finally got there, and presented the sheet with a stamp on it. Heart in mouth, I asked if this was what he was looking for. He just said yes, stamped the form, and told me I could leave. I was sure he knew which piece of paper the stamp should had been on, but gave us no help at all, which was typical of the unhelpful, arrogant bureaucracy that we constantly encountered during the seventies and eighties.

Brent and I finally left the docks half a day behind schedule tired, hot and despondent. The coach and the lads would now be on the ferry to Calais. Our horse travel documents required that we rest the horses at Dover Lairage (dock stables for animal quarantine) and have the horses re-vetted next morning before travelling onto Belgium. We stopped at several services to relay messages about our delay to Lou at Bunny; who then relayed it to the Lairage, vets and our B&B, about our delays and give them new expected arrival times. We arrived at Dover just before midnight: thankfully the Lairage was open 24 hrs, so it was a quick unload, feed the horses and off to our B&B a mile up the road. Our accommodation was regularly used by people using the Lairage, so we got clear directions and the owners were used to people coming and going at strange times. We arrived at about 1 am. There was a note on the front door telling us how to find our room, and that breakfast was from 6 am. Unfortunately, the vet was arriving at 5 am so no breakfast. We fell into our beds, exhausted and hungry. We had been on the go for twenty hours and not eaten for twelve hours. After three hours' sleep, that felt as if I had just closed my eyes and the alarm had gone off immediately, we wearily went off to meet the vet, followed by yet more long waits at customs. We finally caught the 11 am ferry and devoured our free lorry driver's breakfast in the ferry's lorry driver's lounge, followed by a doze to catch up on much needed sleep. When we landed, the customs formalities were thankfully quick and we were finally on our way to Leuven. It was now 2 pm local time and hopefully we would arrive in Leuven about five pm.

The trip went well except for grinding our way around the Brussels Ring Road. Not long after leaving Brussels we joyfully saw a sign for Leuven. Ironically, as it happened, I smiled at Brent and fatefully said, "just half an hour and we will be sipping a lovely cold Belgian beer". Five minutes later there was a huge bang and I swerved onto the hard shoulder braking as hard as I dared without tipping the horses over; our second blowout of the trip. We had packed two spare wheels at the start of the trip in case of such an eventuality. It was the passenger side rear wheel that had blown which would have been fine if we were in England, but of course we were now driving on the opposite side of the road, so we were exposed to the traffic as we tried to change the wheel. We were just a couple of feet from the carriageway. It was a terrifying experience, but finally we completed it without any harm to ourselves. I was certainly very glad of the red warning triangle that we had to carry for continental driving.

We finally arrived at the Castle just before 6 pm and were received like conquering heroes. We had been out of communication since Portsmouth, so the lads and Ashcile were all getting very worried that we were not coming at all. As was always the case in Belgium, food and beer appeared from nowhere and Brent and I started to feel human again. Somehow, the Belgians managed to get us two replacement tyres on a Sunday to replace our blown-out spare wheels.

Things were starting to look up! All we had to do now, was two afternoon shows and two night shows. A minor problem was we had never done a night show before and we had no time for rehearsal. The horses had come through all the traveling better than the troupe; they seemed to relish it all and were full of energy.

One of the things that the horses had to do in the night show, was to ride through a wall of thick smoke to enter the arena. To make matters worse, the lighting engineers had also placed a high-powered floodlight behind the smoke so that it glowed a bright white. We were very worried that the horses would not go through this wall of smoke, but our fears were unfounded as the horses galloped through without hesitation. The effect was very spectacular, as the smoke clung to our costumes and gave the knights a sort of ghostly appearance.

As I was leaving the backstage after our first afternoon show, I noticed some men bringing in a large square box filled with earth; they deposited it in the middle of the backstage area, just where we assembled to make our entrance into the arena. I asked them what it was doing there and they explained it was for the fireworks display after the show. It sounded great so I asked what time the display started as I didn't want to miss it. His reply dumbfounded me; it was just 30 secs after we left the arena!! I could not believe that nobody had consulted me about it. Even worse, they refused to change the timing! They had spent a fortune on this grand finale´ and it had to happen before people started to leave the grandstand. Our only option was to gallop across the field behind the back stage, and put as much distance as possible between us and the fireworks. It was an exhilarating but also terrifying ride; six of us galloping flat out across an unknown field in pitch black dark, just praying that there were no hidden rabbit holes or mole hills. When the first firework exploded, we stopped the horses and turned to watch the magnificent display. Amazingly the horses, were not bothered about the bangs and flashes at all! We all had a great bond with our horses and they trusted us completely. I cannot speak highly enough of those magnificent animals. We, on the other hand, were on such a high whooping and hollering! It had been like a cavalry charge and we had survived. Now all we had to do, was do it again the following night. We were playing to capacity crowds every show and the audience were so enthusiastic, lifting us to ever increasing highs. The extremely hot weather was also taking its toll. We used to call it "the second show blues". When you've pumped massive amounts of adrenalin to keep you going past the point of exhaustion during the first show, then the adrenalin drops, and you are completely exhausted, just when you are about to do a repeat performance! When you have been there, you can understand how pop groups doing world tours, resort to drugs to keep themselves going. We never used drugs but on that last night in Belgium we were all close to cracking. Battered, exhausted, and the adrenalin just wasn't working anymore. There was a bottle of duty free whisky being passed around back stage before we did our final performance. I, like a lot of others, took a good swig just before going on. The show was about to start, and first on was Brian, as knight marshal/commentator, but he was missing, so we started a frantic search. Almost immediately, one of the lads beckoned me to come over and whispered to me. "You're needed around the back". I found Brian hitting his forehead on a steel scaffolding tube; tears running down his face. I asked him what was the matter, and why was he hitting his head? He told me he simply didn't have the energy to go out and perform again. He was hoping that pain might start some adrenalin flowing so he could go out and face the audience. If the commentator felt like that without a battered body, how must the rest of the lads be feeling? I told him that we all felt like that and we were relying on him to get us started. I fetched the whisky bottle, we both took a swig, and then he took a deep breath and said, "Let's do it". I returned backstage, gave the lads the thumbs up as Brian walked out to a trumpet fanfare and started the show. Once the roar of the crowd hit us, our energy came back, and we did another cracking show.

The trip home was uneventful and I spent the rest of the week in an exhausted stupor, just doing the essentials. But there was no time for complacency, as we had a big show at Bosworth Battlefield, just five days later. The weekend after was the August Bank holiday, when we had a show in Cheshire on the Saturday, followed by two days at Belvoir Castle. This was normally the end of our busy season and time for a well-earned rest; but oh no! As soon as we finished the Belvoir show, we dashed back to Bunny, packed all our kit into the same packing case we used for Cyprus, dashed home for a shower and change of clothes before setting off for Heathrow at 2 am. to catch the early flight to Lisbon.

We spent a week in Portugal at the Quinta Hispanol, an hour and a half north of Lisbon just outside the town of Torres Vedras. It was a relaxing trip for the lads but very stressful for me. There is a chapter on our trips to Portugal which follows when all will be revealed. What I can say now is, we returned to England but our equipment didn't, and we had our final show at Belvoir Castle in exactly seven days. Thankfully, we had taken our chainmail as personal luggage and we also had some weapons, flags and the tilt that we hadn't taken to Portugal. What we didn't have were tents, a quintain, horse costumes, and various essential weapons. I spent two days phoning Portugal hoping to get the kit released, but then realised it wasn't going to happen, so I switched to digging out old bits of kit and tarting them up to use for the Belvoir show. The one thing we were short of were tents, but luckily my good friend Terry Goulden at Art and Archery had two medieval tents; all I had to do was to drive down to Ware in Hertfordshire to pick them up. The show went ahead at Belvoir although we had to omit some of the specialist fights due to lack of weapons, and replace them with sword fights; in fact, nearly every foot fight was a sword fight. The audience didn't seem to notice and neither did Belvoir; so, everyone was happy.

Next morning, I received a call from Heathrow - our kit had arrived. I was very keen to regain possession of our kit so I set of early the next day to collect it up. I arrived at Heathrow about 10am after battling through the rush hour traffic, but it took me another hour to locate the freight office that was holding our box. When I presented my paper work, I was informed that I had just missed the customs officer, and that I could not collect my box until he had examined it with me being present. The customs officer only visited twice a day and his next visit could be any time from that moment until 4 pm. This meant I had to sit outside the freight office until he turned up. Bored, hungry and thirsty, I waited outside the office until at ten to four he arrived. He asked me if this was my box, did I pack it and did its contents match what was listed on the Carnet. I replied in the affirmative, he stamped the Carnet and said that I could now take the box.

I had assumed a freight office would have had handling equipment to load heavy freight such as our box, but no! I asked for some help to load the box but was rudely informed that it was not their job. I finally managed to prise open the lid and then load it into the back of the truck bit by bit, whilst the man behind the desk kept reminding me, that I had better hurry up as they closed at 4.30 "sharp"! I managed to load everything with minutes to spare, just in time to start my homeward journey at the start of the London rush-hour. An exhausting stressful end to an exhausting stressful season!

Chapter 6   New Horizons 1989-2006

Portugal

Yes! Dad had actually, got us a job in Portugal! Hooray! We were like zombies by now, but we just kept going somehow. Three days jousting, then pack up all the kit that night, before going home to pick up passports and say goodbye to loved ones. We had only been home ten days in the last month! We just kept drinking and laughing, and boy did we laugh! It kept us going!

We catnapped during the night drive to Heathrow, but didn't get any real sleep. At Heathrow, it was manic. Unloading the kit box and getting all the customs papers signed and then onto our own check-in. We were taking all our chainmail and costumes as personal luggage, which along with a week's clothes, was way over the baggage allowance, so we were going to have to pay excess baggage, which by my calculations was about £400, a lot of money in the eighties! We deployed Pete (aka Mr Sex or Satan) to chat up the check-in girls, with tales of working on films and television. It was a very successful ploy and we managed to check all our bags in free of any charges! (We tried the same ploy on the way home at Lisbon Airport but the Portuguese girls were much sharper.) By the time, we had finished checking in, the lads were getting side tracked with shops and bars, so I rounded them all up and collected all their passports to go through passport control, as a group. When we arrived at the passport desk, they had formed an orderly single file queue behind me. At first I was impressed, but soon became worried about the sadistic smirks on their faces. Just as I presented all our passports at the desk they started; "Daddy, Daddy want wee wee", "Daddy, Daddy want ice cream", "Daddy, Daddy want toilet", "Daddy, Daddy I've poohed my pants" and so it went on. Even the stern-faced passport officer laughed saying "don't envy you, overseeing this lot!"

As soon as we boarded the Portuguese plane we experienced a huge cultural shock. It seemed as if everyone on board was smoking, including the flight attendants! The cabin crew were very slovenly and spent most of the time sitting at the back of the plane smoking. When we arrived at Lisbon I had to go to the customs office to clear our kit box. Three men were standing around my box in wrinkled uniforms, hands thrust in their pockets; each of them sported a bushy black moustache, and had a cigarette hanging from the corner of his mouth. It was just like a Mexican revolution movie scene! They didn't speak any English but looked at the customs papers that I offered them, and then gestured to me to open the box. When I raised the lid they obviously didn't like what they saw. Swords, battle axes and spiked ball and chains were well out of their comfort zones! I was getting very bad vibes about the looks they were giving me. Luckily, I had my briefcase with me which contained some publicity brochures and photographs of us jousting and fighting. These changed everything! I was offered cigarettes and from the now friendly sign language, I ascertained that they wanted to know if I was in the photographs, and whether they could they examine the weapons. After gesturing yes to both questions I became their best buddy, and spent the next half an hour smiling whilst they chased each other around the room with a variety of the weapons. When they tired of playing knights they resealed my box, stamped my carnet and escorted me to the exit with lots of smiles and pats on my back. I was greeted outside by some very worried lads who wanted to know why I had been kept so long by customs. I just said that everything was fine and that things happened a little more slowly over here.

Our next culture shock was seeing the huge shanty town not far from the Airport. Thousands of people lived in houses made of old packing cases and rusty bits of corrugated iron and there were piles of rubbish everywhere. Poor people living in abject squalor. None of us had any idea that this still existed in Western Europe; the mood in the mini bus suddenly became very sombre.

When we finally reached the village of Carreiras, where the Quinta was situated, it was mid-afternoon and baking hot, well over 40°C. As we drove through the centre of the village there was a group of about twenty women bent over communal sinks all doing their laundry by hand scrubbing, and then laying the washed clothes out flat on raised stone areas to dry in the sun, something you would have expected to see in rural India rather than in Europe. We finally drove up the drive to the Quinta Do Hespanhol Estate; it was very like one of my favourite films starring Russell Crowe called "A Good Year" about a high-flying City banker who inherits his uncles neglected Chateau in Provence. Like the one in the film, the Quinta was in a time warp, as was much of this area of rural Portugal we had travelled through to get there. The rambling gardens were overgrown, although close to the house they were well tended. The swimming pool was empty of water but now contained lizards and dried eucalyptus leaves from the huge trees that lined the drive. The eucalyptus trees gave the Quinta its own unique fragrance.

The next morning I was up with the lark as usual and took the opportunity to do some exploring, and was truly amazed at what I found.

In the first barn, that I entered there were about twelve, huge, round tanks, six on either side of a central passageway. Each tank was plastered on the outside and was painted white. At the base was a small hearth to light a fire. I decided they were wine fermenting vats; each one must have held 2000 gallons. So, this was wine making on a grand scale! In the next barn was a huge stone wine press with a roughly hewn, tree trunk of gigantic proportions providing the pressing weight. To lift and lower this massive piece of timber was an equally impressive wooden screw mechanism, not unlike a ship's capstan. I stood for several minutes trying to take it all in. I then realised that there was something else in the shadows; it was a Rolls Royce, relatively modern, but covered in dust and about two inches of pigeon shit. I wandered on trying to get my head around what I had seen. It was such a magical place, and so quiet. We were treated like honoured guests and ate with the family. A loud gong was rung to announce lunch or evening meal that could be heard anywhere on the estate. There was always lots of wine on the table, but the family never indulged, however we were always encouraged to drink our fill, and very nice it was too!

The plan had been to spend the first five days at the Quinta selecting the horses and then training them to joust. Except for using the Polo Ponies in Cyprus, we had never tried to do a show without our own, highly trained horses so this was a big gamble, a step into the unknown. The lads were keen to get started, so early next day we unpacked all the kit and got ready for an intensive schooling session on our new jousting horses. They didn't arrive. We waited until mid-afternoon but still no horses, so we decided to go and set up the tents in the arena. I left the lads with cold beers that we had been told to help ourselves to at any time by the family, and went to find Dad, as we had not yet, been shown our arena. Finding Dad proved quite a challenge; first I was told he was having his siesta which seemed quite normal to the Portuguese, but finally I found him having a gin and tonic with Granny Perestelos, a charming English lady who had her own cottage in the grounds. I should explain that Dad had gone out a week earlier than us to check that we had suitable horses and make sure everything was ready for our arrival; much to my horror he seemed to have to have gone native within a week, what with a siesta every afternoon followed by a couple of gin and tonics in the garden! Worse was to come when I asked for the directions to the arena; he became very evasive, not only about the arena but also about when the horses were going to arrive. He finally told me where the arena was located but added that I was not to bother going there as it was not quite finished. I was furious! He seemed to have arranged nothing in his week at the Quinta except the lads' hotel, but he didn't even know where that was located, just it's name. I set off with the knights to find our not quite finished arena. We scrambled up an old goat track through spiky scrub and boulders to where we discovered our "not started at all arena". What we saw was a steep sided valley covered in thorn bushes, brambles and boulders. We looked at each other in disbelief. What had Dad got us into this time? I was starting to learn that time in Portugal was not the same as the UK; things happen, but not at the stated time.

The bulldozer arrived the following day to start work on the arena but the horses did not arrive until the day before the show. The lads had nothing to do for four days so moved their office down to the local bar in the village. They spent so much money in this tiny bar that the owner must have thought he had died and gone to heaven. When we returned the following year, he had doubled the size of his bar and built on a pool room! Wicksey offered his services driving a hired transit van and made several trips with members of the family to collect things from Lisbon that were needed for the opening celebrations. Every time he returned, the van had more dents and bits missing. When we commented about his careless driving he explained he was just following orders. When he was told to park in a space that was obviously to small his co-driver told him to ram the cars front and back until there was enough space. Apparently, this was customary practice in Lisbon. On one occasion, he arrived at a narrow street with cars parked either side of the road. When he stopped, and told the co-driver that the van would probably hit some of the wing mirrors, she said, no problem they shouldn't be parked here, so he went up the street removing car wing mirrors as he went! I had to take the van into Lisbon to do a TV interview at the station's studio, right in the very centre of Lisbon. It was a very nerve-racking trip; my guide, who was supposed to know Lisbon like the back of his hand, got us lost several times, topping it all by telling me to turn right into a one-way road with eight lanes of traffic coming head on at us. I vowed never to drive in Lisbon ever again.

When the bulldozer finally arrived on the second day that we were at the Quinta it carved out a flat area for the arena and steps into the hillsides to make a three-sided grandstand. It was a magnificent, natural amphitheatre of red soil that made it look stunning. The only minor problem was that the arena floor was littered with hundreds of fist-sized stones that had to be cleared by hand. Not the most pleasant task in temperatures of 40° plus.

Our horses finally arrived on the day before the show leaving us little time for training them. However, they seemed unfazed by the small amount of jousting we could practise with them. The next evening, we did our show and true to Portuguese custom, everything was late except us; we sweated in our armour for over an hour, awaiting the arrival of the coaches bringing the guests. By the time, we started the show the temperature had dropped from mid-40s to 39°c. I was commentating, and you may be wondering about the language barrier, but there was none. Most the wealthy Portuguese spoke perfect English, most were educated in England, and it was a tradition that many had English wives. There was even a very successful Portuguese newspaper printed entirely in English. The show went extremely well and clouds of red dust that followed the galloping horses, added to the dramatic effect that is until we got to the Grand Melee´. Six horses galloping around the arena for several minutes together, stirred up such a dust cloud that neither audience nor I could see anything that was happening. I knew what should be happening in this dense, red fog so just made up the commentary as if I could see what was going on. After the show, several of the audience congratulated me for being able see through the dust and tell them what was happening. The Melee` took much longer than normal because the knights couldn't find their next opponents in the dense red dust! I had to delay the final salute for several minutes until the dust cleared, so that the audience could see the Knights. Everyone, including the audience now had a red tinge, something that didn't go down well with the finely dressed ladies in the audience. How the lads managed to perform in the heat and dust is just beyond me.

We returned to the Quinta many times over the next few years to perform corporate events and even does some stunt work on a film. What follows is a resume of some of the happenings that occurred during these trips.

On our first trip to the Quinta we were treated to any amount of free beer at the house, but after a couple of days we decided it was only fair to buy same cases to replace what we had drunk. Pete Webster, aka Satan, nominated himself to negotiate with owner of the village bar to purchase a couple of cases. Satan spent over fifteen minutes haggling intensely with the bar owner to no avail and in the end, we shouted at him "just buy the godamm stuff". We later worked out that the beer cost about 12p per bottle and the bar owner was trying to explain to Satan that you got 16p back when you returned the case plus 1p per bottle. Throughout the argument, Satan was convinced he was trying to rip us off, when the poor man was really trying to save us money.

On one of the other trips we were having a meal in our hotel with the public relations company we were working for. Dad was seated next to a very tall, elegant lady. The lady really was very tall, and Dad had to look up to talk to her, he was also visibly very pleased to have been seated next to her. After a series of nudges and whispers the whole troupe were watching Dad's performance as the meal progressed and the wine took its effect. As we watched the tableau unfold, someone commented that he looked like the cat that had got the cream; the comment was passed around the table much to everyone's amusement. Not long after Gilbert Harvey let out a "meow" sound which caused the table to erupt into laughter. However, it went straight over Dad's head, his only comment being "keep the noise down you silly buggers". More "meows" followed and even the mimicking of a cat rubbing against you for attention didn't provoke a comment from Dad as he was much too occupied with his quest. Gilbert then summoned the waiter and had a quiet word in his ear; a few moments later the waiter reappeared placing a saucer in front of Dad which he duly filled with milk. The table exploded in uncontrollable laughter, tears running down our faces. Dad looked at the milk with a puzzled look and at the table, of lads crying with laughter. He still didn't get it, but was now annoyed at the level of noise erupting at the table saying to us all. "For god's sake, get a grip on yourselves! You are acting like a bunch of little kids" which of course only intensified the laughter. Nobody had the guts to explain the joke to him, and we were happy to let him believe we were laughing because we had had too much to drink. For the rest of the tour all the lads greeted him with the enquiry phrase "what's new pussy cat?". Towards the end of that week Dad had a quiet word with me; he was worried about the mental state of the troupe and thought they all needed a rest because they kept saying Meow and calling him Pussy Cat…

On another occasion, we were invited to a VIP reception which was part of the launch of the Opel Corsa car in Portugal (that was being held at the Quinta). As we were the main entertainment at the event, we were on meet and greet duty. The event was held at the nearby seaside resort of Santa Cruz, in a cliff-top night club overlooking the Atlantic Ocean. It was a lovely warm evening with a cooling Atlantic breeze. Trays of ice cold cava complimented the sumptuous buffet that was laid out for the guests. It was a very up market affair. As the night wore on it became quite hot inside the venue, and a lot of people drifted out onto the terrace to take advantage of the cool sea breeze; you could also hear the Atlantic rollers crashing against the cliffs several hundred feet below. I had stayed inside and was seated at a table with a group of the organisers discussing the next day's event, when one of the lads came in with a worried look on his face and told me that I was needed outside urgently. I excused myself from the meeting and followed the messenger. Once out of earshot I hissed in his ear that it had better be important as the people I was talking to were the event organisers. The reply came back that it was exceptionally important; it was Wicksey threatening to throw himself off the cliff on to the rocks below; I was their last resort to try and talk him out of this dreadful act. I knew Wicksey had been depressed a few years earlier, so I knew that I had not only a very serious situation on my hands, but that I was way out of my depth to try and talk him down. The single good thing about the situation was that only the jousters were present and the part of the terrace where Wicksey had taken refuge was hidden away from the main party. At least I didn't have to deal with a huge crowd of onlookers. He was balanced on a stone wall about one and a half metres high with his back to the sea. To this day, I can still hear the crashing of the waves far below and remember the strong gusty wind that caused him to wobble and put out his arms to try to keep his balance. I asked him tentatively as to what had brought on this desperate decision, and then went on to tell him how much we love his company, how we needed him for the show the following day, but it seem to be to no avail. Suddenly he said something like, "it's no use," and stepped back off the wall into the abyss………. I stood rooted to the spot my stomach and mind reeling trying to come to terms with what had just unfolded in front of my eyes; there was a deathly hush all around me. Eventually after what seemed like an age, but was probably less than a minute, I forced myself to walk and look over the cliff. What would I see? I steeled myself, trying to imagine what I would have to witness; would it be a battered body on the rocks below or just the swirling black ocean crashing against the cliff. I took a deep breath and peered over the wall. Immediately, I flung myself back, it was almost as though I had had a massive electric shock. Had I seen what I thought I saw? I looked around. It was surreal. Everyone was laughing and then Wicksey popped his grinning face up from behind the wall, standing on the tiny concealed ledge which lay on the other side. I slumped down into the nearest chair, totally exhausted, looked up, smiled and just said "You f****** bastards".

Looking back, I should have been proud of them. They had all joined the jousting troupe with no acting skills or sense of theatre; they had learnt their skills on the road over the last ten years and now were pushing the boundaries to see just how far they could go with those skills. Wicksey had played his part so convincingly, although when I later examined the ledge he had landed on behind the wall, it was only a few feet wide, but with the amount of drink we had consumed, and the strong gusting wind, it must have been very close to a great prank, becoming a real disaster.

Our second trip to Portugal was to do some stunt work on a medieval film being shot at the Quinta. This time it was just Dad, my brother Stu and me all travelling together; Dad in his usual supervisory role, Stu and I doing the work. Ever since Dad had first visited Portugal, he had been avidly learning Portuguese from tapes and books. We landed at Lisbon about 11am and hired a car to drive up to the Quinta. It was about 12:30 by the time we left the Airport so we decided to stop for lunch on the way. We pulled into a lovely, sleepy town and made our way to the town square, always a good starting point when looking for a restaurant. We soon found a very traditional restaurant packed with farmers, all tucking into wholesome local produce, not a tourist in sight. The only problem was that the menu was in Portuguese and nobody spoke a word of English. "No problem" says Dad, "I will translate the menu for you". After careful studying of the menu for about 10 minutes he started his translation; soupo, that means soup, he also managed to translate bread and butter, which we had already worked out for ourselves. The waiter was hovering, so Stu and I opted for sign language pointing to the table next to us, where they seemed to be having a nice stew. Dad painfully ordered off the menu in his best Portuguese. When we enquired as to what he had ordered he told us it was a special beef dish. Our two stews arrived very quickly, but it was not until we had almost finished our meals that Dad's meal arrived with great ceremony. It was a full ox tongue laid on a plate, complete with all the hairy bits. Dad was aghast! There had been a terrible mistake; he called the waiter over pointing to the menu saying this was what he had ordered, "Si" said the waiter pointing to the huge, hairy tongue wobbling on Dads plate. Stu and I were crying with laughter as Dad insisted that the stupid buggers had made a mistake (Dad was never wrong). He made a half-hearted attempt at eating it but then said he thought it tasted off, so left most it, but never admitted that he didn't understand what he had ordered. As we drove on he was still going on about his grasp of the Portuguese language when he managed to shoot himself in the foot for the second time. As we drove into the next small town there was a sign painted on a wall saying Farmacia with an arrow pointing up a street. "Look" shouted Dad. Directions to the local farm shop! Stu and I just looked at each other shaking our heads - even we could make the connection between farmacia and pharmacy. Dad's mastery of the Portuguese language nearly had fatal consequences for Stu and I later during our stay. The Perestelos family had arranged for Stu and myself to do a sword fight at the very prestigious new Amoreiras shopping centre in Lisbon to help publicise the Quinta. We hadn't brought any swords on this trip as we we're just riding and doing stunt falls so John Prestrelos offered to lend us two, very fine and valuable 17c duelling swords, that hung on the Quinta's dining room wall. The plan was to have lunch at a very excellent restaurant at the shopping centre, use their toilet to get changed in, and then perform the sword fight for the press on the marble staircase outside the restaurant for the press. In true Quinta style, we were very late, even by their standards. We arrived at the shopping centre three hours late; the restaurant was closed; the Press had gone home and the shopping centre was in the process of shutting down. Undeterred, they announced that we would still go ahead with the fight and that they would photograph us themselves and send the photos to the press with a story; all was not lost. We found some public toilets to get changed in as the centre was now virtually empty. Stu and I had just stripped down to our underpants when a cleaning lady shuffled in with her mop and bucket. She took one look at us screamed and ran out. At this point you must wonder what the rest of the party were doing waiting outside the toilets. Seconds later, a security guard came running in and on observing two, near naked men, with two gold, inlaid duelling swords lying on the floor, immediately drew his revolver and gabbled at us in very rapid Portuguese. We kept saying we were English to no avail, but we soon got the message; he wanted us to face the wall arms and legs spread wide. We were now screaming for Dad or someone to come and explain to this very agitated, gun-toting guard that we were actors and had permission. Looking back now the poor man must have thought we were either mentally deranged terrorists about to go on a sword-wielding, murdering rampage or a couple of gays about to indulge in some bizarre sexual fantasy in a public toilet. At last, Dad appeared and we pleaded with him to explain to the guard in Portuguese what we were doing. Then came the now immortal words, that Dad said to the guard in his finest Portuguese." These'o my son'o they'o doing'o a sword fight'o on the stairs'o". We both thought, "Oh my God we are going to get shot for sure now". Thankfully at that moment one of the Portuguese members of the group arrived and sorted things out. We went on to do our sword fight on the now deserted staircase without mishap and surprisingly they managed to get a picture and a write up in several of the national newspapers. I think they felt quite bad about the whole affair, so took us out on a tour of Lisbon's upmarket watering holes. Our favourite was a beautiful, white marble piano bar with pots containing huge green ferns, it was super chic.

 Portugal doesn't come alive until after midnight, so it was very late when we got back to the Quinta. All the rooms at the Quinta were taken so Stu and I were sleeping in an annexe. Next morning, we were woken by rapid knocking on our door. We both rose with thumping hangovers and quickly looked at our watches to see if we were late for our filming. No, it was only 8 am, not even dawn on Portuguese time! Even stranger, when I opened the door, it was John Perestelos's wife looking very concerned; she apologised for not checking on us sooner and enquired if we were alright. We were very confused because although we had consumed a fair amount of alcohol the previous night, we had not expected the lady of the house to come and check up on us. As usual we had got it totally wrong. She informed us there had been a strong earthquake about 4am which had caused some structural damage to houses. They had checked everyone in the Quinta was ok, but had totally forgotten about us in the garden. To her relief, we were blissfully unaware of an earthquake at all. We had slept right though what was a very frightening earthquake.

Whilst on the subject about this eventful trip, I must mention the magnificent and beautiful horses we were given to ride in this film. They were high stepping, black Lusitano stallions, brilliantly trained in high school dressage including rearing to command. As I rode around the scrub covered boulder-strewn hills getting to know my mount, I felt like Clint Eastwood in one of his famous spaghetti westerns.

Another thing to mention was the contrast between late summer and spring. In September on our first visit, all the vegetation was dead and everywhere the red soil was baked dry and dusty. Now in April, it was full of green grass and beautiful flowers of every kind in full bloom. Such a profusion of vivid colour!

It was in Portugal that we discovered a drink that would almost kill one of our members. It is called Aguardente Bagaçeira: or in the bars "bagaço". I found this description for this deadly drink that wreaked havoc with the jousting troupe; we like the locals drank it as a shot, necking it in one. However, I found this description on the Internet that describes it better than I ever could.

"After a fantastic picnic among friends, we gathered at an outdoor café to finish the afternoon with a stiff drink called bagaço. The boys ordered two very full snifters of a crystal-clear beverage that I had never heard of, nor did I have to chance to ask just how potent it was before it was passed around to "enjoy" a healthy swig. Erring on the side of caution, I took a tiny sip, but that's all it took before my eyes popped wide open, and my face clenched and shuddered in pain. I rapidly slammed my fist on the table until the wave of fire passed; and when I came back from the fifth dimension of hell, all that was left was the delicate essence of fruit."

We had discovered this deadly drink on the last day of our trip and only indulged in "just the one". On our second major trip, Satan moaned all the way to Heathrow that he shouldn't be making the trip; his wife was very much against it, he was short of money and very busy at work (Pete was a Plumber and had his own business). We arrived as usual, late in the afternoon and after a late siesta hit the town about 7pm, with Satan who was still complaining that he couldn't afford to go drinking. The plan was to just have a few beers and get an early night, as we had a show to do the next day. Not wanting to leave Satan behind we offered to pay for his beers and he reluctantly agreed to join us. We were all having a lovely relaxing evening and were on about our fourth beer, when the man with no money came dancing out of the bar with a huge tray of Bagaço. He had an evil grin on his face and proudly said, "Look what I have found lads". We all protested; it was much too early for that kind of stuff but as he pointed out, it would be a shame to waste it now that he had bought it with his own meagre amount of money. We were all ceremonially presented with a glass and on the count of three all downed it in one. Tim Badder, a renowned beer monster was immediately sick in the street and the rest of us were left coughing and choking; by the time we had recovered, the man with no money was dancing out of the bar with a second tray of Bagaço. Most of us resolutely refused a second. Tim Badder, a man never known to run, sprinted down the street shouting "no no no". Someone else did have one and passed out in the street immediately. A now deflated Satan was moaning about what he was going to do with the rest of them. Someone foolishly suggested he had better drink them himself as he had bought them. We never saw Pete again that evening.

Next morning, we were all having breakfast in the beautiful wood panelled dining room of our hotel, when I noticed Satan was missing. I was not perturbed as he was renowned for oversleeping. However, we did have a big day ahead and a tight schedule. I sent Andrew Ducker, his roommate, to go and wake him and "to get his ass down here pronto". Ducker returned, reporting that he was up but didn't look great. This however was normal for Pete. Peter appeared about ten minutes later dressed in nothing but a crumpled tee shirt and his underpants; he was walking like a man who was a 100-year-old and appeared to be almost blind. The wealthy immaculately-dressed Portuguese having their breakfasts looked horrified, as did all of us.

I told Ducker to tell him to get out of the restaurant immediately and get some clothes on! I was then treated to probably the most embarrassing few minutes of my life, as Pete slowly groped his way around the wood panelled walls searching for the door. The nearest way I can describe it was that he looked like a "highly drugged up Golem out of Lord of the Rings". None of us wanted to be associated with him but in the end, I gestured to Ducker to get him out as fast as possible. Ducker returned shortly after and came straight to me with the words, "You'd better come boss; he's in a bad way". I collected Stu, who was his best mate and went up to his room; Ducker was not exaggerating - he could barely speak or move his body; everything was locked solid. Suddenly he muttered he was going to be sick so Stu and I carried him to bathroom, ejecting Ducker from the toilet seat where he was about to start his morning ablutions. Pete then spent the next ten minutes being violently sick. We made him drink as much water as possible and then put him back to bed leaving Ducker to look after him.

We went to the Quinta, set up the arena, worked the horses and then returned to collect Pete and Ducker. The Satan part of Pete was dead and he was still very ill, although some movement in his body was starting to return; however, his hands were still clenched in a fist. We took him to the pub where we took it in turns to walk him around and feed him water. There was a strong body of opinion that favoured a hair of the dog, but I vetoed that as I'm sure it might have killed him. Except for regular bouts of vomiting he gradually started to improve. I should say at this point, Pete was a key part of our show. When we flew to Portugal we only took key personnel, no reserves; without Pete, it would be very hard to do a show as we didn't have any more riders. We prised Pete into his armour and costume. The plan was that he would ride in, continue for as long as he could and then fake an injury. Unfortunately, Pete's state didn't go unnoticed. John Perestelos commented to Wicksey as Pete rode in, that he didn't look well. Quick as ever Wicksey told him that Pete had been up all night with a tummy bug. The show progressed with Pete making regular vomiting visits to the tents. Pete even managed to do a joust and a fall; the lads carried him back to his tent after his fall and he was immediately sick again but this time he stood up made a roaring sound and announced, "Satan is back to normal". The show was a remarkable success and we all breathed a big sigh of relief as it had been a very close run thing, both for Pete and the show….

We had another drink related incident with Pete and the dramatic effect that it had on his character. This trip we were staying in some brand new, high-class apartments. We had split up into groups that night. I was enjoying a quiet nightcap with the oldies, Brent (aka Hairy Chest) and Scotch Jimmy, when one of the lads found us and told me that I was needed back at the apartments. When I arrived, the lads were all grouped around the elevator. I assumed that it had broken but no, it was Pete again. They said he had gone mad, completely lost it. I was about to enquire in what way, when the elevator doors opened revealing Pete standing totally naked; he leapt in the air flinging his arms and legs wide apart, screamed "Aargh", closed the doors and was gone to another floor in a flash. It took over fifteen minutes to finally catch him, by which time he had traumatised two elderly Portuguese couples trying to get to their apartments. Even when we managed to get him into his apartment he escaped though his window and was swinging on the drainpipe outside, several floors up. Luckily, we managed to talk him back in before he fell to his death or suffered significant injury.

The music of our Portuguese adventures was Dire Strait's songs like, "Money for Nothing", "Sultans of swing", and "So far away", come to mind. It was to the music of "Money for Nothing" that we had one of our wildest, craziest moments. We had tired of touring by this time, so had started to insist on a free day after our last show to relax and see a bit of the places we were visiting. We had a hired mini-bus for the duration of the tour so decided to go out to the coast, have a few beers, and take in the scenery. As we meandered up the coast, it was suggested that we should try and find a way to drive onto the beach. After a few failed attempts to get onto the beach, we finally found a road leading towards the sand dunes that looked promising. Just before we reached the dunes we encountered some 45-gallon oil drums that had been painted red and white and had been placed across the road so that we had to weave in and out of them. We performed this manoeuvre at some speed throwing everyone out of their seats, much to the amusement of Stu, who was driving. Having negotiated the barrels, we found ourselves on a large expanse of flat sand. It was ideal for more high-speed swerving and ejecting passengers from their seats. To add a little more risk to this frivolity, and because it was very hot, we had opened the sliding door on the side of the mini bus, thus making it possible for the driver to throw a few bodies out, if he drove fast enough and swerved hard enough. This was great fun and we all clung on for dear life as we enjoyed this impromptu" Helter Skelter" ride. Suddenly there was a shout from the front "Shit there's a f****** plane coming in to land". It was then that we realised that our flat piece of sand was a landing strip, and to make matters worse a Jeep with soldiers carrying guns was also bearing down on us. We turned tail and went as fast as we could, back the way we had come. Unfortunately, in our haste to escape we forgot about the chicane of oil drums. As we approached them an argument broke out as to whether they were filled with concrete or not; the not-filled with concrete camp won the argument so we took a chance and hit the final one on exit. It was filled with concrete! There was a great crash, and everyone was thrown to the other side of the bus with great force, but we kept going and thankfully made a clean getaway. Unfortunately, Brent who was sitting next to the open doorway was hurled across the mini bus breaking his ribs.

The Portugal we visited in the eighties was a very poor, corrupt country, but one which was changing fast, especially when they joined the EU. During the five years we visited Portugal, we witnessed massive change; things were modernising, the standard of living rose and so did prices. When we went over the first time I gave £20 of Escudos to everyone and they lived like kings for three to four days; three years later £20 didn't even cover one day. By year five it was £50 per day. Laws were changing as well and our behaviour had to be tempered over the latter years. In the early days, we happily drove everywhere about four times over the British legal limit; it was not until we happened to ask why they didn't have any drink drive rules that we got a very sobering answer. They had very strict rules but most people ignored them; apparently, the police regularly staged road blocks and anyone caught drinking and driving went straight to prison.

A classic example of corruption was our airline tickets which we received via John Perestelos's travel agency. They always arrived at the very last minute and were only one-way tickets. We had a friend who was a travel agent who could find out how many seats were left on any flight. She twice told me the flight was fully booked, yet days later we got nine tickets to collect at the TAP desk. When I enquired about this at the Quinta, they openly told me they paid someone at TAP to say that there had been a booking mistake and cancel nine peoples' reservations. The lax way TAP was run got me into hot water with Lou who had asked me for some perfume from duty-free. As we came into land at Heathrow, the cabin crew still had the duty-free trolley in the isle and were trying to serve people as fast as they could; my perfume was stuffed into a plastic bag and I paid for it as we touched down. My trips to Portugal were never popular with Lou, so I was hoping that the expensive perfume would be an olive branch. Unfortunately, I had the right brand but the stewardess had given me men's aftershave instead of perfume, so I was in more hot water!

Air transport in the 80's would be unrecognisable today and we would have not got away with the little surprise that Dad gave us regarding airline tickets. John Perestelos's travel agency had asked Dad for the names of all the lads, so that they could get tickets issued for their return journey. Unfortunately, Dad gave everybody's first names or nicknames instead of their surnames, which the travel agency was obviously expecting. When we arrived at the airport there was a travel agent there who, ceremoniously handed out our airline tickets. To our horror, he started to shout out our names, Mr Stuart, Mr Sam, Mr Wicks, Mr Slim, Mr HC hairy chest, even Mr Satan, and so it went on. Amazingly nobody cross-checked our passports against the ticket names and we all got home without a hitch. I tell a lie. We did have one hitch twenty minutes before our flight. I told every to drink up and set off for the departure gate; Stu and Ducker took the view that I was being needlessly over-cautious and that there was plenty of time. They assumed that the time on the ticket was the time you boarded the plane, not the take-off time. Everyone was boarded and still no sign of Stu or Ducker. We were convinced that they had missed the plane when over the tannoy came "sorry for the delay we are still awaiting two more passengers", the plane, actually waited for the jammy sods to arrive.

You may be wondering by this point how on earth we didn't get arrested in Portugal. Well, two of the lads nearly did. Pete and Gilbert were walking back from a bar through the back streets of Torres Vedras, which were a bit like a labyrinth and of course they were well lubricated. On their journey, they came across a large house with lots of plants in pots outside. They paused and studied the plants concluding that they needed totally rearranging. Unfortunately, the budding garden designers failed to notice that the big house was a police station and the officers inside were watching their every move. The police finally had enough of their redesigning and apprehended them; as neither party, could speak each other's language and the only common word they both understood was the name of their hotel; the police decided to let them go.

The horses we used for our shows in Portugal were always beautiful Lusitano's, but they never came from the same source. I suspected that the reason could be that owners might not have been paid; the more shows we did the more random the origins of the horses became, with one horse from this man, two from another and so on…

On one of our last shows Dad informed us that one of the horses would have to be ridden from the owner's farm as he had no means of transport. Ducker volunteered to collect the horse as he fancied riding a flashy horse over the mountains. He was driven to the farm early in the morning so that we could train the horse and then rest it before the late afternoon show. Time ticked by and there was no sign of Ducker and his horse. He finally arrived many hours later, just in time for the show. Apparently, the owner had made Ducker muck out the stables, clean it's tack, and groom the horse to the owner's exacting standards before allowing him to leave. Moreover "the just over the hill" turned out to be just over several mountains. Poor Ducker arrived not only exhausted, but with two blisters on his backside.

There are so many more tales; I could write a whole book just on Portugal but before I move on I must mention the port shop that was just down the road from our hotel. When I'm in a foreign country I love to visit their markets and food shops to get a real feel of what people's lives are like. As I strolled down into town from our hotel I noticed a shop with crates of fruit and veg outside on the pavement. There were several items that I had never seen before, so I decided to see what other unknowns awaited me inside the shop. It was very dark inside and my eyes took a moment to adjust. When they did, it was as if I had found Aladdin's cave! Huge hams hung from the exposed rafters, as well as many different salamis. The counter was made of old dark mahogany with a top of a lighter coloured wood that had been well scrubbed for many decades. On its top sat a beautiful set of Edwardian grocery scales. As my eyes came into focus, I could see that the shop went back further and I could just make out hundreds of old dusty bottles, some wine but mostly port, most of which had multiple price labels, on them reflecting their increasing value as they aged. As Portugal was not involved in the Second World War, their cellars had not been plundered and some of the ports went back to the early nineteen hundred's, although these were way too expensive for us. The shop became a pilgrimage for the connoisseurs of our troupe, and this was where we always bought our duty-free allowance.

I never made our last trip to the Quinta. I broke my ankle the day before we were about to fly so Ducker took my place and went with Stu. It was a small promotional job requiring just two people.

Times were changing. The once young lads who came to the fore after Tony left, had now all grown up and they either had their own businesses or were in demanding, executive jobs. As we entered the nineties, jobs became much less secure, but also very rewarding if you put the time and effort in; however, you couldn't afford to stagger into work on Monday mornings, battered bruised, and hungover.

 At our Christmas party in 1988, which was held in the Red Lion Pub at Costock (now closed and demolished) I made a toast. *"Thanks for another great season! Let's hope the next one is as good!".* To my surprise, it was met with a muted response. During the evening, several of the main characters approached me and said they no longer wished to do the jousting if we were going to be doing the same number of shows. They didn't want to stop altogether, but they now had other more important commitments. Time was becoming valuable to them, they wanted to be paid for travelling to shows that required an overnight stay. However, I soon discovered that this didn't apply to exciting foreign trips or filming!

Recession

At the end of the eighties and early nineties things were changing; economically and socially, there were fewer independent shows willing to risk money on big expensive main attractions. However, the film industry in the UK was starting to boom, as were the new independent television production companies.

Writing this book has meant doing a lot of research and I have been astounded by the amount of information that is out there. Having written the previous paragraph, I was inspired to research the economic data for the period that this book covered. I was astounded to discover that the number of shows we performed, almost exactly mirrored the rise and fall of the UK's GDP. Moreover, our trips to Belgium only occurred when there was a weak pound. Sometimes, no matter how good your shows are, if there isn't the confidence, or money out there, you just won't get the bookings.

1989 was the start of a very dramatic recession. After years of growth through the eighties, everything came to a grinding halt; people stopped spending and that included having jousting at their events. There were still all our regular shows,

Belvoir, Bosworth and Lincoln. These were enough to cover the overheads. We also picked up two new venues that helped us keep going over the next few years. They were Margam Park in South Wales, and Harlaxton Manor not far from Belvoir Castle.

Margam Park was run by Glamorgan County Council, and attracted huge and enthusiastic crowds. We also found, some very good overnight stabling not far from the show ground. The down side to the show, was that the nearest hotel was at Port Talbot, home of the famous Steel Works. Lou did, however, find us a very charming hotel that offered a good weekend rate. During breakfast, the manager entered the room and apologised for the late arrival of the Sunday papers, and informed everyone that they had now arrived. The papers would be brought to the tables of those who had ordered them. The clientele was obviously very well-heeled, and their choice of newspapers reflected this. The manager worked through the Sunday Times, then the Sunday Telegraph, with people raising their hands to indicate they had ordered that paper. At the end of the process he looked a little embarrassed and finally muttered that he also had a Sunday Sport; as if it was obviously a mistake, a small gasp of shock could be heard across the room. It must be a mistake! Surely nobody would dare to own-up to having ordered such a near pornographic publication. "That'll be mine!" boomed a voice from the far side of the breakfast room. Everyone turned towards the direction of the voice. It was Wicksey, who was now striding across the room grinning from ear-to-ear and quipping, "You lot don't know what you are missing!"

We only did one full show at Harlaxton Manor, but returned many times to do sword fights at banquets. This stunning, beautiful stately home had now become an American

University Campus for the University of Evansville. We performed on the front lawn with the manor as a back-drop, making it rank alongside Belvoir and Lincoln Castles as one of my favourite venues. To say we went down well would be an understatement! The audience was made up of mainly students and they were predominantly female. It was a little like going back to the sixties when girls screamed hysterically at pop groups. When we finished the show, the lads were mobbed for autographs, photographs and kisses. Although that was the only full show we did there, I sent groups of lads over to do foot fights inside the house, for end of semester functions. These were very popular with the lads, and I never had trouble getting people to go there. It was not unusual for the lads to disappear for several days at a time, whenever they performed there. Sadly, their exploits became common knowledge at the university and the powers that Be put a stop to the sword fights, and extracurricular entertainment. But that was several years down the line, but as the saying goes, all good things must come to an end!

De Rode Ridder

The recession also brought a drop in the value of the pound, which in turn opened the door for another trip to Belgium. However, this show would make us even more famous in Belgium than we already were. The Belgians love their cartoon strips in their newspapers, and one of the most popular was the "De Rode Ridder" (The Red Knight). The Rode Ridder stories were fantasy. The medieval knight had all sorts of adventures involving, Dragons, Ghosts, Aliens, and anything else that was fantastical. The common theme for all the stories involved scantily dressed damsels in distress, with large bosoms bursting out of see through tops. They were the nearest thing to pornography that could be published in a daily newspaper. Each story was made into a cartoon book at the end of the story, they were in great demand and highly collectable.

Ashcile had managed to persuade the writer, Karel Biddeloo to make Horst Castle. the birth place of the Rode Ridder and base several stories there. This boosted the visitor numbers to the Castle immensely. One of these stories also involved the Knights of Nottingham, and Karel travelled over to Bunny Hill to sketch the main characters including myself. We had now become strip-cartoon characters! Not only were we strip-cartoon characters, but we were going to come alive, and recreate the strip-cartoon to a live audience.

When the Rode Ridder first entered the arena, the heavens shook with the cheers. Whatever he did in the show brought forward a massive roar from the crowd. The day after the first show we were front page news in all the Flemish newspapers. It certainly blew away the recession blues. The Rode Ridder stories began way back in 1949, and over the years have had several writers and illustrators, and their appeal has spanned many generations. After the shows, we would sit in the castle courtyard relaxing with a beer; families would quietly approach our tables and say, "we are sorry for disturbing you but we felt we just had to thank you, seeing the Rode Ridder come to life, has meant so much to us all. Please if it doesn't trouble you, may we have your autographs so that we can remember this day?". They were so humble and obviously greatly moved by the show, and it made us very proud of what we had done.

Boon

Early in 1990, Bill Hammond and I got a day's work as extras in a television production called "Box Thirteen". It was a boring days' work that took place in an old closed school; as usual, the extras were treated like cattle, herded into a room and told to "wait until called". "Waiting" was sitting on the floor as all the rooms were empty. There was much coming and going by stressed production staff, but nothing else seemed to be happening. We gradually gleaned snippets of information. The star was not feeling well, hence the delay. Eventually we all trouped out into the playground, and watched a group of firemen climbing a ladder. One of the firemen seemed to be distressed and out of breath. The director shouted "Cut" and thanked everyone. Five minutes of actual work in a twelve-hour day! We returned to sitting on the schoolroom floor, while we waited for transport to take us back to the studios. As we sat waiting, a production assistant came and asked Bill if he had a motorcycle licence, and when Bill answered in the affirmative, he was asked to follow the assistant. Sometime later he returned looking a little bemused. When I enquired, what was the matter he said, "I think I have just been offered the job of doubling for the main actor, riding a motorcycle". At the time, we both thought it was a lucky break of maybe two or three days' work at a much higher pay rate.

It turned out to be the making of Bill. The series was later renamed "Boon" and was to run for seven series. Bill became a full member of the cast and was paid a very generous sum of money for the privilege. The best was yet to come for Bill, as he was only required to be on set for the motorcycle scenes. The production had moved from Birmingham to the new Central studios in Nottingham, so filming was always close to where Bill lived. With a solid income, and plenty of spare time, Bill started buying and renovating cottages, which after seven years became a very successful full time business.

It also proved very good for us too, as Mike Elphick, the main character loved horses, and endeavoured to have one or more in as many programs as possible. In the programme his alter ego was that of a cowboy sheriff. With Bill's contacts, we were able to secure the contract for supplying the horses. Mike always wanted the same horse to ride and had a fond attachment to her. The horse's name was Zara. We nearly didn't use her as she was easily spooked at home, but on set, hardly anything "fazed her" except for the sound man's big hairy microphone, which terrified her.

Not only did we supply the horses, but I also got to do several riding stunts as well. One stunt was the opening sequence for series five. This involved riding my jousting horse Drummer at night along the raised loading bay of a disused factory close to the River Trent. The loading bay was five feet high and very narrow, it was pitch black, except for a wall of backlit smoke swirling around for dramatic effect. It was very dangerous, but Drummer was, as ever, rock steady, and we pulled it off in five takes. We built up a very good relationship with the production crew over the years, and they eventually wrote a special episode that involved a travelling jousting troupe. This involved all the jousters performing our show. The sequence was filmed in the beautiful grounds of Holme Pierrepoint Hall and was great publicity for the jousting troupe.

The Robin Hood Pageant

During the eighties, I also built up a good working relationship with Nottingham City Leisure Services and the Publicity Departments. They were keen to promote Nottingham as a tourist destination, and saw Nottingham Castle, Robin Hood and the Sheriff of Nottingham as a central part of this strategy. It started with providing mounted knights as an escort, for the Sheriff and Lord Mayor when they were making press statements. This attracted a lot of press and television coverage, and was a remarkable success. Later they started having parades for the Sheriff and Lord Mayor from the Castle to the Council House in the Old Market Square. I suggested that both officials could be mounted and offered to train them both in basic riding skills. This was embraced enthusiastically by all parties. Again, they had a massive publicity coupe with crowds turning out in their thousands to watch the parades. I went onto train numerous Sheriffs and Mayors to ride, until budget cuts forced the cancellation of the parades early in the new millennium.

I was always campaigning to perform a joust at Nottingham Castle but this always brought a very hostile reaction from the Parks Department who would not allow a single hoof to be placed on their hallowed turf. When the parades from the castle to the square started, there was uproar from the castle staff, who complained about everything we did.

It came to a dramatic climax, one bank holiday Monday, when we arrived at the castle gates with our horsebox and were told we couldn't enter. When the Lord Mayor arrived in his chauffeur-driven, official limousine, there was chaos. The Mayor was furious with the "Jobs Worth" who was barring our entrance and causing a major traffic jam; all he kept saying was, "nobody has informed me to allow any lorries or horses through this gate, so you can't come in". The normally quietly spoken Mayor raged at the gatekeeper, informing him that if we were not allowed entry immediately, he would be out of a job the very next day. We were finally allowed in! The parade started half an hour late, with the Mayor vowing this would never happen again, and that he was going to make it very clear to the Parks Department that they did not own the Castle but the City Council did!

Bob Chaffin was a rising star in Leisure Services, and we both shared a dream of holding a jousting tournament based around Robin Hood at the Castle, but such was the Parks Department hostility, that we were seriously drawing up plans to try and stage it in the Old Market Square outside the Council House, when the Lord Mayor incident took place. True to his word the Lord Mayor championed our cause.

The council overruled the Parks' objections and in 1990 the Robin Hood Pageant was born. We had done a daytime joust the previous year, but it was a pre-show publicity stunt, on the evening before the show, that stole the show, attracting worldwide interest in Nottingham. The stunt involved all the jousters, plus Robin Hood's Minstrels. Half of us were the Sheriff with his guards, whilst the other half focused on Robin Hood and the Outlaws. The plot was that the Sheriff had captured Robin Hood, and was parading him around the market square in chains, before taking him to the Castle for execution. But before he reached the Castle Green, the Outlaws would stage an ambush, free Robin and set fire to some buildings. A huge crowd assembled in the Market Square and followed us up to the Castle. The darkness blotted out the modern-day city, creating a fantastic atmosphere. The Knights carried flaming torches on horseback, (idea borrowed from "By the Sword"). The Outlaws were armed with flaming arrows which set fire to the special straw huts that we had constructed on the "hallowed" green. The flames were much bigger than we expected and lit up the whole Castle. The crowd cheered and cheered. The press and television cameras went into overdrive.

The Council had a massive success on their hands, and of course it was all their idea!

Bob and I didn't mind, as we had got what we wanted. In 1990, we staged three evening shows Thursday-Saturday, as well as two day-time shows on the Saturday and Sunday. I wrote a special script for the evening shows. There were special effects, plus full theatre quality sound and lighting. We even had a huge mock castle backdrop, allowing us to have a proper backstage area (idea borrowed from Belgium). Every evening show was sold out, and 22,000 came to see us over the four days. The next year it was 30,000!

We could never have pulled-off the night shows off without the huge help from wives and girlfriends, who miraculously changed the costumes of both, horses and riders, dozens of times, in extremely brief time frames, and managed the back stage to the second. Another hugely influential person was Rob Wilkinson, who we first met when we did a Summer Ball with him that was held in a local farmer's grain store. Rob handled all the sound and lighting for the night shows, which was a hugely complicated task requiring great skill and technical knowledge.

The pageant is still on going to this day and our show remains the main attraction. The night shows stopped in 2000 due to budget cuts but have now been reinstated, albeit on a more modest level. We attracted people from all over the world. A group from Japan flew over every year to watch the shows, they always brought me a gift from Japan. It was very touching when they all bowed to me before presenting their gift. The pageant is now recognised as a major tourist event for Nottingham that boosts the city's economy between Goose Fair and the Christmas period.

The Crash

1991 was the deepest part of the recession that the country was experiencing and we struggled to find bookings, other than our regular venues, however, the ones that we did get were very memorable. I did some cut-price deals for local shows, and it was like going back to our roots of the early seventies.

The first of these shows was not local however. It was at a small village situated between Stansted Airport and Braintree called Stebbing. They were raising money to fight the expansion of Stansted Airport. There was nothing grand about the show; we performed in a farmer's paddock, with a bit of a hill on one side for the audience to stand on. The audience numbered less than a thousand, but were very enthusiastic and appreciative. What was so special about this show was that we were welcomed into their community. We travelled down the night before the show and slept on camp beds in the scout hut. We were split into groups, and took our meals with families in the village, before being invited to the village pub, for a bit of a get- together. The pub was bursting at the seams, full of raucous laughter and much back slapping. It was as if we had lived here all our lives; the pub was still partying until the early hours when we staggered back to our scout hut, although some of the lads ended up at a pool party and didn't return until dawn. It was also a very beautiful village full of thatched cottages and narrow streets. It made me realise, that doing big grand shows was not what it was all about, and that these small community shows left you with a warm glow of satisfaction, very different from the adrenaline rush of huge audience shows.

The following week we did two more community shows. However, the first was a very grand affair. At that period, Lou and I used to visit the Cuckoo Bush Pub in Gotham. We had made friends with many of the locals who drank there. Many were from the local farming community who had a very vibrant social life. There was always something being planned that involved eating and drinking. Every year things got a little grander. The two Ploughwright brothers, Paul and Simon, and another friend, Rob Wilkinson, were always very much the centre of these activities.

One evening in the "Cuckoo", Rob asked me if I thought it was possible to do a jousting show inside a barn. It was for a Ball that he was planning with the Ploughwright brothers. Always up for a challenge, I agreed to meet them and have a look at the proposed venue. I was shown into a very dark series of interlinked barns that were used for storing grain. It was early summer and they were now empty, and cleaned out ready to receive the next year's harvest.

The plan was to hold a Black-Tie Ball in the barns; the entertainment was to be provided by a top London pop band, a disco, and hopefully the jousting. It was going to be an all-night affair and to circumnavigate the archaic licensing laws, it was to be ticket only, and all the food and drink was to be free. It was certainly going to be a challenge! The area we had at our disposal was narrow and had concrete pillars at regular intervals down one side of the arena. It was very dark and the concrete floor was very slippery. We eventually solved the problems, and rehearsed with the horses so that we all knew where the dangerous pillars were.

Although we performed early in the night, the immaculately-dressed audience had already made effective use of the free bar, so they were extremely raucous and bawdy. The experience that the lads had performing, for diverse types of audience really showed. Within a minute of starting the show, they started to improvise with the audience putting a much bawdier adult theme to the show. The audience went wild and we all had a fun time pushing the boundaries of our show. By the end of the show I realised, that we were not only a family show, but also had the ability to entertain adult-only audiences. Some of the "off the cuff" comedy was outstanding. We did the show in exchange for free tickets; there were two tickets for each person who performed so that we could bring our partners. After the show, it was a race back to Bunny with the horses, a quick shower and a change into our tuxedos. It was a great night; the band was outstanding and everyone was in a great party mood. There was one bit of high drama. As Lou and I entered the Ball, the ultraviolet light illuminated her underwear as if she were naked and caused her major consternation. Lou's lifelong friend Vanda, who had come with us came to the rescue. I have been informed that ladies often put an extra pair of knickers on over their tights to hold them up tight. They were of a colour that wouldn't show up under ultraviolet light; so, they raced off to the ladies, giggling, so that Lou could borrow Vanda's spare pair. They returned, now crying with laughter; Vanda in her rush to get ready, hadn't put on her extra pair of kickers - in fact she hadn't put any on at all!

They both had to drive back home to fetch alternative underwear after which order was restored. They both still cry uncontrollably with laughter whenever we reminisce about that night. I had ordered a taxi for 3 am as I was driving the coach next day, however it never arrived and neither did two others I ordered. I had driven down in the old Land Rover which I intended to leave there until after the weekend but at 6 am I loaded a group of drunken ladies in ball-gowns into the back of the filthy Land Rover, and drove the few miles home. Thankfully at 6 am on Sunday morning the roads were empty.

I collected my "wrecked" jousting troupe from Ploughwrights Farm at 8 am. Most were asleep on the coach, but a few diehards were still drinking whatever was left to drink at the bar, still wearing their DJ's, the rest were sleeping in theirs!

Our Sunday show was the Oxford Country Show. The drive down was a nightmare. The previous night, I had had only one and a half hours' sleep, coupled with an eight-hour drinking session. I was so tired that my neck muscles kept going slack as I fought drifting off into sleep, whilst driving. Twice I had to pull over and have 15 minutes' sleep. We arrived at the show ground just before midday, just as the mobile bar was opening. As I shook the lads out of their drunken slumbers there were moans and groans as the hangovers kicked in. They staggered over to the bar, most still wearing wrinkled DJs, and enquired as to what was the strongest drink that the barman could offer them. Jack Daniels was the reply, so they ordered thirty doubles (two each). Unfortunately, the bar did not have that amount of "JD" so the shortfall was made up with double brandies. Thus fortified, we set up and performed two great shows, albeit with extra alcoholic top ups during the day. It was a real farming show with Terrier and Ferret racing which was great fun. The show was run mainly by young farmers who thought it was wicked that we had come straight from an all-night farming Ball to entertain them. The Young Farmers are a National Organisation; which is renowned for its wild work hard play hard ethos. We were now cult heroes in their eyes, so finished the day off with another drinking session with our newly-found friends. Thankfully I had a relief driver to take the coach home and slept soundly all the way home.

A weekend to remember!

The last of our cheap community shows brought us firmly down to earth. It was at the local village of Keyworth and I took it on for the nostalgic reason that it had been the venue for one of our first public shows way back in 1971. Keyworth is a very large commuter village and the show was on the village playing field. When we arrived our designated parking, the area was already full of cars so we had to park the horsebox and coach in a side street close by, causing chaos and bad feeling with residents. Luckily there was a tractor and trailer on site, so we able to slowly but surely ship our equipment to the arena. Being some way from the show site, communications were not good, so when we arrived ten minutes before our start all dressed and ready to perform, we were told the show was running an hour behind schedule, so we all had to troupe back to our cul-de-sac to disrobe. Eventually, we did our first show which went down very well. Our second show was last in the programme which was now running two hours behind schedule. It was nearly dusk and nearly everyone had already gone home, so with the light fading and everything being packed up we did our final show to about fifty people.

Bring back the big shows run to the exact minute!

The highlight of this difficult year was another tour to Belgium. The shows were still organised by Ashcile but this time they were at the very grand seaside town of Knokke-Heist. We took the overnight ferry from Felixstowe to Zeebrugge and then it was just a ten minutes' drive up the road, but being holiday time, it took almost an hour. Knokke-Heist is known as the Monte Carlo of the north. I don't think that there is an English equivalent even on the south coast. It was very grand, super upmarket hotels, very expensive, and the place to be seen. As we crawled into the town we just couldn't believe the number of "super cars" we saw.

Life soon came down to earth with a bump, when we arrived at the show ground it was flooded! Latitude wise, Knokke is about the same as London and the saying in Belgium is whatever weather England has, Belgium gets it the next day. Not only was it flooded but the site was on what is called "Polder land", strange grey clay-like soil renowned for becoming very boggy, and very slow to dry out. All the grandstands where built, as were all the banqueting tents but the arena was unusable. We had arrived at the beginning of a heatwave and the ground was drying but very slowly. Ashcile and I inspected it three or four times a day. I had travelled over with the horses on the Wednesday, three days before our first show, in case severe weather delayed the sailing; the coach arrived on Thursday with some late comers making their way by car on the Friday. It was a long tense time. Ashcile was continually asking me if we would be able to perform at the weekend, but all I could offer was "we must wait and see". Friday was supposed to be a rehearsal/press day and Ashcile was desperate for us to joust for the press, as ticket sales were not looking good. I had to inform him that if we tried to joust with the ground a wet as it was, it would make the arena unusable for the shows when the ground dried out.

In the end, we came to an uneasy compromise. We would canter around the drier edges of the arena with flags and charge at the cameras with lances for action shots. Ashcile was very angry; he didn't understand horses or ground conditions and I thought it was the end of our working relationship. What he wanted was a cast-iron guarantee that we would be able perform the shows, and that depended on the weather and the way that the ground drained. That Friday, the centre of the arena looked like a dried-up pond; no standing water but lots of gooey mud. After the press morning, I asked the Knights to walk the arena with me to see if it was going to be fit to perform on the next day. We finally, after much deliberation decided that some parts of the arena would be workable the next day, but the centre where the tilt would normally be, was unusable. We would have to reconfigure the show using several islands of dryer ground. The only place we could have the jousting was very close to one of the grandstands but a long way from the other three so we would have to use small patches of dry land near the other grandstands for foot fights to balance the viewing.

Ashcile was over the moon. The show could go on! Organising a show like this would have cost many thousands of pounds and I think it would have bankrupted him if we had to cancel. It was an extremely hard show for the Knights as they had to remember where all the wet patches were, as they were so deep that they could have brought a horse down.

The first show was going well and we were near the end. I rode out for one of the last jousts of the show and had the accident with the breaking lance that was mentioned in the Belgium chapter. Luckily there were no evening shows and I recovered in time for the Sunday shows. We were now in the middle of a heatwave that dried the arena and made it fully functional for the last two shows. The only problem was that when the sun shines everyone wants to be on the beach, not paying to watch a jousting show. Attendance was not bad, but not the sell-outs that we had had in Horst and Leuven. Ashcile was very down, and we all thought that this would be our last trip to this lovely country.

It was a sad year after all those previous record-breaking years.

Early in 1992 we received a chance call from Kilkenny about having a jousting show for a festival that they were planning. It was Saturday lunchtime; I was teaching and Lou was running the bar which as usual was packed. She nearly told them they had the wrong number as they asked to speak to another jousting troupe but then thought I had better speak to them, so sent someone to takeover my ride so that I could speak to them. This chance call was to start a friendship that continues to this day.

It also messed with my mind very seriously!

In England, we had been at war with the IRA for twenty odd years, all sorts of atrocities had been committed by the IRA in England and Northern Ireland. In my warped English-media, oriented mind, Eire was a place where it rained constantly and was full of English-hating terrorists. Because of this, plus the fact that our international tours had exhausted me both mentally and physically, I really didn't want to go on a tour to Kilkenny, deep in southern Eire. However, I couldn't resist another challenge; I really didn't feel any enthusiasm to visit this wet English-hating place and why on earth did they want to hire an English jousting troupe anyway? So, I sent my brother, Stuart, who was itching to do more in the organisation of the jousting. He managed to get a lift with his girlfriend's father who was a regular visitor to the Emerald Isle, so kept the cost to a minimum in case we didn't get the job. He returned with glowing reports of parties and meeting horse-racing legends at these parties but not much information about the people who were hiring us, and whether they were trustworthy or not, but to be fair, it was not easy to understand the commercial makeup of something called the Kilkenny Confederation. I entered detailed negotiations with this Confederation and after much wheeling and dealing with ferry companies and other ancillary service, we finalised a deal. On Wednesday June the17th at 4pm we left Bunny Hill for a new adventure!

1992 started much better than the previous year. There was a trip to Portugal at the end of April, to launch the new Opel Corsa in Portugal. We were in Portugal for a whole week, and then three days later Stu and I travelled to Frankfurt in Germany. This time it was to launch a new flight service from East Midlands Airport to Frankfurt. It was organised by East Midlands Airport and a new organisation called Profile Nottingham which was part of Nottingham City Council. We travelled in style. First, we flew on the inaugural flight from East Midlands Airport to Frankfurt with a hot breakfast and free drinks all the way and then on arrival we were whisked off to stay at the fantastic Frankfurter Hof Hotel. This hotel, is without doubt the most luxurious hotel that I have ever stayed in. The corridors outside of the bedrooms were about eight metres wide, and I imagined Hitler or Goring (in years gone by) sweeping down these curving corridors followed by a huge entourage spread out behind them. Stu and I shared a small suite and revelled in the style and luxury. The only down side was that it was room only and there was no way we could afford to eat or drink in the hotel. The up side to this was that

Stu and I ate our first Thai meal ever and this introduced me to what is now my favourite cuisine. It was a very easy job as all we had to do was dress up as Robin Hood and The Sheriff of Nottingham, and perform a sword fight at the press launch. The most exciting bit, though, was a tour of Frankfurt Airport, which I believe is larger than Heathrow. We were taken airside into the huge hangers to see the servicing of jumbo jets and see their state-of-the-art, computerised baggage-handling equipment. They employed so many people it was like a town, with services like doctors, dentists, and various restaurants all airside for the staff, and never seen by travellers. It was during this tour that I almost insulted our hosts. They were proudly showing us the new Terminal that they were in the process of building; it was due to open in four months' time, so, I asked what would have been a very normal question in the UK. I simply asked it the project was running to schedule; the guide looked at me as though I had asked an incomprehensible question. After he had recomposed himself he replied, "Of course, why would it not be on time?" He obviously had no concept of the English way of working, where nearly every large project was always months behind schedule!

Ireland

We travelled to Kilkenny on the ferry from Fishguard in South Wales to Rosslare on the southern tip of Ireland. The longest part of the trip was down to Fishguard from where we took the overnight ferry. We landed at 6 am and immediately noticed how mild the weather was compared to England; I think it could best be described as balmy. To our amazement there were palm trees growing everywhere, and another surprise came in the part of a cheerfully smiling customs officer who greeted us, not like the stony-faced ones we had to deal with when leaving the UK. He stamped our papers and cheerily said, "just park your lorry over there. The vet will want to have a quick look at your horses and then you can be on your way. He shouldn't be long, he knows y're here, so, get yerselves a cuppa tea and have a relax." True to his word a cheery vet appeared after a short while, popped his head inside the horsebox, counted the horses and commented that they looked a good bunch of "Osses", then signed our papers, and we were on our way, in less than half an hour, unlike the three to five hours we had to wait at Dover or Felixstowe when travelling to Belgium! However, we did find navigating a little difficult as most of the road signs were to Dublin, and that the distance to Dublin kept varying greatly, as did the distance to other places mentioned on the signposts. This mystery was solved later when our hosts explained that when the south joined the common market, they changed from miles to kilometres but to save money, they had kept all their old road signs only putting kilometres on new road signs. This also applied to speed limit signs as well. It was the Irish way of doing things we were told. We were to gradually learn that there was an Irish way of doing most things.

After a short stretch of new road from the docks, all marked in kilometres, our A road changed into what I would call a good B. Road in England and was mainly signposted in miles. Although it was only fifty odd miles it was very slow going with steep hills and very winding roads, and it took us over two hours to reach Kilkenny. As we ground our way up one of the steep hills at a snail's pace there was a sign saying "Slow, Road works ahead". We laughed as we really could not go any slower. As we rounded the next bend another sign stated that the roadworks was funded by the EU. This massive project turned out to be pile of gravel tipped at the side of the road and fenced off with reflective barriers; there was no sign of any work being carried out, in fact there was grass and weeds growing all over the pile of gravel suggesting that it had been there many months or even years! Our second experience of the Irish way, and we had only been in the country for one hour.

It turned out that the Confederation celebrations that we were part of, were to commemorate the three-hundred-and-fifty-year anniversary of the confederation of Kilkenny, which was an Irish parliament that governed Ireland between 1641and 1649. Nearly all the organising committee had some connection with horses so our stabling and all horse arrangements were excellent; it also turned out that a lot of them also owned pubs, hotels and nightclubs. This meant I had a very happy jousting troupe.

Our stables for this first trip were at the Deer Park on the edge of Kilkenny, less than a mile from the show ground, which was inside the grounds of Kilkenny Castle. They were first class stables and facilities; the owners were very friendly and couldn't do enough for us. The accommodation for the troupe was at the Glendine Inn at the opposite end of town, known locally as Brannigans after its owner Michael Brannigan who is now a good friend of twenty-five years standing. The accommodation was perfect for us; Michael was used to having stag parties and travelling sports supporters. Whenever he had a group booking, he would not take any other bookings even if he had spare accommodation, so that they could let their hair down without upsetting anyone. Fortunately, he afforded us the same privilege. Breakfast was when you woke up and the bar never really closed. I came down for breakfast one morning at about nine o clock to find Andy Ducker drinking a pint of Guinness at the bar. When I asked if he had already had breakfast, he just said "this is my breakfast".

The other very Irish thing about Brannigans was that he ran his own illicit, bookmaking service from behind the bar, and the racing channel was streamed into a small side bar. This was like heaven for my brother Stu.

Michael Brannigan was renowned for falling asleep behind the bar, so after he had gone to sleep, we just helped ourselves keeping a tab on what we had. Kick and Rush joined us on this first Irish trip and many others. On this first trip, we always finished the night with a sing- song. The news of this strange English group spread like wildfire through the town and by the second night the bar was heaving with partying Irish.

When we arrived in Kilkenny, the celebrations had already started and I was taken for a guided tour of the town by the lady who I had dealt with to set up the trip. As we walked down the street, it was heaving with revellers all in various states of inebriation; as we crossed John's Bridge there was a lady lying on the pavement completely unconscious, skirt up over her waist showing all her underwear. I felt dreadfully embarrassed for the town official showing me around, as it seemed that the whole town was drunk. When I enquired if we should help the unfortunate lady she flippantly replied" Oh no, she will be just fine! She's just having a wonderful time!"

Their generosity knew no bounds, everyone wanted to buy you a drink, and the lads soon discovered that wearing your jousting sweatshirt got you into nightclubs free of charge, often with a free drink as well. It was a time of newly-found freedom in Ireland and very akin to the swinging sixties that I had grown up in. We had a crazy taxi driver called Kevin who seemed to work 24 hrs a day; he knew all the best pubs and everyone in Kilkenny. One day driving through the centre on town, we asked him about the fabled illicit drink called poitín that the Irish made from potatoes. Our question was, if it was still made is there anywhere nearby, that we could taste it. He spun around in his driver's seat and loudly screamed "Jesus lads, have you never taste poitin! I have some in the boot I'll get it for you; you need to try it now!" We were halfway around a traffic island at this precise moment. Kevin slammed his brakes on and leapt out of the car, causing traffic to swerve and hoot loudly. He threw open his car boot and after much rummaging, and lot more horn tooting, he reappeared brandishing a plain bottle of clear liquid. "Here lads, will you take a pull on this." He thrust it into our hands, and then launched his taxi forward without any indication, causing more swerving and blaring horns, which was countered with rude hand gestures and verbal obscenities. The poitín hit your mouth like eating a hot chilli and burnt its way down to your stomach producing a warm glow throughout your body and in less than a minute, made your brain start to swim. Kevin looked over his shoulder grinning and said "Fecking great isn't it!" By the end of our first trip to Ireland, I was given the name of someone who could get me a bottle or two of the magic spirit, whispered with a nod and a wink.

The script for the show that we did in Kilkenny was altered as in Belgium, but this time it was our idea. Knowing the rivalry between the English and the Irish, we made the Black Knights Camp English and changed the Good Camp to local Irish names. The show went down a storm. We estimated that there was over 10,000 people in the audience and they loved the show, we had never had such an enthusiastic crowd but we also got some very strange reactions too. Our first show was on the Saturday afternoon and it was going very well with loads of cheering. I was commentating and about halfway through the show, I made an innocuous comment and everyone leapt to their feet waving and cheering. I was a bit bemused by this but put it down to language or cultural difference. However, it happened several more times during the show. I was now very confused so I asked Ray the guy who had supplied the sound system for us if he could explain the unexpected wild cheering. He just laughed and then explained that Kilkenny were playing in the All- Ireland Hurling Championship final in Dublin, and everyone in the crowd had brought transistor radios with them to listen to the match whilst watching the jousting. The wild cheering had nothing to do with the jousting, but because Kilkenny had scored. Kilkenny won the final, so there was an even bigger party that night in town. Ray, the sound system man, became a good friend of mine and my source of poitín! He has now progressed to having a very successful music bar called Mat the Millers, plus several other enterprises. I always look him up for a drink when I visit my other Kilkenny mates to this day, 25 years later…

In all the forty plus years of travelling with the jousting show we have never found so many kindred spirits for drinking and having fun. We have forged great friendships that have stood the test of time, and like a family the numbers have swelled over time expanding well outside the bounds of the jousting troupe.

The Ireland we knew in the early nineties has gone now. The EU and the Euro saw to that! I deeply regret I never went over with my father on his horse-buying trips so that I could have experienced more years of the old Ireland. But here are some of my recollections of those few last years of wonderful old Ireland.

On our first two trips, you could stand outside Brannigans, which is on the edge of Kilkenny on the Castlecomer road, and wait ten minutes to see a car come past and it would probably be an old beat-up Morris Oxford with a smokey exhaust. However, two years later, you would see a car about every ten seconds and it would probably be a Golf gti or a BMW.

On our first couple of trips if you were caught drunk driving, the Guardia would take your keys and drive you home; they even gave us lifts back to Brannigans as we staggered the mile or so back, from a night out in the town centre. These days the drink drive laws are stricter than England and they regularly hold road blocks and breathalyse everyone. Kevin, the taxi driver, found Harvey Broadhead staggering down the Waterford road at 6 am. When Kevin asked where he was going he said that he was heading back to Brannigans, whereupon Kevin informed him that he had walked three miles in the wrong direction and told him to get in the car. Kevin turned his car around and took him back to Brannigans free of charge.

To spread the cost of jousting, a lot of the big hotels and bars took it in turn to feed us at lunchtime or in the evenings. It was a fantastic way to get to know the different bars, restaurants and their owners. I personally made a lot of friends in Kilkenny this way. The first year, we got to know Eamon Langton who owned a pub called Langton's - a pub of the like I had never seen before. As you entered, you were faced with a cosy upmarket bar, however at the rear of the bar a corridor led onto a large glass panelled restaurant of unusual design. Walk further down the corridor and you could pay to enter a nightclub. None of us had seen anything like it anywhere else in the world. The most astounding thing though, was the range of clientele. In England, different generations would have their own clubs and bars. Here in Langton's, teenagers mixed happily with much older generations. One night in Langton's Night Club, I met a group of people in their late fifties happily sitting dressed in cavalry twill trousers, tweed jackets and ties, mixing effortlessly with the younger generations.

The other nightclub in town was Nero's, which was done out like a Roman villa. Like Langton's, it was attached to a restaurant and bar called Kyteler's, owned by John Flynn. The bar was reportedly the oldest pub in Kilkenny. John gave all the jousters free admission to Nero's, so this was the lads favoured haunt, although it was not to my liking as it was very hot, very crowded, and very loud; I was getting old!

As always when on tour we had to have an office and this was the Caisleán (castle) bar which happened to be the closest bar to the Castle grounds where we were performing, although as Stu chose it, I think it had more to do with its racing connections and its close proximity to a bookmaker's shop.

Another venue that fed us was the Club House Hotel; it was very different from the other venues. It was a lovely, old hotel with carpeted stairs and a quiet air that none of the others had. Unfortunately, we dined there in the evening after our first successful show so arrived rather drunk and noisy. Most of the clientele were well dressed in suits or jacket and tie, whilst our gang turned up in jeans and jousting sweatshirts. We were escorted upstairs to a dining room by a very well dressed waitress who kept looking over her shoulder with a worried look on her face; surely there must be a mistake? Could this unruly mob really be dining in the Georgian dining room? I think that was the only time we visited the Club House on our first visit but it would play a major part in our successive visits and its owner, Jim Brennan, along with his family, would become close, personal friends with my family. It is a friendship that continues stronger than ever, even to this day, but more about that later.

On that first trip, there was a lot of media presence and I was accosted by one of the organisers outside the castle bar, with a television presenter in tow. The organiser asked where I had been, as she had been looking everywhere for me. I explained that I had been doing a sound check and was now on my way for a pint of Guinness before starting the show. The organiser then said that she'd like to ask a big favour, would I do an interview for television instead? Knowing how pushy and self-important TV news presenters can be I said. "No problem. Let's do it now." To my amazement, the presenter said "he could not possibly interfere with a man and his glass of Guinness. Please go, relax and enjoy it." He would set up just inside the Castle gates and wait for me until I was ready. The Irish way again!

We did have one disaster during the show, but thankfully it was not too serious. Our erstwhile lorry driver Scots Jimmy was working the tape machine for the fanfares to enter with. Mine was the first as I entered as knight marshal. I waited and waited but no fanfare was forthcoming but I could see Jimmy getting more and more irate by the tape machine, so I abandoned my entrance to see what was wrong. As I arrived all Jimmy could say was - "It's not working Sam. It's not working!", in his strong, Glaswegian accent. By the time, I got to him, he had already stopped the tape so I rewound it back to the start and try and find the fault. I pressed the start button to see if the tape had jammed and to my horror, Jimmy's voice boomed out over the PA system

"Hey Sam, it's not working I canna get the fanfare ta work"

I thought that the tape machine was fool proof, as the play and record buttons had to be pressed simultaneously, and were split up by the rewind buttons, so it was a two-handed job to set the record mode into operation. How Jimmy had managed to do this we never found out, but my opening fanfare was lost for the whole tour. The lads found it hilarious as it added to the never-ending catalogue of funny mistakes Jimmy made. They played the recording repeatedly just to annoy Jimmy. Luckily, I stopped the tape before the full recording was broadcast to the audience as it included several strong swear words. Even when I had made a new tape the lads kept the old one to play at random times for amusement.

Our itinerary for the homeward journey was not ideal as we had to be at Rosslare Docks by 7 am at the latest, to complete the veterinary checks for the 9 am ferry. This meant departing from Kilkenny at 4.30 am. We had been asked by our hosts at the stables to leave the stables completely cleared out before leaving, so with the feeding, bandaging and mucking out, we needed to be at the stables for about 3 am .I knew that if the lads went to bed it would be a nightmare to get them up and going at that time in night, so against my better judgement and on their suggestion, I agreed to finish off this most successful trip with a mega party at Brannigans, both for the troupe and also all the many new friends we had made over the last few days. Kick and Rush agreed to play yet again and Michael Brannigan just said in his soft slow Irish drawl... "Urr can do whatteeverr urr like lads, it's beeen greaat having you".

Everyone packed and loaded their kit onto the bus for a quick getaway. Then after a farewell tour of as many of the one hundred or more pubs in Kilkenny as they could fit in, they returned to Brannigans about 10 pm to start really partying until we left for the stables at 2.30 am. We left Brannigans led by Kick and Rush playing us out and onto the Coach, cheered all the way by our lovely Irish friends. It was without doubt, the most emotional end to a tour ever. We all felt that we had joined a very special family.

When we arrived at the stables we split into two groups, those with horse experience fed and bandaged the horses ready for travel. The non-horsey lads mucked out the stables. These were simple jobs when you are sober but not so easy in the middle of the night after an eight-hour drinking session. The bandages were fumbled partway through bandaging a leg, and unrolled themselves across the stable floor. Re-rolling the bandage became a major test of coordination, and getting the bandage evenly overlapped so as not to cause pressure points on the leg tendons was a near miracle.

The mucking out section didn't fare much better. There were several near accidental stabbings with the muck forks, and many fallings over whilst wheeling overfilled wheelbarrows. One lad even launched himself off the top of the raised ramp into the muck heap below along with his wheelbarrow. It was some time before anyone noticed he was missing. Although it was dark outside with no lighting, dawn was just breaking by the time we were about to leave and someone noticed an upturned wheelbarrow in the muck heap and then a body sweetly snoring away in a drunken slumber. He didn't smell so sweetly on the two-and-a-half-hour coach trip to the docks. Scots Jimmy and I were driving the coach and horsebox, and although we had stopped drinking a couple of hours before setting off, we had not slept for about twenty hours, so with a day's drinking behind us were not really fit to drive, certainly not in England but this was Ireland so we did it "The Irish way"

About halfway through the journey to Rosslare docks, the sun was rising and driving conditions on the bendy Irish roads became easier, but it was then that I saw a signpost to New Ross which I remembered passing through on the way to Kilkenny. The road looked rather narrow but there was no indication as to where the road that we were on now went to. I shouted to my brother Stu, who was sitting behind me and was supposed to be helping me navigate, but who was in fact now sleeping soundly. After much shaking, he finally came around and I asked him if we should take this turn to New Ross (part of his brief when he did the pre-show visit was to check the route). When he was finally back in this world, he declared he had no idea as he had slept all the way back from Kilkenny to the docks. Our little convoy was nearly blocking the road and I had no wish to meet an early morning Garda patrol in my state, so we took the sign posted road. After a couple of miles, I knew we were wrong! The road narrowed to a single track with passing places and there was wild boggy-looking moorland either side. We were climbing up a steep hill that looked as if it might be a mountain. I wanted to turn around and go back to the other road but it was far too narrow even at the passing places for our large vehicles to turn around, so we soldiered on at a snail's pace, always upwards. My biggest worry was meeting another vehicle coming the other way, but at this hour of the morning it was thankfully very unlikely. We finally reached the summit of our climb and started to descend, which brought as many new problems as it solved. All the time I kept looking at my watch knowing we were running more and more behind schedule. After what seemed a life time in a barren landscape with absolutely no sign of life, we came across another solitary signpost pointing to New Ross. After several more painfully slow miles of deserted moorland, civilisation started to appear, and finally we found ourselves in a housing estate but with no idea where to go to next. It was at this moment of utter despair and panic that Lady Luck smiled on us in the form of a milkman. He, like ourselves, was astounded that we had driven a coach and horsebox over the mountain road. With true Irish hospitality, not only did he tell us how to find the Rosslare road, but stopped delivering his milk and guided us through the back streets of New Ross onto the main Rosslare road. I will be forever grateful to this kind and generous man.

We had less than an hour to get to the docks, and I was very unsure whether we would make it in time. It was some time before we came across a sign giving the mileage to the docks. It was not good news but if we got a clear run we might just make it. As hope started to grow, I think the adrenaline that had been pumping over the mountains dropped and I suddenly became extremely tired. I was so tired, that my neck muscles gave way and I kept drifting off to sleep for split seconds. I looked around to see if anyone could take over, but the whole bus was comatosed and I certainly didn't have any time to stop and wake anyone to take over. I slapped my face hung my head out of the window and sang loudly. Thankfully, after about fifteen minutes, that seemed more like an hour, the tiredness passed. Every signpost told the same story, we might just make it but now the traffic was starting to build. We finally rolled in five minutes late but as luck would have it the ministry vet hadn't arrived. We had made it!

On the ferry, everyone was suffering terrible hangovers. However, those of us who drank Guinness discovered the perfect cure; it was Guinness Export, sold in half pint bottles with a bright orange label. It had a silky-smooth taste and best of all it was eight percent proof. A genuine, "hair of the dog". The ferry trip was three and a half hours, so we able to have a good big fry-up and do some recovering before the long drive home.

I had made a lot of contacts during our first visit to Kilkenny and two seemed good prospects for further shows in the future. Lou and I decided to visit a Bronze Age living history site that was keen to do a history of Ireland festival. This was just outside Wexford, not far from Rosslare, and then we were to move onto Blarney Castle famous for the Blarney Stone that visitors kiss to gain the art of eloquence. The trip took place in the winter of 1992/93 and the plan was to take the overnight ferry to Rosslare do my two visits and stay near Blarney before moving up to Kilkenny and to have a day's hunting with the Kilkenny Hunt. The trip started very badly. About lunchtime on the day we were leaving I started to get a sore throat, by the time we boarded the ferry I was feeling dreadful and running a fever. All I wanted to do was lay down and sleep. We decided that we would book a cabin as soon as we got on board so that I could rest. Then we got our first shock; the ferry was a relief boat and didn't have any cabins, in fact it didn't have much of anything. To make matters worse there was a storm raging in the Irish Sea. During the voyage the boat would leap into the air and then come crashing down into the sea making a deafening booming noise. It was impossible to stay lying down on the bench seats at all as the boat bucked and rolled towards Rosslare. To make matters worse the heating wasn't working! I felt worse than shit by the time we landed. Both meetings proved to be a waste of time; however, I did get to kiss the Blarney Stone.

I concluded my business just after lunchtime and set off to find our hotel which was close to Blarney Castle. By this time lack of sleep and the bug I had caught were making me feel dreadful. All I wanted to do was to go to bed and sleep. To make matters worse, I had run out of the cold and flu tablets that had been keeping me going. We were in the middle of nowhere, with no idea where to find a chemist so headed straight to the hotel. The hotel was a no more than a pub with rooms and as this was the middle of winter I don't think that they had seen a tourist for several months. The room was freezing and the bed felt damp. Lou went downstairs to ask for the heating to be put on but was told it didn't come on until six o'clock as they were not used to guests arriving so early. However, she did notice that there was a cosy bar with a roaring fire downstairs. We decided to go to the bar and await the heating coming on. I had heard that most bars in Ireland served hot Toddies (for the uninitiated, a hot toddy consists of a large whisky, brown sugar, a wedge of lemon studded with cloves and topped up with boiling water). Thankfully this bar specialised in them. After an afternoon of hot toddies, I staggered up to bed as soon as the heating came on. Almost immediately I fell into a delirious sleep and boy did I sweat!

We had been accompanied on this trip by John Cook, my good friend and racing mentor. Our plan was to drive up to Kilkenny after my meetings and all go fox hunting with the Kilkenny Hunt. Michael Brannigan had arranged everything for us including the hire of horses, but my participation in this event was looking highly unlikely. Next morning the fever had broken and although very weak I was feeling much better. After we arrived in Kilkenny, it was a quiet afternoon with me showing Lou and John the around the town. By evening I was sure I would be fit enough to hunt next day.

The day's hunting was like nothing any of us had experienced in our long English hunting careers. We returned to Brannigans that night, faces covered in dried blood from numerous bramble scratches and having jumped so many terrifying obstacles, which before that day, I would have deemed unjumpable by any horse. I was addicted, and returned as often as I could afford it for the next twenty years!

We returned to do another joust the next year by popular demand and the format was basically the same. There were two minor changes, the first was our stabling which was at a racing farmer's yard near Gowran Park race track, and the other was that the jousting arena was moved from the far end of the Castle park to much closer to the Castle, making it much easier to access from the town.

Stuart and I came over with the horses on the overnight ferry on the Wednesday arriving in Rosslare at 6 am Thursday morning. We quickly cleared the docks and so on our way making good time, as this time I had purchased a good road atlas of Ireland. The road to Gowran was much more direct and we arrived in the village just before 8 am. We had hardly slept at all on the ferry as we had found some enthusiastic Irish drinking partners in the ferry bar. By the time, we reached Gowran, our mouths were like the bottom of a parrot's cage, so we decided to stop and ask directions to the farm, and see if we could find a café to have a cup of tea and hopefully some breakfast. We parked the lorry outside a large pub painted black with beautiful scrolling gold writing that announced, "Thomas Kavanagh Imbibing Emporium", which I think is the best description of a pub I have ever seen. We wandered around the sleepy village but with no sign of a café anywhere. Eventually we found a post office, ideal for directions and local knowledge. The farm was only a couple of miles up the road but we were not expected for at least another hour. Having gained directions, we were then quizzed about our life history (a normal occurrence to any stranger in Ireland) by the Postmaster. The post office didn't sell any snacks or soft drinks so having finished our CV's I enquired if the was anywhere nearby where we could buy something to drink. The Postmaster replied

"Jesus lads it's a bit early for that, but if you're that desperate you could try around the back of Kavanagh's pub. There's some stairs at the back, if the door is open at the top they will be cleaning. Tell them I sent you and they will fix you up with a quick one". I explained that we were thinking more of tea or a soft drink not an alcoholic drink, and he directed us to a paper shop on the Kilkenny to Carlow road.

Most of the lads arrived the next day in the coach and the usual group of self-employed arrived about 9:30 pm the evening before the first show. The shows went well with huge crowds again. When the last show finished, we had to pack all the kit so it was quite late and almost time for our evening meal. I sent Jimmy off with the horses back to Goran which was about a 45-minute round trip by the time the horses had been unloaded. We were being fed on that evening by Kyteler's and we expected him to be a few minutes late for the meal but had warned the kitchen and it was not a problem but by the time we had finished our second course I was getting worried.

Jimmy had broken down on the way back from the farm in the middle of nowhere and had to walk back to the farm to contact us (still no mobile phones). By the time we found out, the light was fading so there was nothing we could do that night. It was lucky we had decided to stay an extra day before going home. Early next day, my son Mark, who was fifteen and on his first trip to Ireland, accompanied me to the dead horsebox. We found it on a narrow lane and on a blind bend. Not the best place to breakdown. Luckily, we had a full set of tools and overalls and it wasn't long before we discovered that it was a fuel problem. I was very aware that Jimmy would have tried to restart the lorry several times and that the battery could be dangerously low. Luckily, I had replaced the battery with a new one at the beginning of the season. I thought it would be a simple job of changing the fuel filter. Again, carrying a spare with us paid dividends, but having fitted the new filter we still didn't have fuel although we had plenty in the fuel tank. I traced the fuel line back and found another filter this with a glass bowl and a gauze filter. To my relief this was well and truly "gunged up". After cleaning this I thought our problems were over, but no; after endlessly working the lift pump by hand to purge the system of air we still didn't have any fuel. It finally dawned on me that the core problem was the fuel tank itself. I had never taken a tank off before but with the help of a bit of hose pipe and an empty five-gallon oil drum, we siphoned the fuel out of the tank and then removed the tank. We took it back to the farm and flushed the tank out. To our horror, it was full of dead leaves and I knew exactly how they got there. During the shows, the horsebox had been parked under some lovey big old trees and around the base was a thick bed of old leaves. We had been plagued over the show days by a group of very scruffy young Tinker children who hung around the vehicles. We were forever chasing them away, but as soon as your back was turned they were back again swearing and hurling abuse at us, along with the odd stick or stone. The Castle Warden warned us that they would steal anything they could lay their hands on. I was sure that leaves in the fuel tank was their revenge, as it was a well-known dirty trick amongst country folk.

By the time, we had flushed out the fuel tank it was about 1 pm and Mark was desperate to get back to join the lads, who were being taken on a trip out on the coach to some more remote country pubs, so I took him back to Kilkenny as he had more than earned a bit of fun. I was quite confident that I could now finish the job on my own. I skipped lunch and worked on and by 3:30 pm the lorry was up and running. It was about 4 pm when I got back to Brannigans, filthy, covered in black grease and stinking of diesel. My plan was a hot shower, a couple of quiet pints, followed by a very good late lunch! I wandered into the bar feeling relaxed after a long hot shower wondering of what I could do to make the most of my well-earned afternoon of freedom. I was about to order a Guinness, but the barmaid beat me to it. "Mr Brannigan needs to speak with you. It's urgent! I'll get him". My heart sank. What on earth had happened. Michael sauntered though to the bar smiling and announced "I'm to take u to Kells to drive the bus home. They're all too drunk to drive".

I was not amused, I had just spent 7 hours lying on my back covered in grease and diesel, whilst they were off enjoying themselves, and Jimmy the Driver who I was paying to drive, had irresponsibly got drunk, dropping me right in it. If I had not stopped for a drink in Brannigans, I too would have been unfit to drive very quickly once I hit town. It was a good twenty minutes' drive to Shirley's Bar in Kells. During the drive, and with the help of Michael's slow Irish drawl I slowly calmed down. We arrived at Shirley's Bar to be greeted by the sound of Hippy Steve's washboard playing and loud singing, my fifteen-year-old son looked like a grinning snake as tried to say a slurred "Hello Dad", and slipped fluidly off a bar stool onto the floor. Jim Brennan, owner of the Club House Hotel, came up to me and said it was all his fault that they were in such a mess, and not to blame the lads. Mark and his two mates, Tom Arris and Jamie Tom, who were of a similar age, were so bladdered that they could hardly stand let alone walk. Kells was a lovely sleepy village in the middle of nowhere and I have visited Shirley's Bar on many occasions since with Jim Brennan, often after hunting, sitting in front of the roaring coal fire chatting to the locals.

I had hoped to drive the bus straight back to Kilkenny but Jim said there was one more pub we had to visit before returning to Kilkenny, and that I would love it. The pub was called O'Gorman's and apparently was very special. It was so special that Michael Brannigan said he would have to drive on ahead and see if we would be allowed in. He didn't say it, but I think it might have had something to do with us being English. I drove the bus down a narrow lane, so narrow that the bus filled the whole lane. I kept praying that we wouldn't meet another vehicle coming the other way. What we did meet was a herd of cattle being herded along by an elderly man in a faded bib-and-brace overall. We slowly chugged along behind him at a snail's pace until they turned into a farm yard that had a small cottage at its entrance with a peeling sign on its side saying "O'Gorman's". I drove the bus hard into the hedge opposite the farm gateway allowing cars to squeeze by and was met by Michael Brannigan, who said were going to be allowed in but we must calm down and be quiet. Mark and co were banned and told to stay on the bus. Jamie Tom had been sick on the bus and the lads told them in no uncertain terms that it must be cleared up by the time they returned. The bar was so small that we could not all fit in, it was big enough for about ten people, fifteen at a squeeze. The seating was a plank of wood balanced on two, rusting five-gallon oil drums. There was a shelf that held an array of canned food which seemed to have been there for some time and were showing signs of rusting, the only thing out of place with this 1920s look was dozens of bright red packets of Marlborough cigarettes which just didn't fit in with the rest of the shabby bar. Someone commented that nobody had seen Marlborough cigarettes on sale anywhere else in Ireland. Behind the bar stood a fearsome old lady, you just knew you had to behave! The bar was so small that some of us had to stand outside in the yard. The gent's toilet was the crew yard complete with thirty odd cattle. The Ladies toilet was in a small stable just across the yard. The toilet itself, consisted of a five-gallon oil drum with its top cut off and a toilet seat balanced on top. There was no lock on the door, but the fearsome old lady accompanied every lady using her salubrious facilities, standing outside on guard arms tightly folded. The old lady was soon joined by the farmer we had seen herding the cattle down the road. He set to pulling pints of Guinness still dressed in his bib-and-brace overalls complete with, still steaming cow shit! Environmental Health the Irish way!

Whilst this collage of old Ireland played out there was another drama playing on the bus involving the drunken teenagers. Whilst they were trying to clean up Jamie's mess, he was sick again, but thankfully this time into the hedge-bottom. Jamie was then desperate for a drink of water. Not daring to show their faces in the pub, Tom set off with an empty litre pop bottle to find water in the farmyard; he searched everywhere but could not find a tap. He finally found a water trough in the cattle crew yard. However, it was not a conventional water trough fed by mains water; it was a metal beer barrel cut in half and the two halves sunk into the manure. I can describe them in such detail as I observed them whilst relieving myself. There was a shiny film on top of the water, probably cow saliva, the odd dead fly, and some straw floating around as well for good measure. Having failed to find a tap; Tom filled his empty bottle from the above described trough. Jamie apparently guzzled it down with relish, fortunately he was immediately sick again. At this moment, we all arrived back at the bus, and heard the tale with horror, rushing back to the bar to get bottled water for Jamie to wash his mouth out. Thankfully except for a hangover, Jamie didn't have any adverse effects. Just another normal day at the office!

The following year we performed our Robin Hood Show which we had developed so successfully for the Robin Hood Pageants in Nottingham. It is the only time that we have performed this show abroad and we were not sure how it would go down. We need not have worried. The story of Robin Hood was just as well known in Ireland and I now believe this to be true in many other countries around the World. Where ever I go in the world, and say that I come from Nottingham, I get one of two replies; either "Ah, Robin Hood" or "Ah, Nottingham Forest football ".

Not only did we do the show, but the lads came up with a new idea of Hunt the Outlaw. Robin and his men would hide in the woodland inside the castle grounds. The Sheriff and his Knights would enlist the help of the children of Kilkenny to capture Robin. The hunt was advertised on the jousting posters and we were amazed when a small army of children turned up for the hunt. The script was very simple; Robin and his men would creep up and indicate to the children not to tell the Sheriff and then capture one of the sheriff's knights. The children quickly understood the game; one by one the Sheriff's men were captured and the hapless Sheriff never even noticed. The final act was that Robin appears before the Sheriff, who then orders the children to capture him. They, of course, now work for Robin, overpower the Sheriff and tie him to a tree leaving him in the woods shouting for help. Unfortunately, we had not anticipated the enthusiasm of the children; they set upon the Sheriff like a pack of wolves thumping and kicking him. They were not doing severe damage so Robin and the Outlaws encouraged them, and telling them to tie him to the tree. In a flash, they had him bound to the tree and were now beating him with sticks and even quiet sizeable logs. The Sheriff was now screaming for help and Robin and his Outlaws had to step in and rescue the Sheriff! Not the end we had planned! The poor Sheriff was really battered and bruised from the onslaught, another few seconds and I think he would have been a hospital case.

By the third tour, the Humphrey family and Brennan family had become great friends and I took both my children Mark and Emma over to spend time with Jim's children, Ian and Michelle, who were of similar ages. This was the cementing of our friendship, but it also came close to ending it as well. Michelle was the eldest, followed by Mark, then Ian, and then Emma. Mark and Michelle were sixteen, Ian fifteen and

Emma fourteen. One evening Kick and Rush were playing in Brannigans bar so the whole jousting troupe was there including Mark and Emma. Michele, however, had been grounded by Jim for coming home late the previous night, so wasn't present. Michelle however, was a very strong willed young lady had other thoughts, so she climbed out of her bedroom window and then shinned down the drainpipe to join the others. I knew nothing of this until Jim arrived to apprehend his runaway daughter. I had no problem with underage drinking and would rather them feel comfortable drinking in my presence than secretly with a gang of other kids. Jim, however, held very different views and exploded when he caught Michelle with a half of lager in her hand. I tried to intervene and explained that both my children had beers as well, but they were being very responsible, and that I was keeping a close eye on them all the time. We had a standoff with our views for about five minutes, but with the help of Michael Brannigan and other jousters, we finally won him around. The compromise was that Jim would stay for a short while to watch the band and then take Michelle home. I seem to recall it was quite a long time once Jim got into the party mood.

Jim Brennan is a marvellous host, and this shows in the warm welcome you always receive at his hotel, called The Club House Hotel, which is situated just a few hundred yards from the town centre. After our first three big events Jim organised all the other events himself, and accommodated us in his lovely hotel, feeding and watering us very generously. The Club House had originally been a Gentleman's Club for wealthy fox-hunters visiting this excellent hunting area. Kilkenny held the same status during the 1800's as Melton Mowbray, being a Mecca for the fox hunting aristocracy. One aristocrat is on record for riding his horse up the stairs of the

Club House and into the Georgian dining room which is on the first floor, and then jumping a large fire guard for a bet. The dining room is small and intimate so this would have been a stunning feat of horsemanship.

Although this incident is not directly associated with jousting, it gives an insight as to what it is like to visit Ireland and have Jim Brennan as your host.

Lou and I were doing our weekly shop one evening in Sainsbury's when the phone rang. It was Jim asking if we fancied coming over tomorrow, as he was sponsoring a race at Gowran Park. We were somewhat surprised so told him we would call him later when we had time to study our diaries. At first, we both agreed it was crazy, but by the time we reached home it was a possibility, and another hour further on we had rearranged our schedule and booked flights for the following evening. When we called back, Jim had already made plans. Besides a day at the races he had already booked a table on the night of our arrival. This was at a new restaurant in Thomas Town, some twenty minutes south of Kilkenny. He had also arranged a morning's cub hunting for me before going to the races, so I was to bring my hunting clothes. We landed in Dublin about 7 pm, hired a car and then drove down to Thomas Town, arriving at about 9:45 pm, which was later than we had anticipated. To arrive at a country restaurant in England at that time and expect to be fed was nigh on impossible. We were ravenously hungry and very worried that we had missed our meal. When we arrived, we were relieved to find Jim had informed the restaurant we would be late, everyone had ordered except us so as soon as we had chosen from the menu they were ready to go. We were joined by Patricia's sister Kitty and her husband, who had also just arrived for a quick visit from Spain where they now lived. We left the restaurant full of food, wine, and brandy. It then dawned on us that we had a twenty-minute drive along treacherous winding roads back to Kilkenny. To make matters worse it was foggy. Halfway into the drive, the guiding lights of Jim's car vanished leaving us on a road we had never driven on before and no signposts to guide us. We finally made it to Jim's house just after 1am to be informed that we needed to be up at 5 am to go Cubbing. So, after barely four hours sleep I was trundling along in a Land Rover and trailer towards county Tipperary. About 9 am I was on the top of a mountain, taking in the breath-taking views and solitude, when my phone unexpectedly started to ring, completely spoiling the moment. It was a girl from the BBC costume department wanting my measurements for a forthcoming job we were about to do. There were some measurements that I didn't know off hand such as my arm length so I told her I would phone her back tomorrow. At this point she became very self-important, restating that she was calling from the BBC and they were not in the habit of waiting for actor's measurements! Knowing how left wing and anti-hunting most BBC staff are it gave me immense pleasure to inform her that at this precise moment in time I was sitting on a horse on top of a mountain in Ireland hunting foxes and didn't have a tape measure to hand so she would just have to wait until I returned home tomorrow!

While I was away hunting, Lou was catching up on her sleep. Later in the morning Jim took her to see the future Brennan family home which was a very large but dilapidated Georgian country house set in twenty to thirty acres of parkland. Lou was then taken on a sightseeing, stroke shopping trip, and to look at a potential hunting horse for me. before meeting us for lunch at a restaurant in Kilkenny. The horse was owned by Pat Loughlin who was a Horse Dealer, Publican, and Undertaker. This seems to be a strange combination of vocations to the

English but certainly the Publican and Undertaker often go hand in hand in Ireland. It's a complete service burial and wake all under the same roof. Lou told me about the horse over lunch and it sounded quite promising so I brought along my riding clothes to try the horse after the races. The races involved more eating and drinking than racing, but it was some great "crack" as most of Kilkenny seemed to be there. To make things even better Lou won a Waterford Crystal vase in the raffle.

It was nearly dark when we arrived at Pat's pub. I had changed in the back of the car into my riding clothes so, as to waste no time. After a quick look, over the horse, Pat had him trotted up for us straight up and down the middle of the village Main Street in the now fading light. Thankfully only one car appeared and patiently waited for us to complete the trotting up process. By the time, I had ridden the horse it was pitch black. The big problem I now had was that I had not come to Ireland with the intention of buying at horse. The highly efficient, Irish bush telegraph had heard I was visiting and Pat had contacted Patricia to say that he had a horse that might suit me. Again, it was Jim who showed what a great friend he is by casually saying in the car on the way to look at the horse, "Don't worry about the money, I'll pay Pat you can pay me next time we meet up"

I bought the horse and named him Connolly which was the name of Pat's pub or to be more accurate his pub is called Connolly's. We of course had to have a couple of drinks to seal the deal before leaving.

After visiting several more pubs we finally ended up in Langton's nightclub. Leaving Langton's became a problem. It was after midnight and we had to leave at 5 am to drive back to Dublin Airport. The problem was our hosts had stolen our car keys to prevent us from leaving the party. After much argument and pleading we finally got the keys, but once again, it was nearly 2 am before we got to bed. So, for the second night running we had less than three hours' sleep. We had planned to work on our return to Bunny Hill but fell into bed about 11 am and didn't wake up until 5pm. That was a day out with Jim Brennan!   The best, but we have had many others of a similar ilk.

Although we only performed in Ireland for five years, the friends and business relationships we made over there remain extremely strong. I don't think a year has gone by since 1993 when some members of the troupe or people from Kilkenny have not been visiting one another. During those five years, we saw the next generation start to make its impact on shows and the social side of the troupe.

The key members of this next generation were Edward Kopel, Tom Arris, and my son Mark. They re-invigorated the shows and the camaraderie of the troupe. During one of our last official trips to Kilkenny, they were in their late teens and early twenties. In the Club House Hotel after a show, they were challenged by Pete Webster (Satan), who was our unofficial entertainments manager, to a tequila drinking competition in the hotel bar. The bar was packed, and everyone was chanting and cheering on the contestants.

The Tequila shots were ceremonially brought forth on a silver platter, and on the count of three, necked in one gulp. Satan let out his famous Lion roar and shouted "another" bringing a spontaneous cheer from the crowd, as the challenge was laid down. After each shot, Pete roared again and laid down the challenge, glaring straight into his challenger's eyes. As the contest progressed, the chanting grew louder and more rhythmic. All the contestants had consumed four or five pints before the contest, so when they reached tequila number six, Satan turned to me and said, "I've got to hand it to the young lads, they can certainly hold their drink, I'm getting a bit wobbly and they all look fine" After two or three more Satan reluctantly threw in the towel and conceded victory to the younger generation. He staggered away shaking his head muttering, "I don't know how they drank that much and are still standing. I must be getting old".

What Satan didn't know was that the younger generation only drank two shots, and then had their glasses fill with Irish red lemonade, which looked identical to the tequila gold that Satan was drinking. Shortly after the drinking competition, Jim took Stuart and Satan to Dublin Airport which was a four-hour round trip. When they arrived at the airport, Jim told Satan about the trick the younger lads had played on him in the tequila drinking competition. Mark received a text from Satan which simply said, "You bastards! I'm going to kill you." This provided much joy among the perpetrators.

After Jim left for the Airport, his wife Patricia offered to take us out on the town. We decided on a quiet night; find some bars we had never been in, and hopefully find some Irish music. We were all tired after the travelling and performing, so we slowly worked our way up Johns Street from bar to bar. Halfway up the street we passed The Perch Bar and Patricia commented, that was one bar in Kilkenny you really didn't want to go in. So, she was horrified, when we informed her that we had already spent a night in there. I can only remember two things about The Perch Bar. Firstly, it had an old fashioned, English public telephone that used old pre-decimal English pennies, that you had to purchase from behind the bar to make a call. The phone had A and B buttons that you pressed, A for answer and B to get your money back if nobody answered. I believe they became obsolete around the mid-sixties in Britain! The second thing I remember was that it was raided by armed Policemen. I don't know why it was raided but we were held for some time, as the last thing they had expected, was to find was a group of English lads complete with their own band, Kick and Rush, singing merrily away with the rather dubious locals. They eventually let us go, but we're still very confused as to why they were there in the first place.

We finally found a bar at the top of Johns street that had a very good Irish band playing, and settled there for the evening. The band were very good but it soon became clear that that both the band and audience had strong IRA sympathies. Towards the end of the evening, I had to swap my drink from Guinness to gin and tonic, as after seven hours drinking pints of the black stuff I was well and truly full to the brim. I knew it was a dangerous gambit as Irish single measures are equivalent to double an English measure, but hey-ho, it was almost closing time. What I had not factored in was the arrival of Jim Brennan, who had not had a drink all day due to his driving duties, and was now in overdrive, catch up mood. We lamely protested that we were tired, and had already drunk our fill, but it fell on deaf ears. After two more in the music pub, we then stood to attention for the republican anthem, which the band played at closing time. It was a very, uncomfortable moment and brought home to me that there was a section of the Irish population that still had a strong hatred of the British. It prompted me to research the history of Ireland and it made very uncomfortable reading. After leaving the pub, I thought that might be the end of the drinking session, but oh no. Jim announced we were off to a new nightclub owned by his friend Pious Phelan. Jim was known everywhere in Kilkenny and when we arrived at the club, the doorman greeted him with "good evening Mr Brennan" and waved us all in free of charge. I spent the next three hours dodging drinks and trying not to fall over. I remember holding onto to a hand rail thinking I can't manage to drink anymore, when I heard the DJ. announcing that the bar had closed and this was the last record he was playing. All I wanted to do was crash into my bed as we had a 5.30 am breakfast booked and a long drive to Dublin Airport. It was now 3 am, so I thanked Jim for a wonderful day and bade him good night. "Oh, no you don't, we're off to the private bar for a lock-in. The night is young". It was a beautiful little bar packed with after-hours drinkers, which was great as after one more drink, I managed to escape without being noticed and stagger back through the deserted streets back to the Club House Hotel.

My alarm woke me at 5.15 am after just two hours' sleep. I was still feeling very drunk. I ran a very, hot bath to try and sweat some of the alcohol out of my system. I then went to wake Mark and Edward who were sharing a room; both were renowned, heavy sleepers. I arrived at their room to find Mark curled up like a cat on the windowsill of the stained-glass window, that was opposite his room. When I shook him to try and wake him he fell off the windowsill with a crash onto the floor which sort of woke him. After much hammering on their bedroom door I finally woke Edward who was in the same incoherent state. The only slurred words I could get out of either of them were "tequila" and "Patricia." I eventually got them down for breakfast and some strong coffee. Thankfully, we had all packed the previous day so all we had do was get in the car and go.

As I looked across the breakfast table I saw that Mark had slumped, face down into his breakfast. At first I thought he was asleep but then I noticed movement, his nose was touching his breakfast but he was slowly and carefully trying to saw through his soft fried, egg yolk, unsuccessfully with an upside-down knife. After a painfully slow breakfast, I finally got them both into the car and set off for Dun Laoghaire docks situated on the south-east edge of Dublin, to catch the fast HSS ferry back to Holyhead in Anglesey. We had only gone 400 yards and were just crossing John's Bridge when Mark started to regurgitate his breakfast out of the car window! He continued until we reached the train station at the top of the street, a full quarter of a mile further on. There was a petrol station open on the edge of Kilkenny and we pulled in to wash down the car and the hire tow-a-van before proceeding. My passengers then slept all the way to the ferry terminal. I, didn't have such a blissful trip, as a Garda patrol car pulled in behind me and followed me all the way to the town of Carlow, some 40 minutes away. I was sure he was going to pull me over and I was sure I could smell the alcohol on the nervous sweat that had formed on my brow. It was a long thirty miles but thankfully he turned off just as we entered the town. When we were on the ferry, I lost Mark and Ed, but eventually found them playing on two game machines. I was astounded that they had the mental co-ordination to play them with such monumental hangovers. They later said that they were not actually playing the games but just hanging onto the handles to stand up. They slept all the way from Holyhead to Bunny hill and were almost fully recovered by the time we got home. I was totally knackered as they were supposed to be sharing the driving. The reason for Mark and Ed's demise was that after I left the Kilford Arms, they challenged Patricia to a proper tequila drinking competition. We learnt much later that Patricia was ill for several days after the "Tequila Night"

Although that was the last public show we performed in Kilkenny, we did return to perform at Jim's daughter,

Michelle's wedding. We performed on borrowed horses, to the wedding guests in the paddock, adjacent to the family home. It was something we were all proud to do. This party lasted for over four days!

America and Canada

As I mentioned earlier when I took the call from James Zopie in November 1996, I turned down the offer of working in Colorado, and taking part in a real jousting competition for money.

The reasons were many and complicated. The main reason was that I was burnt out and didn't have the energy or desire to take on another big, very risky project. Mum and Dad had retired at the beginning of the nineties and I had to re-mortgage our house to buy the business. Taking over the sole running of the business was a great strain on both Lou and me. This was compounded by me being away on foreign tours and the addition of many TV and filming contracts, that took me away for much longer than the tours. I was also having a lot of trouble getting the lads to take on foreign tours as they too had family and business commitments. Many of them could only spare the weekend to fly out, do the show and fly back again, to be back at work for the start of the working week. Probably the biggest problem was that our insurers had refused to insure us for foreign trips and had served notice that they were not going to take on our public liability insurance for the next season. This was nothing to do with anything we had done, but the was consequences of the

Lloyd's crash, which resulted in insurers pulling out of any perceived, risky business. We were to suffer the same problems with the Riding School business and it was an enormous stress right through the first decade of the new millennium. Without public liability insurance, you cannot trade!

As I spoke to James Zopie, I knew it would be impossible to get public liability for such a risky business, but I knew there would probably be a few individuals who might want to take up the challenge, so I gave him Phil's number as he was the most senior jouster, and the one most likely to want to test himself against the Americans and Canadians. To my surprise, Phil agreed to go, and raised a full team to compete. Insurance was still a big problem, but after much searching, Lou managed to find an extreme sports insurer who was willing to offer personal accident insurance if anyone were injured. All the contestants signed waivers against the other contestants to cover severe injury, or even death whilst jousting. My legal friends in Britain told me that they were not worth the paper they were written on under UK law but were unsure about American or Canadian law. They were all taking a huge risk, and as the prize money was many thousands of dollars, everyone was going to be hitting as hard as they could.

The team, which included some squires had all their flights, car hire, and hotel expenses paid for. Any winnings were pooled and shared by the whole team. It was the first trip to Canada, that the lads had a stretch-limo provided for them. I know they loved that and had great fun with it.

From 1997 until 2000 the team went every year in September to Estes Park to compete at the Longs Peak Scottish Highland games, and in 2000 they were invited to compete in Canada by the Canadian team. The venue was near Toronto at a place called London. The following year the lads asked me if I would like to go and do some commentating in Canada. I was honoured to be asked as I knew how proud they were of doing these trips off their own back. I had just had my fiftieth birthday, which was a bit of a milestone, and I always fancied looking at Canada, so I said yes!

It was a budget flight from Manchester to Toronto and then about an hour's drive to a small town called Orangeville. The competition took place at fair grounds, where they hold livestock sales or have equestrian activities, such as rodeo. We stayed in a motel/conference centre that was surrounded by forest. The town of Orangeville was about five miles from the fair grounds. The Canadians were very different to the Americans we had met; much more social and they loved to drink beer that had a decent amount of alcohol in it, unlike the weak, cat's piss that you get in America.

I couldn't wait to see this real competitive jousting. They had two sections in the competition, light armour and heavy armour. The light armour section wore chainmail or in our case, theatrical mail that was lacquered knitted string, that offered no protection at all. The heavy armour section was full plate armour. The biggest difference between the two disciplines was with the light armour you aimed at the opponents shield, whereas with heavy armour, you aimed at the body. The first time I saw a heavy armour joust it took my breath away to see the wooden lances shattering on the opponent's body, but after watching it for several hours it became boring….

Our style of jousting was very different to the Americans and Canadians. We were lightweight riders on fast, lightweight horses. Our opponents all weighed in at over 20 stone and rode slow, lumbering, cart horses. Their riding skills were below ours and they needed rails either side of the lists to keep their horses straight and stop them from running out. Many of their horses, although supposedly fully trained, failed to start and had to be led in by squires. Many contestants could not even turn their horses around at the end of the lists without help from a squire. Our lads, on the other hand rode hired local horses which had never jousted in their lives. They hurtled down the tilt at a gallop and had spun around at the end, and were ready to charge again before their opponents had managed to pull up! Our opponents lowered their lances at the start of the run, whilst our Knights dropped their lances at the last moment and twisted to hit them side on instead of head on. The differences in style was like American football is to English rugby. It caused endless arguments and blighted the competitions in both America and Canada. To prove a point, Phil borrowed a suit of heavy plate armour and rode against the current champion. Phil had never ridden in full plate before and never jousted in this discipline. After two brutal strikes shattering lances on each other's bodies, Phil cleanly unseated the champion. The champion was very magnanimous and took the microphone to congratulate Phil and stated that it was the hardest anyone had ever hit him in his life.

Unlike in the UK where we did two forty-five minute shows, this went on for most of the day, five or six hours. There were two other commentators as well as myself and it was our job to try and make things exciting and entertaining for the spectators. We didn't really commentate very much but acted more like the football pundits on British television talking about the background of each knight and his horse. By the end of the tournament, after talking five to six hours every day, we had all lost our voices.

The highlight of the day was the medieval games. Although slightly different from our games, our lads really excelled at them. There was a medley of games that was timed and Phil brought the audience alive with his astonishing, full gallop speed halving the fastest time. It was a fantastic display of horsemanship bringing the audience to their feet cheering and clapping. I was saddened by the amount of back biting and quite frankly mardy behaviour of our friends from across the pond. The east coast knights didn't like the west coast knights or the Canadians, and that was a mutual feeling across the board. They all took it very seriously and in the main were trying to make a living from jousting competitions. Then we came along drinking, partying pranksters who just didn't give a shit. Worst of all they didn't understand our sense of humour, so we were always upsetting someone.

The other jousters seemed to live a puritanical existence; hardly any of them drank and most were religious; their religious views varied greatly depending on where they hailed from. We however, soon found a lively bar in Orangeville which we frequented most nights. Pete's latest strange, party trick of the moment was to squeeze the juice of an orange over a woman's feet and then lick it off! To make matters worse the feet had to be unwashed! This strange behaviour was loved by the Canadians and a large cheering crowd quickly developed in the bar whenever he performed his ritual and a line of eager ladies all wanting their feet to be licked. Demand was so high Pete had to make a trip to the supermarket to buy more oranges.

The lads were invited all over the place, and some went out to a posh country club. As they left, they decided to take a short cut across the extensive lawns rather than following the long winding drive. It was only when they came to a sand bunker that they realised they were on a golf course, luckily, they were in a four-wheel drive!

A little further on they came across a dead raccoon on the road and for some unknown reason decided to bring it back to the hotel, where in true jousting madness they sat the dead raccoon in a chair, bought it a beer and talked to it as if it was one of them whilst they drank and played table tennis with some astonished young locals until the early hours. Phil and I had rooms with an interconnecting bathroom. The idea was that I could keep an eye on him in case he had an epileptic fit. We had both gone to bed long before this gang returned. Sometime in the middle of the night there was a knock on my door! It was a couple of the lads who said they just wanted to check Phil was alright but didn't want to wake him. I had been in a deep sleep so let them in and fell straight back to sleep. Next morning, I had forgotten all about their visit until the bathroom door burst open, followed by Phil in a terrible rage threatening to kill me. Apparently, they had brought "Rac" as they called him and put him in bed with Phil, all tucked nice and warm. The first thing Phil saw when he opened his eyes was a racoon with its teeth bared, staring at him just a few inches from his face. There was also the smell and the fleas to contend with. As usual Pete and Wicksey were prime suspects and everyone except for Phil, has it as number one in the list of best pranks ever played!

The same year I got my first invite to join them on their annual trip to Estes Park, Colorado. I've always had a love hate relationship with America. The scenery is stunning and so varied, but America is not at all like the America portrayed by Hollywood. It doesn't seem to have a soul like European countries. Tremendous poverty and bigotry is hidden by its glitzy image. This is my own opinion and maybe I just chose the wrong states to visit, but I have been to West Virginia, North Carolina, Colorado, Florida, and passed through Virginia, Tennessee, Ohio, and New York. Then again maybe I just like to look behind the scenes.

To say my first trip to Colorado was eventful would be a massive understatement! The lads always spoke of Denver and Estes park as if they were one of the same and as I was going as an ancillary I didn't do the usual detailed research I would have done if I had been in charge. Also, they had been their many times before. The event was always held during the second week in September. My only research was to lookup the weather for Denver which was 90deg F with high humidity, so it seemed sensible to travel in a T-shirt, shorts and sandals. Like the trip to Canada I had no responsibilities so I could, in theory, relax and enjoy the trip. However, the truth is I have never discovered how to relax.

 We had a good trip to Heathrow and arrived ahead of schedule and were directed to a group check-in, where we collected our tickets. When they called out Sam Humphrey I never gave it a thought until the check-in clerk looked at my passport and said I must have picked up the wrong ticket. Although I have been called Sam since I was four years old my real name is Mervyn as was in my passport. I tried to explain that it was my stage name, but no, I could not travel on a ticket that didn't match my passport. To complicate matters further the tickets had been purchased by the organisers in Colorado. After much waiting and talking to various airline officials they came up with a solution. If we could get in touch with the original purchaser of the ticket, then they could change the name on the ticket. Luckily, we had that on file. The next major problem was making contact as it was 4am in Colorado and we had less than an hour to change the tickets.

It seemed so hopeless that I was already starting to make enquiries about how to get back home. Luckily, we had the organiser's mobile number and she answered it! Although she was very angry, she could satisfy the authorities, that it was a genuine mistake. I was flying to Denver.

On the plane, we had a pleasant surprise when we looked at the film menu there was a film called "A Knights Tale" available to watch. None of us had heard about this film but when we watched it the jousting scenes were exceptionally dramatic and brutal. It was so lifelike that we were all jumping up and down in our seats and cheering much to the consternation of the cabin crew and fellow passengers who could not see or hear what we were watching. After watching that film, the lads were so pumped up they were ready to take on the world, let alone the Americans and Canadians.

We landed at Denver Airport at 6pm local time 1am our time! Most of the lads had seats together but I was several rows further back. As I started to shuffle down the aisle I passed the lads still seated and playing cards. I jokingly asked them if they were not bothering to get off the plane to which Wicksey replied that there was no hurry, they were going to play a few more hands and wait for the aisle to clear. As I shuffled ever nearer to the exit there seemed to be a disturbance up ahead. Then I heard someone say something about the plane being on fire, which I took to be a joke about the slow rate of our exit. Then someone leaned over and looked out of a window and shouted, "There really is smoke coming out of the engine!" Suddenly the cabin crew realised what was happening and started to shout at everyone to move faster. As I exited the plane I could see the plane's wing and engine engulfed in black smoke and flames. This was a major fire and the rest of the lads were going to be probably the last to get off. I felt so helpless as we were hustled up the gantry and into the terminal building. Once inside I could pause and wait. It was probably only a matter of a minute or two but it was the longest wait of my life. Finally, the lads appeared, much to my overwhelming relief. They were all shouting that we had to move quickly as the plane looked as if it could explode at any minute. Then someone shouted, "We've lost Wicksey." Wicksey was asthmatic so there was a very real concern and we started to look for an official to inform them we were missing one of our group. There seemed to be no cabin crew in sight, but then Wicksey appeared out of exit gantry pushing someone in a wheel chair. His story was chilling. He was the last to leave the aircraft. Even the cabin staff had legged it, and he had found the person in the wheelchair still on the plane so had pushed him out and up the steep gantry ramp to safety. Wicksey was the hero of the day!

We made our way through the painfully slow US. Immigration and then endured a further long wait at the luggage carousel, but no luggage came. We were then taken to a side room and told to wait. After well over an hour we were finally told our luggage would not be available until the next day. So, we then had to queue up to give our onward addresses to the British Airways representatives, so that they could forward our luggage. This produced another problem. The lads knew we were staying at the YMCA near Estes Park and knew how to get there as they had stayed there on their previous trips. However, we didn't have any room numbers as they were allocated when we arrived. This caused all sorts of problems but finally, we were permitted to leave, and then it was onto the car hire which took another hour. Most of us were dressed in shorts and T-shirts but thankfully it was still nice and warm. I had expected a short drive to the accommodation, but was deflated when they told me it was a two-hour drive (Should have done better research). I also wasn't aware that Estes Park was high in the Rocky Mountain national park at an altitude of 2,300 metres. We finally arrived in Estes Park at about twelve thirty and nobody could remember which road out of town the YMCA was on, I also discovered that just out of town meant five miles out of town. After some trial and error, we found the road and the YMCA. It was now 1am and reception was closed, we had been travelling 27 hours my body was shaking not only from sleep deprivation but it was also freezing cold. Wicksey went off and about half an hour later returned with an official he had managed to wake, who gave us our room keys.

Next morning, we awoke to the sound of The New Zealand Police Pipe Band rehearsing in the car park outside our lodge. IN SIX INCHES OF SNOW!
Not what you want to see when all you possess is shorts and a T-shirt. A lucky few had jeans and a jousting sweat shirt. By mid-morning we got the news that our cases would not be coming and to go and buy some clothes; BA would compensate us.

The YMCA was not like any YMCA I had ever seen. It had accommodation for many people in log cabins and large accommodation blocks for groups such as ourselves, all set in 850 acres of mountain wilderness. Herds of elk wandered freely in the grounds and we had to be very careful at night as bears came down into the main complex to raid the trash bins. We ate breakfast there every morning before going down to Estes Park and the food was superb. Sadly, in later years we were given an allowance for accommodation and had to find our own hotel.

Our baggage finally arrived late on the third day after our arrival. We were getting very worried as all the chainmail and costumes were in our bags and the tournament was due to begin the next day. The Knights had been busy selecting their steeds from the local trail riding centre; without their good will and trust we could never have competed. The wonderful thing about horsemanship is that good horsemen recognise other good horsemen, in many cases you don't even have to get on board a horse to prove yourself; it's the way you handle yourself and the way you move around horses. This was the case at the Estes Park Trekking centre, they made dozens of horses available for the lads to try out. Even so to select and train horses to joust against international opponents who have spent years training their mounts in just two days is a monumental feat of horsemanship. When I went to watch, the lads working the horses it looked more like a rodeo than jousting!

The competition was an immense success from our point of view as we won lots of prize money which was redistributed back to the town community via western shops and the Wheel Bar! On the day that we were due to leave, I was up early as usual and wandered up to the small Resident's Lounge where there's was always a pot of hot coffee for you to help yourself to. Each accommodation block had its own concierge, who after we'd stayed there for a week, knew us well. I cheerily wished him good morning, thanked him for all his help, and told him we were all sad to be leaving. He replied by saying that he thought we might be staying a little longer as he had just heard that a bomb had gone off in New York and that the airports were all closed. It seemed an over the top reaction for a bomb, and I assumed he had got his facts wrong. I was not at all perturbed.

Thirty minutes later as I went for my second cup of coffee he informed me that all flights around the world had been grounded until further notice! I raced back to inform the lads, as they stirred from their slumbers. They all thought it was a windup so I decided to drive up to reception where there was television. The scene that presented itself to me will stay with me for ever. The lounge was packed with people; some sat rigid, as if frozen, tears rolling down their faces, others wailing and rocking backwards and forwards, some were just totally hysterical. I was rooted to the spot as I watched a replay of the first plane crashing into the Twin Towers. It was about 7:45 our time but 9:45 in New York.

Getting any information from BA was impossible but we did manage to contact Denver Airport who confirmed that all flights were cancelled for the next 24 hours. Although we had mobile phones they didn't work in the United States so all calls had to be made from pay phones. We had to amass a mountain of coins as it was normal to be on hold for 30-45 mins before someone spoke to you. We had very little help or communication from the organisers in the initial stages but the YMCA informed us we could stay in our rooms and have breakfast until the flights started again which was such a relief. It was about midday by the time we had confirmed that there was no chance of flying home that day, however that was the only concrete news we could get. Worryingly, nobody could give us any indication when flights would resume.

So as in all times of crisis we went to the pub! Nobody had thought of breakfast so we soon moved to the bar diner just down the road. It was at this bar we experienced the first act of kindness from the people of Estes Park. As we sat staring out of the window onto the Main Street watching cars driving past flying the Stars and Striped from their car windows and still trying to get our heads around what was happening, three huge bowls of corn chips covered in melted cheese were placed on our table by the manager who said that he had just heard about our predicament and how sorry he was. A small gesture but it meant a lot to us.

We were stranded for six days. There were no phones or televisions in our accommodation and our only means of communication was by pay phones, that often were out of order or cut you off mid-call. Several hours were spent every day on pay phones trying to find out if were going home the next day. We soon worked out that it was easier to ring home and get information from our loved ones than try and phone British Airways. It was a very scary time with all sorts of rumours flying around the town. The most frightening development was on the second day when large numbers of cars started driving around with flags clipped to their rear windows saying, "Nuke the Bastards"; a view which also seemed to be supported by the majority of the town residents. We now started to have visions of being stranded over there in the middle of a nuclear war. At the time, it felt very real!

After a day in the pub and shopping, we decided we had to get out and about and do something. The stables who rented the horses to us for the jousting arranged for us to go for a ride into the mountains. It was real Boulder Country just like the old black and white cowboy movies. The girl who led the ride was an excellent rider who lived on a ranch in Missouri and had taken this job for the summer to earn extra money. She was thrilled to be escorting people who knew how to ride and as it was her last week at the trekking centre, she broke all the rules by galloping across the high meadows and scrambling over and around the huge boulders. We climbed so high above the town that it was like skiing when you look down at the village from the top lift and she took us to a fabulous viewing point on the edge of a cliff that had at least a thousand-foot drop. She then told us of an incident that occurred the first week she came to Estes Park whilst out riding on her own to familiarise herself will the trails and terrain. Having paused to admire the view, a bear suddenly reared up and started to push her back to the towards the edge of the cliff! She genuinely thought her end had come. Suddenly without her doing anything, her horse reared up, laid its ears back, and charged straight at the bear. To her amazement, the bear turned and ran.

During the ride, we realised that Pete (Satan) had gone missing. Our poor guide was beside herself as she was responsible for our safety and this was the first time all year she had managed lose a group member. We spread out in pairs looking for him, and shouting his name. There was no response but about ten minutes later he suddenly appeared grinning his head off. For a moment, we didn't register it, but to our horror he was only wearing his Stetson cowboy hat, but nothing else! Our guide became very agitated, almost hysterical, she certainly didn't see the funny side of it at all! Again, it brought home to us, just how conservative American country values really are. We took Pete behind a large boulder and got him reunited with his clothes. When we quizzed him as to why he had stripped naked he replied that the grandeur of the whole area had just overwhelmed him, and he had this mad urge to ride naked through it all. We used that as the excuse for his weird behaviour but all of us really thought it had more to do with our attractive female guide. If that was the motive, he had made a serious error of judgement because she was very upset about the whole incident. Luckily, she had calmed down by the time we returned to the stables and saw the funny side of it.

Our next day out was golfing. Both Mark Lacey and Dave Ironmonger were keen golfers and they persuaded us to all to have a go. Golfing is much more relaxed in America and there was no problem playing in jeans or shorts. As with everything in America you could easily hire all the equipment. This was to become one of the funniest days of my life. We laughed so much we had tears running down our faces for most of the round. It took ages for us to get kitted out with golf clubs and sign all the forms that made us responsible for any damage to the clubs. When we were ready to go out onto the course we almost lost our nerve, and hung back until there was a good gap between us and other players both in front and behind.

We all towed our golf trolleys up a steep bank to get to the first tee, and parked them. Unfortunately, we didn't look where we parked them! Several ran back down the bank and crashed, others just tipped over spewing their clubs out, which then slid down the bank. It took us ten minutes to sort out the piles of mixed up clubs and return them to the correct bags. A slapstick comedy sketch couldn't have done it better. We finally got around to teeing off. Balls travelled from about five yards to over one hundred yards. Wicksey hit one of the strongest shots. It sailed high into the sky to gasps of amazement but it then veered sharply to the left leaving the golf course and landing in the nearby housing estate. We moved on quickly so as not to be associated with the wayward ball that, hopefully, hadn't done any damage in the housing estate.

My son Mark (Mookes)was the next to strike a powerful ball. This one landed in the middle of a herd of elk. Even after much egging-on, brave as he was, he declined to go and try to retrieve his ball, as it was the rutting season, and the bull elk can be very aggressive. We progressed at a very slow pace, and soon golfers were asking to overtake us, the only thing we excelled at was losing balls.

I think it was the fourth or fifth green that we started to come back in the direction from where we had started. We now had groups of golfers playing towards us on our right.

It was at this moment my brother Stuart gave his ball a right good whack! Like Wickes's ball, it sailed high into to air, but this time it curved right, right into the middle of a group of lady golfers who were none to chuffed about it. They shouted something about, the need for us to have shouted four, so we apologised and said we couldn't remember if it was the fourth or fifth thingy, so hadn't said anything. Our pace quickened considerably in case they too caught us up. We came to a grinding halt at the sixth Tee when we ran out of balls!

Fortunately, there was a river running across this bit of the course and as the water was crystal clear we could see right down to the bed which was covered with golf balls! Mookes was the youngest and was also wearing shorts so we made him wade into the water and replenish our stocks of balls. He whinged a lot, as the water was icy cold straight from the snow topped mountains, but he was out numbered, and we told to man-up, and not be such a wimp! It soon became clear, as to why there were so many balls in the river, because on the next tee you had to knock the ball over the river.

That was just plain stupid!

We lost most of our newly found balls in the river, so had to deploy our ball recovery system for a second time, (more whinging).

Re-stocked with balls we came to the seventh tee. This ran alongside the main freeway, and had high safety nets to stop any wayward balls landing on the traffic. The net gave us great confidence, to whack our balls extremely hard and our golf skills seemed to be improving, until, I think it was Wicksey, sent another ball skyward and curving sharply to the left! It easily cleared the safety netting, and landed right in the middle of eight lanes of traffic! There was much honking of horns but thankfully no multiple pile up. Our pace quickened again to distance ourselves from the near disaster. Thankfully that was the last major highlight of our three hour nine-hole golf experience. When we got back to the golf shop they gave us a discount to show their solidarity with our plight.

Wicksey, Dave Ironmonger and I also went fishing, we hired rods which included a fishing permit that allowed us to fish, virtually anywhere, for free. We never caught anything but fished three lakes high in the Rocky Mountain National Park. The scenery was breathtakingly beautiful. We never saw a living soul and the peace was deafening! It kept me sane.

Our last fishing expedition was to a small river in the National Park. We had been warned to keep a sharp lookout for bull elk, as mentioned previously they were very dangerous during the rutting season. We could hear them bugling nearby but they never came close enough to bother us. The banks of the river were very overgrown with bushes and finding a spot to fish from was not easy. Eventually we found a suitable spot, Wicksey was about twenty yards up stream, so it was easy for us to chat to each other while fishing. After about an hour Wicksey said in a quiet voice, "Sam I know you hate snakes, but I need some advice."

"What about?" I said in a tense worried voice. Snakes terrify me and I suddenly realised that I was fishing in raw wilderness where you would find snakes! I had been so wrapped up in the beautiful scenery and fishing, that I had completely forgotten about snakes. Wicksey replied "Well I've just noticed that there is a huge snake curled around a branch just a few yards from my head; and it's looking at me!"

"Shit" I exclaimed, as I quickly scanned the floor, and trees around me for snakes, whilst reeling in my line as fast as I could. Wickey's voice broke my panic, as he repeated, "Sam did you hear me. What should I do?" I told him to get his line in and move very slowly away from the snake, I would meet him back at the car - we were getting out of there! Thankfully I never saw a snake but my heart was beating ten-to the-dozen. I really, really, hate snakes. Just writing about this has made feel funny. That was the end of our fishing expeditions and back to the safety of the Wheel Bar.

Our last outing was back at our show ground where we were invited to a bar-b-cue in our honour and to watch a cattle-cutting competition. The competition was one of the most amazing feats of horsemanship I have ever seen. There was a small herd of cows in the arena with numbers stuck to their backs. Four cattle had the same number one, another four number two, and so on. The judge would shout a number and sound a klaxon to start two riders. They had to disengage the cows with that number from the herd and corral them in a separate pen. It was a whirlwind of galloping and sliding stops, but after about just 30 seconds they had achieved the task. Just amazing truly amazing!

Everyone in America seemed to be very jumpy about what had happened so we decided to post our weapons back to England rather than risk trying to take them back on the plane. It was nearly Christmas before they arrived.

 Although I write about a few amusing moments, being separated from your loved ones, and your work, hoping you are going home tomorrow, but not knowing when that tomorrow will come, caused a lot of anxiety and stress.

We continued to visit the championships until 2005. Over that period, we again went riding as a group, but this time in the National Park. We drove up to the Alpine Visitors' Centre which is at 11,796 feet. Most of us walked to the trail head summit which was only about a quarter of a mile further on and over 12,000 ft. The air was so thin that Stuart and Wicksey couldn't walk more than ten yards without gasping for breath. They opted to sit the walk out in the visitors' centre, which turned out to be a wise decision as the trail was peppered with small crosses of people who had died trying to walk to the summit. It was certainly hard going and we had to stop to rest about every ten yards gasping for breath.

Another place we visited was the local gun shop. I had been to several American gun shops before but this one was something else. It was very small but had some very strange things for sale that gave us an insight into the psychic of the local people. The first thing that caught our eye was a water-cooled WW1 machine gun. The owner explained that it wasn't an original just a working replica that fired 200 rounds a minute but it was really, just for kids to play with as its calibre had been reduced to .22. A .22 round still carries a warning of "dangerous within one mile". The other item of interest was a long thick tube with a trigger at one end. The owner nonchalantly told us it was a 50 calibre snipers rifle used for smashing through engines and taking out armoured cars. We asked, if he ever sold any of these deadly weapons. "Oh, yes four or five a year". We then asked what they used them for, his reply was, "they don't say! And agh don't ask!"

No wonder America has a gun problem!

We continued to go every year to the Tri Nation Competition until 2005. My brother Phil won the championship and so did my son Mark, who won it twice. The rest of the lads also did very well achieving top four placings. Our reasons for stopping were many. The trip was long and tiring and the Americans and Canadians were always complaining about our style. We only wanted to fly direct but they had a deal with United Airlines via Chicago and we tried that several times and always lost our luggage adding hours to our journey. After 9/11, the security was horrendous. Phil had his Zippo lighter confiscated on one trip. He had travelled out with it without any problem but they took it off him coming home, he was furious as he had had it for many years and it was greatly cherished by him. He was so angry we thought he was going to get arrested.

The straw that broke the camel's back was when the organisers insisted that we fly United as they had found a direct flight. When I investigated, it was via Washington and we had to sit on the plane for several hours at Washington making it a fourteen-hour flight against the direct BA fight of ten hours. They still send us an invite every year to compete which is nice, but at this moment there is no enthusiasm to go, although we have some exciting young talent coming through in the next generation, so who knows?

Chapter 7   Horses

I could not write this book without mentioning our horses. Like many that joined the jousting troupe they were square pegs being forced into a round hole; very talented but needing a bit more out of life. A large majority of our jousting horses were rejects from the main stream equitation of today. However, the modern rider tends to forget that the main job of a horse for the previous three thousand years was military.

(The *history of Dressage dates back to classical Greek horsemanship and the military who trained their horses to perform movements intended to evade or attack the enemy whilst in battle. The earliest work on training horses was written by Xenophon, a Greek Military Commander born around 430 BC.) source* www.equine-world.co.uk

At the beginning of World War Two in 1939, the German army still had 3 million horses in service, so you can understand we were not going back so far into history to find our training methods. Dad's famous show in the early days with his stallion Amber Solaire (Fred) was based on classical dressage movements used in battle.

I apologise for my digressions, so back to our horses! As you can imagine a vast number of horses passed through our hands during the 35 years covered by this book. Like many of the lads that joined us, not all of them took to it, but some loved it and became stalwarts of the show. In the early days, Dad's stallion, Fred was without doubt the star of the show and had his own fan club. These stunning displays of horsemanship wowed both the general public, and also fellow horsemen. Their finale was a huge vertical rear that finished with the horse dropping onto his knees to bow to the audience. Dad would step off his horse take a bow and then step back into the saddle whilst Fred held his kneel. Then on Dad's command, he would spring back up on to his front feet. This display that lasted 15-20 minutes and covered up the very weak show that we had during our first two years. Luckily, we had no competition to be compared with and soon learned our trade up at Gwrych Castle in 1972.

My first jousting horse was Charlie, a black horse, who was much bigger than the stamp of horse we finally settled on. He was the only black horse we have ever had for the part of the Black Knight. It was important in those days, as the horse costumes didn't have any hoods. The early costumes showed the neck and head of the horse and allowed their character to be seen by the audience. Charlie was about 16.2 hands high, a thoroughbred cross, extremely fast, packing a hard punch when we were jousting for real. Unfortunately, it was a long way to fall off him, especially when we went to Wales and did regular falls each day! Charlie was a very spooky horse and needed strong, determined riding. His spooky character was the reason I got to ride him. His owner, was a wealthy lady who he regularly unseated whilst out hacking. He would regularly return home minus his rider and we would have to send out search parties from the stables to find her. He was the horse, that dumped me in the mud on my entrance at Gwrych. Like a lot of horses, he didn't like me doing falls from him on a regular basis and started to stop or shy away just before impact, which makes it hard to perform a fall that looks natural and credible. About half way through the season at Gwrych, I had to send him back to Bunny for a rest.

After Gwrych, the next few years saw very few shows and I have no recollection of any outstanding horses. I do remember that Tony's first ride on a horse called Edward was at Hastings in 1977. Edward was a strong three-quarter bred bay gelding and I remember it because Tony did a fall from him. Edward panicked as Tony started fall and shot off like a scalded rabbit. Tony hit the ground at such speed that he bounced over twenty yards before coming to a battered halt. To make matters worse, the ground was rock hard. Tony's first words were "that horse is f***ing mental," after which they forged a long and happy relationship.

About the same time, we acquired a young grey horse called Jontie. He was a very placid, easy going horse and took to jousting with great ease. Jontie had very hard feet and never had any shoes on in his entire life. Dad did try to shoe him once for Pony Club Camp, but he couldn't get any nails to go through his foot. Jontie was my horse for most of the years that I played the drunk. He knew the show so well that on the third joust, when I was scripted to fall, he would stop dead just at the point of impact, give a huge buck and send me flying whether I was hit by the lance or not. I have already told the story of what happened when I swapped parts in the middle of the show due to injury. Whenever I did a fall, he would turn around look at me on the floor and then start grazing around my body. Unfortunately, as time went on he found it amusing to ad-lib every now and then depositing me at some inopportune moments. He was so reliable that I became very casual when riding him, and one day when I was demonstrating to some of the younger Knights how to do a fall. I broke a cardinal, safety rule. I performed the fall and then remounted to repeat it. I still had my shield and helm on when I remounted and I forgot to take-up my reins before mounting. My shield clanged as it hit my helm, Jontie spooked and shot forward before I had finished mounting. I crashed head first into the ground and there was a horrific crack from my neck. Thankfully I appeared to be OK; my neck was painful for some time but gradually got better. Some years later I was having an initial body check by a highly-recommended chiropractor before some treatment to my back. She asked me in a matter of fact way when I had broken my neck. I replied that I never had, but she assured me I most definitely had. After more thought, I am sure it was when the above incident happened. Clare has been my chiropractor ever since and has straightened my body out more times than I care to remember. Without her skill, I don't think I would still be walking today. Truly a remarkable lady! Whenever I see anyone mounting a horse without taking up their reins, I tear such a strip off them that they never forget again.

Along with Edward, Jontie was one of the first in a long line of long serving horses that were the backbone of our shows for over two decades.

As Dad's role diminished in the mid-seventies, Stuart took over the role of the good knight eventually changing the name of the good knight, from Robert of Sherwood to Sir Malcolm of Roxburgh. This was after we performed a very successful show at Floors Castle, home to the Duke of Roxburgh. We made up the name of Sir Malcolm of Roxburgh just for that show, but the young Duchess loved the show so much, she gave Stu permission to continue using the name.

 Stu's first horse was Leprechaun an iron grey who like my Charlie was really a bit too big and powerful for the job but he was an impressive animal. Just right for the leading good knight. After several other horses, we bought Cello a flea bitten grey, and formally a high goal Argentinian polo pony. He was light, fast and highly manoeuvrable. When Dad purchased him, Stu couldn't wait to try him out. At that period, Stu was very much into racing and rode with ultra-short stirrups. Dad warned Stu that Cello turned very quickly and that he should lengthen his stirrups, but like all his sons, Stu didn't like being told what to do by his father so he ignored the advice. He set sail up the indoor school at the gallop and asked Cello to stop and turn at the other end just like we would when jousting. Cello stopped and spun around in the blink of an eye, sending Stu, flying through the air, much to the amusement of his father and brothers. Dad muttered very matter-of-factly, "Perhaps you'll listen to what I say one day" as Stu got to his feet dusting himself down. He went on to be one of Stu's long standing mounts. In the Grand Melee' they were magnificent to watch effortlessly weaving in and around the other combatants whilst doing battle.

Another horse ridden by Stu was Darazan, another grey. He was an Anglo-Arab and belonged to my wife Lou who bought him as a hunter and hunted him with the Quorn regularly for many seasons. He was strong enough to carry me and I sometimes borrowed him to hunt on Mondays when he skipped over the big hedges with the greatest of ease. He had a long career with our family excelling at everything him did. He sadly died of a heart attack seconds after crossing the finish line having led his team from start to finish in a Teamchase competition.

Marrick was a naughty nappy horse who when in the riding school would just plant himself and refuse to move. No amount of kicking or whip would make him move. When he decided that he was ready he would set off again as if nothing had happened. He was very talented but it was always on his terms. He loved jousting and again had a long and illustrious career playing every major part in the show.

Sniper was a skewbald coloured mare, very bouncy and forward going. Dad purchased her from a dealer in Lincoln where she had been pulling a milk float. Like many coloured horses, she was an excellent jumper and extremely popular with all the riding school clients. She was mainly ridden by whoever was playing Sir Richard of Gloucester and that was either Pete Webster or Martin Brown. She was quick and manoeuvrable, her crowd pleasing little rear at the start of each run down the tilt was always great for the show. She sadly died after being kicked by another horse when out grazing in the field, a solemn reminder to everyone just how dangerous a kick from a horse can be.

Bess was another horse of the eighties era. She was a super little black cob very easy to ride and she was ridden by many different characters in the show. Despite her small, cobby stature she had a remarkable turn of speed over short distances. We did an advert for Mars Bars called "Mars Make It Happen".

 People could write into Mars with a wish and if they were chosen Mars would make the wish come true. A girl called Gill wrote that she had always wanted to be a knight in shining armour. We trained Gill and her sister to joust and took the horses to Allington Castle on the river Medway to film the joust between the two sisters. My daughter Emma was stunt double for the two sisters and the film was made into a very successful advert for Mars Bars. I think this was the only time we ever got Emma to wear a suit of chainmail. By the end of the process we became good friends with Gill and she later gave Bess and Marrick a retirement home on her small holding in the Malvern hills. Sniper was also due to be reunited with her old mates but sadly passed away the very week she was due to retire to Gill's.

Step was Phil's most dramatic Black Knight horse. A dark bay lightweight thoroughbred. He was so fast he was like a turbocharged dragster running on nitro. When not hurtling forward he danced sideways and spun around with legs going in all directions. Only Phil had the guts and skill to ride him but he complimented Phil's portrayal of the Black knight perfectly.

Drummer was a lovely big grey horse (white), but a little bit too big for jousting. I used him mainly for commentating from horseback when radio microphones became available in the 1990's. He was a strong hunter type and very kind in nature. We didn't joust him regularly but used him for the bigger shows or as a last-minute substitute if one of the regulars went lame. We used him for lots of film work as he was completely safe to put actors on. I did my opening scene on him for the Boon Five series. Once when filming through the night on First Knight down at Stratfield Saye House near Reading, Andrew Drage fell asleep on him whilst we were waiting to do the next scene. We quietly turned Drummer around, pointed him towards the stables and set him off at the walk! It was two very large fields later before Andrew awoke very confused and in the middle of nowhere! Typical jousting humour! I rode Drummer at the Stebbing show and was amazed at the difference a few inches   higher made to the fall. It seemed an age before I hit the ground and it hurt a lot more. He was a real gentleman.

Simpson was a strong, skewbald coloured cob and mainly ridden by the Drunk. As with Jontie, Simpson was a real character and added much to the Drunk's part. He was a real pig for food and would yank the reins out of your hands if you gave him the slightest opportunity and gobble up as much grass as possible before you pulled his head up. He always did this during the opening salute and Sir Frederick (the drunk) would slide haplessly down his neck head first into the ground, much to the amusement of the crowd. Whenever we were loading him onto the horsebox, Simpson would spot a patch of grass and charge off to it dragging the helpless leader with him. I tried to stop him one day after he had pulled over one of the girl grooms. I gathered all the staff together for a demonstration of how to lead and control a wayward horse. He just whipped around using his strong short neck and set off towards the grass. I tried in vain to halt his progress, but the harder I pulled, the faster he went, until he pulled me over flat on my face and dragged me through mud and puddles, until I let go. It was very embarrassing for me, and very amusing for the assembled staff, who to this day, delight in reminding me of the incident.

Tsar was a sweet, little, thoroughbred gelding, ridden mainly by Stuart as the good knight. A bright bay in colour and with a white snip on his nose. Like all of Stu's jousting horses, he was light, quick and very manoeuvrable. Another stalwart of the show for many years.

Declan was another lightweight thoroughbred, again a bright bay thoroughbred, but much more excitable. His legs flew everywhere and he could jump sideways with the slightest of body movement. He was much favoured by Edward Kopel, when he took over the role as Black Knight. Declan and Edward as the Black Knight, can still be seen to this day, featured on a photograph on the side of the jousting horsebox.

Warrior was an enigma when it came to thoroughbreds and our choice of jousting horse. For those old enough to remember the Magic Roundabout on television, Warrior was like Dylan, the dreamy spaced-out rabbit. In the riding school, even good riders struggled to get him into a canter. He was a quirky horse, for most of the time completely switched off, but on occasions could be very stubborn and even rear if you tried to force him. If you pulled him to try and speed him up when leading him, he would run back and rear, snatching the rope from your hands. It was the same when loading him onto the horsebox, you had to allow extra time. He would stand at the bottom of the ramp, wait and when ready, put one foot onto the ramp and then other. The whole process of getting up the ramp could take five minutes, but woe-betide anyone who tried to hurry him.

PJ. was another long-standing stalwart of the jousting-show. He was a 15.3, chestnut gelding, with a flaxen mane and tail. He had a quick, short striding canter which made it easy for the rider to keep the lance level when jousting. He had good bone and was a strong, compact horse capable of carrying the heavier jousters. During his younger days, he was quite excitable, doing little rears at the end of the lists. His strength and easy going nature made him very versatile, and was the first horse many of the younger knights rode when learning their trade.

Bumper was purchased by me as a four-year-old on behalf of Dick Benson as a Point to Pointer. The vendor was very surprised that I wanted to by him, as he had put in a huge spook and followed it up with two equally huge bucks that very nearly unseated me. When I bought him, he didn't have a registered name, which was very exciting for Dick who, being a barrister at the time, loved to play with words. To cause mischief with the racing commentators, he named him Uisge Beatha which is the Gaelic name for whiskey. I truly believe that if I had not bought him he would have been labelled a dangerous horse and could have caused someone serious injury. He was 15.3hh when I purchased him and I confidently expected him to make 16.1, but instead of growing taller, he grew wider and stockier. The last nail in the coffin of his racing career was when he broke down during a fitness gallop as a five-year-old. I was eventually given him by Dick, and he became the most loved horse I ever owned. He was very naughty, impossible at times, but also hugely talented. Many people loathed his rude behaviour but I loved riding him despite his many faults. He came to jousting in his later life when he was slightly calmer. He was so spooky I did not believe he would ever take to it but like so many quirky horses, he loved performing to an audience and he seemed to love charging at horses and crashing into them during the Grand Melee. He was always unpredictable, and as well as spooking he could stop dead from a gallop in one ejecting stride. He continued to joust into his twenties and died at the ripe old age of twenty-six.

Falero known to everyone as Fal is a grey Andalusian gelding. He is only 15.2hh but very strong and compact. He is kept at livery at Bunny and owned by Ceri Walters who kindly lends him to the jousters. He was originally my wife Lou's horse who sold him to Ceri's sister Clare, who then passed him onto Ceri. He made his debut at the last Lincoln Castle show I did in 2004. He loved it from day one, especially all the crowd attention after the show. Fal is a real 'people' horse and is happy to be surrounded by crowds patting him and stroking him for hours-on-end. He has also done a lot of film work including the very successful multi-series television drama "Merlin". Being an Andalusian he has a flashy action and presence which has earned him a very large and loyal fan club. He continues to wow audiences to this day 2017.

Three horses that were not regular jousting horses but did a lot of filming, were Zara, Garth and Smartie. Zara was Michael Elphick's horse in many episodes of Boon, and has already been mentioned earlier in this book. Garth, who belonged to Dick Benson, carried Mike Lane in "By the Sword Divided", and many more films and television series. Smartie was my son Mark's horse, when he was a teenager. Smartie was a cob and like all cobs his world revolved around food. Once in the early hours of the morning during a night shoot on "First Knight", large trays of hot meat pies were being brought around to keep us going through the night. Smartie noticed these and suddenly lurched forward knocking the tray from the terrified caterer's arms. Before we could stop him, he had scoffed more than a dozen of these meat pies. So much for horses being vegetarian!

Although most of the horses have belonged to our riding stables, some have been loaned or lent to us by friends and clients for both jousting and film work, always free of charge. Without their generosity, we would never have been able to do many of the things described in this book. You may wonder why they would be so generous. The answer is that there are many reasons. It has certainly helped sort out many behaviour problems and improved the horse's way of going but I think the main reason is the desire to see their horse reach its full potential and enjoy watching them captivate audiences, whether it be live or on film. Whatever the reason, I say a big thank you to you all, as do your horses who have had so much fun!

Chapter 8   The last Hoorah

My last ten years at the helm seemed to me like treading water; repeated recessions had curbed people's risk taking, and new adventures like Belgium and Ireland were not forthcoming although there were a few highlights such as a week in Jersey that was very successful. In 1993, I set up the first show at Sewerby Hall just outside Bridlington; that show is still running in 2016 and I hope the lads continue on, to reach the 25 years' landmark in 2018. The Robin Hood pageant continues to be a great success and has just completed its 26th year, although it could be in jeopardy due to the planned multi-million-pound redevelopment of Nottingham Castle.

On Sunday, 29th October 2006, thirty-six years after that one-off joust at Wollaton Park, I stepped down from running the Nottingham Jousting Association or as we were now more often called, simply The Knights of Nottingham. It was a cold, damp, drizzling day and I had little enthusiasm for my final show. As we did our final salute the council announced that it was my last show. I got a fabulous cheer from the crowd and to my great surprise the council presented me with a handmade long bow made by my longstanding friend Wib Bond, and a mounted golden arrow for my services to the pageant. I still have the bow which I greatly cherish. The golden arrow was taken away to be engraved and never seen again.

It had looked as if this was the end of the jousting, and I was preparing to sell-off all the equipment, but to my great delight a group of the Knights both past and present decided to take over the reins. They had the enthusiasm and energy to guide the troupe through the deepest recession I have ever known. It was and still is a very difficult trading environment; the big budget shows are no more.

Despite the recession, the troupe is still going strong with an exciting new youthful line-up. The show is like Dr Who; the characters stay the same but every generation, they regenerate into new, younger, re-energised people. I missed the jousting like crazy and it was sad to have finished on such a gloomy day,

I had originally planned to retire from the jousting in 2005 after 35 years at the helm but decided to do another year when Ashcile proposed Bruges. Three years later Ashcile decided to have one last jousting show at Horst Castle, but on the condition that I came and did the commentary. It was an offer I could not refuse as I truly loved that place.
So, in 2009 I set off for another "last" trip to Belgium. The shows were like our first trip; there were no night shows, no special effects. The weather was beautiful and the crowds flocked to see us. Word had got out that this was to be our last show and our Horse enclosure was constantly surrounded by well-wishers wanting to share memories with us. Many brought their children or grandchildren to meet us. It was very moving and it has brought a tear to my eye just writing about it.

The last night at the Castle was beautiful. It was a warm night when you could sit outside in a t-shirt easily until midnight. I sat with Ashcile and his family reminiscing. The shows had been a great success. Everyone was tired but happy. Kick and Rush played several sets, and we all sang along to their well-known songs. They were joined by my brother Phil, Pete Webster and Dave Ironmonger who had formed their own band inspired originally by Kick and Rush.

I remember looking around and thinking how we had all changed since that first trip. The lads were not wild teenagers anymore and most were in their late thirties, running their own businesses; Kick and Rush were knocking on the door of sixty and I was fifty-six thinking more about going to bed rather than drinking all night long. Belgium had been a magical ride but this was the perfect time to end that ride. It was also the perfect time to close this book.

Epilogue   Wicksey

As I was neared the end of writing this book I got an early morning call from Mark. This was quite normal as he calls me most mornings to go over work plans for the coming day. His voice sounded strange, and then he said, " Had I heard the terrible news". A wave of nausea passed through my body, I knew it was very bad news as I had never heard him speak this way, his voice was breaking down trying to utter something so bad that it just would not come out. Hundreds of awful possibilities raced my mind and tears started to well in my eyes. To break the impasse, I shouted down the phone "Mark just tell me" his reply took me by complete surprise "It's Wicksey, he's dead, he committed suicide last night"

It was his fiftieth birthday. He had invited all his many friends to join him for a celebratory few drinks at the Round Robin micro pub in his home village of East Leake. It was a Tuesday night. Lou and I could not make it as I was working that night so sent a text "Sorry mate, can't make it, working. Happy birthday, see you Saturday". He had invited us to a Birthday Barbecue at his home on Saturday. He left the pub in high spirits and reminded everyone not to forget his party on Saturday night.

 After taking an overdose, he phoned one of the jousters who he knew lived a long way away and told him what he had done, knowing he would not have time to reach him. The jouster immediately phoned Mark who was now back at the stables who raced to his house, but it was too late. Mark performed CPR on Wicksey until the ambulance arrived but everything was in vain. He had timed his final call to perfection to achieve his own end.

Wicksey had been in the show for thirty years and played the Black Knight's Man-at-Arms for most of that time. He was a master at whipping up frenzied hatred of the Black Knight from an audience. He was also the life and soul of all our parties and could always come up with a funny one liner, no matter how bad the situation was that we found ourselves in. Whenever we travelled abroad he would buy pieces of unusual art or some expensive clothing to remind him of his trip. When we were on tour he could beg borrow or steal anything that we needed to keep the show on the road. He was proud that he had no shame and was happy to do the most outrageous things in front of complete strangers. Whatever he did he never caused offence and would always end his exhibitions with his trademark infectious chuckle. For all his wild happy go lucky ways Wicksey had a heart of gold always there for people when they were down. I could go on talking about his qualities for pages but I think Jim Brennan summed it up when I phoned him in Ireland to tell him the terrible news by saying, "his generosity knew no bounds in every manner and sense." Wicksey also had may friends in Belgium and made many none jousting trips over there to keep in touch.

We all knew he was vulnerable as he had tried to commit suicide some years before and we kept a watchful eye on his moods. He had recently finished some very expensive counselling and spoke openly of how it turned his life around, stating that he felt completely cured. We never saw anything to indicate anything was wrong.

The jousters formed a mounted guard of honour at his funeral which was attended by over 300 people. His wake was held at the stables in our indoor school and went on until the early hours of next morning. He would have liked that!

Lou and I were away on holiday in Turkey with our friends Vanda and Ian who were also close friends of Wicksey. On the day of the funeral at the exact time we blagged our way into an exclusive private resort on top of a mountain overlooking the beautiful little bay of Turunc. It was a typical Wicksey caper. We toasted him as a way of saying goodbye, with classy cocktails in the outdoor bar that hung on the edge of the cliff overlooking the bay. Very stylish and expensive - just the way he liked it.

Depression is a terrible, over looked illness that is only just becoming recognised and understood. Three other members of the troupe have taken their own lives over the past forty years but all had left the troupe for some considerable time prior to the sad event to pursue other goals. In each case, we were shocked, saddened and surprised that it had happened.

Glossary

Coif — Chainmail head piece covering head, neck and shoulders

Hauberk. — Chainmail knee length coat

Chausses. — Chainmail trousers

Broke down. in horse's legs — Severe injury to leg tendons or ligaments

Put down. — Euthanasia of a horse

Unseated. — Polite term for falling off a horse

Lists. — A defined enclosed are where a jousting tournament takes place.

Sometimes refers to the barrier dividing the horses in an joust

Tilt. — A knight charging another knight at the gallop head-on

Also, sometimes refers to barrier dividing the horses in a joust

Skewbald. — A brown and white horse

Piebald. — A black and white horse

Chestnut. shoes — A very light, brown horse, like light tan

Light bay. — Light brown horse with darker brown points

Dark bay. — Very dark, brown horse almost black

Snip. A small, white area on a horse's muzzle

Cob. A small, strong stocky horse

Please note that this paperback version does not have the list of all the shows we performed over the 36 years. However, the Kindle version does, which is available free of charge to download when you purchase the paperback. I have done this to try and keep the printing costs down as it adds another 45 pages to the book.

I did, however, count up the days I was away doing shows, films and travelling. This amounted to 2 and half years away from home!

About the Author

Sam Humphrey was born in 1951, in West Bridgford, near Nottingham. The family moved to Bunny Hill, eight miles south of Nottingham, when he was four years old. He has lived or worked on Bunny Hill all his life. Horses and the countryside have always been a major part of his life. He married his wife

Louise in 1973 when he was 22 years old and Louise just 18 years old. They have two children - Mark born in 1978 and Emma born in 1979, and two granddaughters, one from each of their children. Their children have both pursued successful careers in the equestrian world.

Sam was educated at the local, village, primary school of Costock and then at Rushcliffe Grammar school. He later studied science and management studies at Peoples College, Nottingham. He left school at the age of sixteen to work in the family, riding school business, and also spent six months working as a jobbing builder with his future brother-in-law, before joining British Gypsum Research Department at their plant at nearby East Leake. He left British Gypsum in 1971 to take over running the jousting at Gwrych Castle and became managing director of Medieval Entertainments Ltd. In 1973, Lou and Sam formed the School of National Equitation Limited with Sam's parents. Sam was again managing director and Lou was company secretary. They became sole owners of the business in 1991 when they purchased the other half of the business from Sam's parents on their retirement. Sam and Lou have also owned a riding clothes and saddlery shop, and have been partners in an auction company specializing in selling horses, saddlery and farm equipment, where Sam was an Auctioneer.

Sam has taught riding all his life, taking his first-class lesson at the age of 10 years, when his father failed to get home in time for the lesson. He has a Diploma in Sports Psychology and uses Bio-Mechanics in his teaching. He has always been attracted to the adrenalin side of riding. As a youngster, he was a member of the Quorn Hunt Pony Club Prince Philip Cup Team for mounted games. As a teenager, he jumped a string of ponies at county level for a local trainer and in the 70's and early 80's he rode in point-to-point races, riding and training his own horses. Later in his racing career, he was granted a National Hunt Amateur License and went onto achieve one of his ambitions of riding around the Cheltenham Race Course. He started hunting with the Quorn hunt when he was five, and has hunted with many fox, drag and blood hound packs both in the UK and Ireland and has been Field Master of three different packs. He has been a keen participant in team chasing since its inception in 1974 until late 1990's.

Although now officially retired, Sam continues to teach and help his son with the family Bunny Hill Riding Centre, which was started in 1955.

Sam plans to write two other books. One about his equine life and the larger than life characters he has met. The other about his life from moving to Bunny Hill until he started jousting. The three books will be a series called The Bunny Hill Chronicles.

Contact:- sam@bunnyhill.co.uk

Printed in Poland
by Amazon Fulfillment
Poland Sp. z o.o., Wrocław